AF323539

JEROME COCHRAN

HIS LIFE, HIS WORKS, HIS LEGACY

Jerome Cochran

Courtesy of The Medical Association of the State of Alabama

JEROME COCHRAN
HIS LIFE, HIS WORKS, HIS LEGACY

BY

JOHN T. MORRIS, B.S., M.D.
AND
BARBARA ANN McCLARY, B.S., R.N.

JEROME COCHRAN
His Life, His Work, His Legacy

Published by
The Mulberry River Press
1316 Legion Drive NW
Cullman, Alabama   35055

ISBN 0–9636529–3–1

PRINTED IN THE UNITED STATES OF AMERICA

FIRST EDITION

*To Miriam Morris, who has been supportive and patient.
She has been helpful in more ways, tangible and intangible,
than she is aware. Without her this book would never have
been finished
and
To Joseph Patrick McClary who has been most cooperative
and supportive and has been our "great communicator"
and transporter.*

Photo by Tom Morris

First Encounter

Jerome, Your peers respected you; vision-driven, duty bound.
Quietly you loved your family, remained a private man.

Your only picture speaks to me. I searched the State for statue
peers proposed to cast of you. No trace was found, no meeting
you in life-like rounded form. Your only portrait speaks to me.

When together we, that day, went through the portals
of your works' seat, A shock! you gazed at us with twinkle
in your bronze-cast eye! Your noble bust enraptured me!

You are home!

Barbara McClary

Contents

continued

Contents

Contents

ILLUSTRATIONS

JEROME COCHRAN

HIS LIFE, HIS WORKS
HIS LEGACY

Preface

While researching another Alabama pioneer doctor, I found the name of Jerome Cochran mentioned and constantly recurring. Some of his accomplishments were noted. I was aware of the name from the Jerome Cochran Lecture series, a highlight event at the annual sessions of the Medical Association of the State of Alabama for all the years I have been a member of that organization (forty plus years). From the beginning I felt that he was a very significant man, and at last, having reached that stage of retirement when I no longer felt guilty for reading other than articles on clinical medicine, I wanted to read more about Jerome Cochran. A man who had done so much for Alabama medicine should have volumes written about him, I thought. Alas, after much searching, I was able to turn up only a few pages of significant biographical material. The best information available, Dr. Howard Holley had included in his book, *The History of Medicine in Alabama.* Dr. Emmett B. Carmichael had written a very good short summary of the illustrious man titled: "Jerome Cochran: The Guiding Genius in Public Health Legislation in Alabama" for *The American Surgeon.* I found enough biographical information in these two sources to convince me that Jerome Cochran deserved to be studied in more depth. Why had the biographers neglected him?

It soon became apparent that there were several reasons for this neglect. Jerome Cochran was a very complicated man, and he seemed to have covered his tracks very effectively. He wrote extensively, but on things other than himself. Most of his writing was published in the *Transactions of the Medical Association of the State of Alabama.* These journals, nearly all of which are over one hundred years old (1996), are usually stored away in library archives and are difficult to get to -- covered with dust and sometimes difficult to read.

The Alabama Department of Archives and History in Montgomery is a veritable treasure trove of biographical material. They have only a slim vertical file on the great man, and it is yellow and faded. Some of it is torn and almost illegible. Some of the old newspapers are so faded they cannot be copied. The pertinent census indices have nothing on Dr. Cochran or his family.

In order to begin this story at the beginning, I made a pilgrimage to Moscow, Fayette County, Tennessee and was impressed by its location between the two forks of the Wolf River, with swampland near the town. There was a large mosquito population, but only the Culex species, harmless to mankind, a significant part of the food chain. The town had not increased much in people population since Jerome was born there in 1831.

I met Mrs. J. R. Morton, who had lived in Moscow all her life, had taught school and had been the principal of the high school there and was the wife of a former mayor. She is the local historian. She knew of the Cochrans, but none of them had lived in Moscow during her life time. She told me that there were a great number of Cochrans living in and about Holly Springs, Mississippi.

There is a small museum in Holly Springs. The curator is very friendly and helpful. She told me of some of the Cochrans living there. I called one of them, Mr. S. Vadah Cochran, on the museum's telephone. He told me that he had seen the house that Jerome had lived in while he practiced medicine in Holly Springs.[1] It was white, as most of the houses were at the time. This house had green shutters on the windows and lots of shrubbery that may have been planted first by Jerome or his wife. It looked better than most of the houses of that era. It has long since been demolished. Mr. Cochran told me of another member of the family, Mary Gregg, who had worked up the genealogy of the Cochran family of Marshall County, Mississippi. Mr. Sam Vadah Cochran was a descendant of Clark Cochran, a brother of Augustus Owen Cochran and uncle of Jerome Cochran. Vadah was therefore Jerome's cousin, several generations removed.

When he became convinced that I was serious about Dr. Cochran's biography, Mr. Vadah Cochran wrote me several letters, and was quite helpful. I did not hear from him for over a year, and so I wrote him a kind of progress report on the biography. I was shocked to receive a letter in December 1995 with the details of Mr. Vadah Cochran's death in February of 1995. Among the eulogies to Mr. Cochran, I found that he was an artist of considerable ability, and he had been a professor at Memphis State University. He also had some local credits as an accomplished actor.

Of course I wrote to Mary Gregg and found that she has done a thorough, historically accurate study of her Cochran ancestors and relatives. The genealogical manuscript she gave to me was the first real break I had found. She graciously consented to having it recorded in the Reynolds Historical Library. of the University of

---

[1]S. Vadah Cochran, personal communication, May 10, 1993.

Alabama at Birmingham.

I next visited Mobile, Alabama. Here I was told by the attendant at the Catholic Cemetery that they had no record of Dr. Cochran's having been buried there. It is a very old cemetery, and all the Catholics who had ever died in Mobile were buried there. Convinced that he was there, I was willing to spend several days, if necessary, looking for his grave.

Fortunately for me, a survey and Cemetery Lot Information Form had been filled out unbeknownst to the attendant. He had found it after my call, and he had it on his desk when I arrived. We easily located the grave plot: section A, Lot 50.[2]

Until this time, the only Cochran children recorded were Jerome Bowling, Augustine, and E. C. Cochran. The grave monument found in the Mobile Catholic Cemetery listed the names of Augustine Schamyl, Ina Lou, Mary Fooshea, Francis Lawrence, Lamoua B., and Louis. These names do not occur in any records I have found. Dr. Jerome Cochran had survived his wife and six of his eight children.

The early deaths of his children must have had a devastating effect on Jerome. Five of them died between 1869 and 1875, the years that Jerome's mysterious disease, contracted on a speech making trip to Nashville, Tennessee, was at its worst. This was also the period of time that Dr. Cochran organized the Medical Association of the State of Alabama and the State Department of Public Health and wrote the laws governing the practice of medicine in Alabama. I can find no record or notations anywhere except on this one cemetery marker about the children and their tragedies.

Mrs. Sarah Jane Cochran's life history is written on this cemetery monument along with those of her children. It is written in very few words: "Wife of Dr. Jerome Cochran, Born Dec 11, 1833 DeSoto

---

[2]The names on the roster are grossly misspelled and inaccurate due to the erosion of the granite monument. I have attempted to trace out each letter and I have double checked for accuracy.

County, Mississippi died January 3, 1880, Mobile, Alabama."

It is said that true love comes with years of sharing each other's dreams and triumphs, years of rejoicing together and years of sorrowing together. Sarah Jane and Jerome had the thrills of watching their children, Jerome Bowling, E. C., and Ina Lou grow up. They shared the horror as one by one their other five little ones were laid to rest in the simple little plot, section A, Lot 50. It is hoped that Sarah Jane shared with Jerome the supreme satisfaction that must have come to him as he shaped the practice of medicine in Alabama for the next millennium.

Sarah Jane did not live to know of Jerome Bowling's success in business. She died three years before he married, and she never knew her grandchildren.

We can find no correspondence between Jerome Bowling and his parents after he moved to Texas, but we feel sure that there was no family rift. Jerome Bowling named his firstborn son for his father. Mr. Jerome Cochran, Jerome Bowling's first born son became a successful publisher in Houston, Texas.

Schamyl Cochran, Jerome Bowling Cochran's next son, graduated from the United States Naval Academy in the class of 1908. While in the academy he answered to the nick name "Shemmy" He seems to have had an adequate sense of humor. It was said that he "knows seamanship like a book. Has also been seen in the first section in mechanics." He served in World War I and retired as Lieutenant Commander in 1926 due to physical disability. He owned the Cochran and Bryan Naval Academy Preparatory School in Annapolis, Maryland. He came out of retirement to serve in World War II. He retired as a Commander.

Walker Cochran graduated from the U.S. Naval Academy in the class of 1913. It was said of him "he should be in a choir, whether he can sing or not, because of his angelic face." His nicknames at the academy were: "Tramp," "Pretty," and "Cockee." His classmates wrote this of him: "His merry heart and generous, kindly disposition have won for Cochran a group of friends who think the world of him. As a dependable man, possessed of grit and a high sense of honor and duty, Walker will win his way in whatever direction his path may lie." He served continuously from 1913, through WW I and through the uneasy peace to 1934, at which time he retired as Lt. Commander. He answered the call to duty in 1940 and served throughout WW II, then retired with the rank of Commander. The name Cochran, throughout a long history, seems to imply integrity, ability, and a certain degree of altruism.

By bits and pieces, Jerome Cochran's chronological biography gradually came together over the years, but I found the real Jerome Cochran in his own writings. Most of his written articles are found in the *Transactions of the Medical Association of the State of Alabama,* 1870-1898, copies of which were made for me by Ms. Faye Harkins, the assistant to the Curator of the previously mentioned Reynolds Historical Library. Another of the very good people who helped me gather data on Dr. Cochran was Fran Edwards at The Alabama State Department of Public Health. She sent me copies of relevant data from the Alabama Department of Archives and other sources that she was aware of, not necessarily from her own section, *Graphic Communications, Bureau of Health Promotion & Information.*

When I thought I had finished Dr. Cochran's story, I read it over and had some of my friends read the text. We all agreed that my story was not up to snuff. I realized that this very important man should have a better biography.

At this point I asked Mrs. Barbara McClary, B.S., R.N., to help me. She became quite excited about Dr. Cochran. She not only read over my references, she delved even deeper and found more information. With her tenacious researches and her Irish gifts for fine writing, she rapidly advanced from editor to co-author. She has made this book a significant study of a great man.

John T. Morris, B.S., M.D

As co-editor and contributing author of Brookwood Medical Center, Birmingham's nationally published professional newsletter,[3] I have gained some insight and experience in the field of editing. As members of the Alabama Writers' Conclave, the oldest continuing writers' group in America, Dr. John Morris and I were acquainted. After a lecture on editing that I gave at the 1995 annual Conclave workshop in Montevallo, John asked if I would edit his biography on Dr. Jerome Cochran, the "Father of Alabama Public Health." I agreed.

John is right. In studying the 18 chapters he had written, I became enthralled with the life story of Jerome Cochran. In doing the extensive corroborative research I felt was necessary in order to do a good job of editing, I found that John's five years of research had yeilded a tremendous amount of information. It was information that he had arranged by topic, and was loosely chronological. But so much of Dr. Cochran's work was carried out simultaneously, that I got lost in the dates and times.

Dr. Jerome Cochran deserves to be known and understood. His story cried out to be told in a chronological manner that covered not only his works, but his life, his family, and the legacy he has left. With so much work to do, John offered me a co-authorship which I readily, and gratefully accepted.

I was particularly awed to learn that Dr. Cochran was baptized less than one hundred years before our first son -- at the same baptismal font.

I am deeply grateful to Drs. Wayne H. Finley, Bill Weaver, S. R. Hill, Michael Maetz, and Charlotte Borst for their painstaking editing of our first completed draft.

The biography does contain many quotes. John and I felt compelled to include whole passages, as these helped us to know Jerome Cochran. We feel that it will also help you to make your

---

[3]Brookwood's professional newsletter, *New Challenge*.

decisions about the type of man he was. The capitalization and spelling inside the quotes are left as is. They are faithful copies, exactly as written. Occasionally we have inserted the authors' [sic] to denote a particularly old-fashioned spelling or term.

I thank John for the invitation and the opportunity to co-author this biography. We both hope you enjoy reading it as much as we have enjoyed putting the pieces together.

Barbara McClary, B.S., R.N.

Additional Acknowledgements

Any work of this nature requires help and cooperation from a variety of sources. We have been fortunate to have received such help from many people. In addition to those previously mentioned we wish to thank the following:

Mr. Marion McGuinn was the Curator of the Reynolds Historical Library during the time we were most involved in this research. He not only helped us obtain key material, he also encouraged us and offered valuable suggestions for the elaboration of the manuscript.

Dr. S. Richardson Hill, whose opinion and judgement we greatly admire, offered good wishes and expressed the opinion that a biography of Dr. Cochran was a worthy undertaking.

Dr. Wayne House Finley, chairman of the Reynolds Library Associates, has never seemed to get tired of my numerous calls. Always friendly and helpful, it was he who suggested that we include a list of the illustrious men who have given the annual Cochran Lectures during the past one hundred years.

We have had the full cooperation of MASA. When we talked to Mr. George D. Oetting, Director of Continuing Education, about a list of all the Cochran Lecturers, he promptly sent us a copy of his list. (*see* appendix). We are grateful to Mr. Victor McClean,

MASA's Public Relations Director, for the portrait of Dr. Cochran used as the frontispiece of this book.

There are many defects in the presentation of Alabama's medical history. One major flaw is that Dr. Howard Holley's *History of Medicine in Alabama* went out of print before I could obtain a copy. I am deeply in debt to Dr. Sue Walker of Mobile, the 1994 recipient of the William Crawford Gorgas Award of the Medical Association of the State of Alabama. She gave me her copy.

It takes only a brief visit to Mobile to understand why Dr. Cochran decided to live there after the war —the people are so friendly and helpful. One person particularly embodies those qualities of friendship, generosity and helpfulness — Dr. Samuel Eichold of the *Eichold—Heustis Medical Museum of the South.* He gave me a copy of Dr. Cochran's Valedictory Address to the Mobile Medical Society, *written in his own handwriting* — a unique document. (See Appendix)

Mrs. Mary E. Dodd, Dr. Eichold's secretary, was kind enough to show me the Museum and the old Medical School building. Another lovely lady who helped us is Ms. Elisa Baldwin, the Archivist at the University of South Alabama School of Medicine. Ms. Baldwin supplied us with the photographs of the old Medical School and the portraits of Dr. Cochran's Mobile friends.

We wanted portraits of Drs. Peter Bryce and James T. Searcy. These gentlemen were close friends of Dr. Cochran. Dr. Bryce taught Cochran psychiatry (and general humanity) when he first came to Alabama. Dr. Searcy gave the first Jerome Cochran Lecture. When we found that our supposed source of these illustrations was not forthcoming, we called the librarian at Bryce Hospital and talked to Ms. Kathy Fetters, the librarian. She promptly sent us a color transparency of Dr. Peter Bryce.

To Dr. Bill Weaver, Chairman of the Publication Subcommittee of the Reynolds Library Associates, we wish to express our thanks for his meticulous examination of a portion of an earlier version of this manuscript, and then our complete manuscript.

PROLOGUE

This story shall the good man teach his son;
And Crispin Crispian shall ne'er go by
From this day to the ending of the world,
But we in it shall be remembered,—
We few, we happy few, we band of brothers.
Shakespeare, *King Henry the Fifth*, Act iv, Scene III

Monday, April 13, 1874

Montgomery: The Annual meeting of the Medical Association of the State of Alabama

It was a sober Jerome Cochran, M.D., Senior Censor, delivering the first annual report of the Board of Censors of the Medical Association of the State of Alabama,[1] who began his address:

"If we look around us, we find at work everywhere in our unfortunate country, the agents of disorganization and destruction.[2] Widespread and paralyzing demoralization pervades all the ranks and classes of our social and political communities.[3] The peculiar civilization which was slowly taking definite shape amongst us, has been broken into fragments by the tremendous revolution through which we have passed; and whether we will it or not, it devolves upon us, out of these fragments, to build up another civilization for

---

[1]Jerome Cochran, "Annual report of the Board of Censors of the Medical Association of the State of Alabama," *Transactions of the MASA,* April 13-15, 1874, pp. 2-22.

[2]The Carpetbaggers.

[3]Reconstruction following the Civil War.

the times in which we ourselves live, and for the future which is to come after us. Whether we build wisely and well, or whether our work shall prove to be far otherwise than laudable and beneficent, depends very much upon ourselves. It is true that many duties and obligations press upon us; and that the burden is hard to be borne. But shall we for this reason lose heart and hope, and lie down by the road-side to perish like dumb-driven cattle, in ignominious apathy and despair? Nay, verily. We are men, and we will bear ourselves like men with manly courage and magnanimity. To fold our hands passively and take things as they come -- this is not our mission; but to shape events for ourselves and to compel circumstances to pursue such course as we may believe to be wisest and best."

Full of conviction, passion, dedication, Cochran tried to motivate the members of the Association. But he was really saying these things to himself. He recognized that most of the doctors gathered at Selma were looking to him to make the Association, under its newly installed Constitution and Bylaws, work. He also recognized that some actually hoped it would fail, and they could go back to the old irresponsible organization.

He reminded the assembled Association that their ranks were riddled with incompetent men. As far as Cochran was concerned, one of the missions of the Association was to rid itself of these incompetents. He believed this could be accomplished by constructing out of the "...scattered members a powerful organization, and through this organization to secure concert of action and the prevalence of wise and prudent counsels."

He recalled to those assembled that "We have just adopted a new constitution[4]. Many of its provisions seem strange to many. Whether it has been in all things wisely planned or not, time will show. For the present, both good faith and good policy demand that we shall all give it an earnest and loyal support....If it fails, it adds only one more to the sum of the failures we have already to lament. If it succeeds, no monuments of marble in our public places -- no

---

[4]Jerome Cochran authored the Constitution and Bylaws.

monuments of affection in our hearts -- can ever adequately express our obligations to those who have originated and carried it into execution. Without pretending to forecast the result, we take leave to press upon the Association the importance of having the experiment fairly made."

During the meeting, the challenge Cochran put forth not only covered the call to professionalize the Medical Association. He also brought to the floor another project in which he fully believed. In the annual session of 1872 in Huntsville, he had submitted a plan for a general system of Boards of Health for Alabama. The plan had been discussed and endorsed. In 1873, at the annual session in Tuscaloosa, the plan was endorsed by the unanimous vote of the Association.

In addressing the issue of public health, he stated:

"A bill has been prepared, embracing the details of this plan [for state and county boards of health,] and was presented to the General Assembly of the State during its last session. It was received with a considerable amount of favor; but for reasons not necessary to be explained, it was never voted on. We believe that this bill, if its provisions should be adopted, is calculated to be of great service to the State, and to the prosperity and influence of this Association. It is therefore presented here in full."[5]

Finally, he presented the third of his great proposals. He had also prepared a bill on a subject "... that is of great importance to the Medical Profession and to the welfare of the people of the State...the regulation of the practice of Medicine so as to secure the just rights of the regular Profession, and restrict the various systems of quackery and irregular medicine within the narrowest possible limits. With this object in view, we [the Board of Censors: Drs. Cochran, Richard Fraser Michel, and George Ernest Kumpe] have prepared the draft of a bill which we submit for the consideration of

---

[5]See Appendix #1, Document A. An Act to establish Boards of Health in the State of Alabama.

the Association. We suggest that it will be best for this bill to lay over until the next meeting of the Association, before it is taken up for discussion. The subject is one of great difficulty, and no decided measures should be taken in regard to it without mature deliberation."[6]

As Senior Censor, he continued the meeting. He reported on formal relations between the MASA and the County Societies. [See Chapter 9.]

The Senior Censor had been delegated to address a circular letter to all who were eligible for permanent membership under the old Constitution explaining the conditions upon which they may become Counsellors under the new Constitution. Cochran then produced a list of names of those who were to be the first House of Counsellors of THE MEDICAL ASSOCIATION OF THE STATE OF ALABAMA.[7]

After the report of the Board of Censors, certain reports on diseases were heard of which Cochran's old friend and teacher, Dr. Peter Bryce of Tuscaloosa, read a report "On State Patronage of Asylums and Hospitals."

Cochran said he thought the Association was under obligations to the reporter [Dr. Bryce] for the thoughtful and carefully prepared report just read. He spoke upon the feature of the report advanced by the essayist -- that of a State Medical School -- and offered the following resolution, which was subsequently adopted by the Association:

"Moved, That Dr. P. Bryce be appointed to prepare, for the consideration of this Association at its next annual session, in the form of a bill for presentation to some subsequent meeting of the General Assembly of the State, a systematic statement of the plan in relation to a State Medical College, and a higher standard of

---

[6]See Appendix #1, Document B. An Act to Regulate the Practice of Medicine in the State of Alabama

[7]See Appendix #1, Report of the Senior Censor on the Roll of Counsellors.

acquirements as a prerequisite to the degree of Doctor of Medicine, and the right to practice medicine in this State."

At 42, Jerome Cochran was tired. He was not well. He had taken on himself a Herculean task, and he prayed to God for strength to carry that task to completion. In his heart he was quite aware there was probably no one who could carry it on if he should fail. The first phase had been accomplished; but Cochran knew this was not enough. The remainder of his program was crucial. Would legitimate medicine survive to foster reason, encourage research, and protect the citizens of the state? Or would the legitimate practice of medicine decline to the level of quackery?

Who was this man who was attempting to revise and improve medical education; improve the quality of medical practice and its practitioners by making them show their competence on examinations given by practitioners who had proved their own competence; create a health department that would protect the citizens of the state by bringing all the legitimate practitioners into its fold?

Who was this man who was attempting to wrest authority away from politicians and give it to the professionals to whom it belonged? Who was this man who was attempting something that had never before been attempted, and, in the process, challenging his fellow physicians to lend their expertise and strength to the task?

Chapter 1

Birth and Early Life[1]

Jerome Cochran, like many of his southern neighbors, was a product of the hardy people who had long inhabited the areas of northern Ireland and the southwest coast of Scotland.[2] Although lacking their physical fierceness, Cochran's personality and career did reflect the influence of his sturdy, opinionated, and stubborn ancestors.

According to Cochran family tradition, two brothers came to the new world before the Revolutionary War and settled, one in Pennsylvania, the other in Virginia. The Virginia family grew rapidly in number and spread over many counties of the Old Dominion and into the states of Georgia, Alabama, Mississippi, and Texas.[3]

Cochran's grandfather, William, was born in Virginia in 1774, but moved later to Georgia where he purchased 200 acres of land on the Little River in Oglethorpe County in the northeast section east of Athens. William and his wife, Betsy, later migrated from

---

[1]*Genealogy of the Cochran Families of Marshall County, Mississippi*, by Mary Owen Sapp Gregg., *See* Appendix 2

[2]"Doctor Jerome Cochran of Alabama," *Representative Men of the South, Memorial Record of Alabama*, Vol. I, Chas. Robson & Co. , 1880, Philadelphia, PA, p.649.

[3]*Ibid.*

Georgia to Jefferson County in Alabama,[4] and in Alabama there is evidence that they owned a few slaves. In Fayette County, Tennessee, there is recorded a bill of sale in which a slave is sold to "Daniel Johnson by William Cockram[sic][5] of the State of Alabama, Jefferson County."

By January 23, 1827, they finally settled in Fayette County, Tennessee, 30 miles east of Memphis, There is a deed recorded on that date where William Cockran bought 500 acres of land from John Wallin, it being part of a former grant to Thomas and Robert King. At William Cochran's death in 1828, a portion of his holdings in Fayette County were inherited by one of his sons, Augustus Owen Cochran.

Jerome H. Cochran was born in Moscow, Fayette County, Tennessee on December 4, 1831, the second child, and the first male child of Augustus Owen and Frances (Bailey) Cochran. His birth must have been bittersweet since only four months earlier the Cochrans had buried their first born child, 18 month old daughter Elizabeth Owen. Jerome, gray-eyed, possibly fretful, was frail and sickly. Moscow, lying between two branches of the Wolf River as it does, with standing water and swamp land, may have been an unhealthy place to live. The children may have been unduly exposed to infectious disease brought in by travellers to the hotel, owned by Jerome's uncle Owen Cochran, six years his father's senior.[6]

Jerome's family lived in Moscow until he was four years old. The 1836 tax list for Fayette County, published in *Ansearchin*

---

[4]Birmingham was not incorporated until 1871, but Alabama achieved statehood in 1819.

[5]Many misspellings are noted in the records of the time.

[6]William and Elizabeth (Betsy) Owen Cochran named their firstborn son Owen J. (1799) and their fourth child Augustus Owen (1805).

News, shows that Augustine O. was taxed on one slave and "1 lot.[7]
Although the Cochrans had been among the founding fathers of Moscow, Tennessee, Augustus Owen saw fairer fields twenty miles farther south in northern Mississippi on land that had been opened in 1832 for homesteading.

The era of the early 1800's in America was one of expansion. Many of the farms in the East had worn out due to too many soil-depleting tobacco crops, the lack of adequate fertilizing, and otherwise poor soil management. The eyes of the Atlantic Coast were turned to the West, and Mississippi was "the West." A mania of land speculation and a fever of adventure struck the country, and the westward rush was on.

At this time, northern Mississippi was a vast fertile expanse of virgin timber land, sparsely populated by Indians and scattered white settlers, with a few trading posts connected by Indian trails or "traces." Some historians claim that DeSoto marched through this area on the way to his death and burial in the "Father of Waters," the mighty stream that he, DeSoto, had been the first white man to view. Fortuitously, in the early 1830's, negotiations had been put through to persuade the Indians to sell their land in Mississippi, and the Chickasaw Cession of 1832 had procured for the white men this vast expanse of rich land in the state. The price of the land seemed high by standards of the day, and the Indians seemed happy with their new lands in Oklahoma.[8] The Indians were further compensated when they later reaped the benefits of the discovery of oil on their Oklahoma lands.

The territory included roughly the present Marshall County, together with most of Benton County, and part of DeSoto County. In 1836 the territory was divided into counties. Of these, Marshall was the largest. This is the year Augustus Owen and Frances (Bailey) Owen bought their land a few miles south of the Tennessee

---

[7]See Appendix #2. *Genealogy* by Mary Gregg.

[8]This was a legitimate buy and sell proposition and not part of the infamous *Trail of Tears.*

border.

This area and its activities deserve a thorough study because Jerome Cochran lived there for the next 25 of the formative years of his life.

Most of the people coming to Marshall County, Mississippi were from Virginia and North Carolina, bringing their institutions, mores, politics, and chattel with them. In the area, there was a beautiful ravine where holly trees abounded, surrounding a group of 30 or more springs, one of which was enormous, 30 feet wide and ten feet deep. It was the source of a clear, swiftly moving creek running to the southwest to empty into the Tallaloosa River.

In the mid-thirties, this site was chosen by a group of immigrants for the founding of a city. They named it Holly Springs, and the first street to be laid off was named Spring Street. The Square soon began to take shape. Due to the rabid land speculation, the first permanent brick building to be erected was a land office.

Holly Springs seems to have escaped the rowdiness and the sordid lawless side of a frontier settlement. When the people moved in, they set up schools and churches before they did anything else. In 1836, a year before the town was incorporated, there was a town meeting. The citizens proposed, financed, and organized an Academy. Over the years many institutions of learning have flourished in Holly Springs. The University of Mississippi began in Holly Springs and later moved to its present site on a campus with total lands amounting to 4,000 acres, near Oxford, Mississippi, just thirty miles due south of Holly Springs.

In February 1838 the Holly Springs and Mississippi Turnpike Co. was chartered to insure communications with the Mississippi River, thus making obtainable everything not made locally. The Mississippi River actually made Holly Springs a cosmopolitan city. There were already three newspapers in 1836. By 1839 there were Methodist, Baptist, Presbyterian, and Episcopal Churches, each one interested in establishing institutions of learning.

With their cavalier heritage, the young blades of Marshall County did not neglect the pleasures of the flesh. An early (1839) market report states, "the stock of whiskey is fair and demand good," at 50 to 60 cents a gallon.   Local sportsmen built a race track and ran big races in the fall and spring. In 1839 the Holly Springs Race Course changed hands. The new managers renamed it the North Mississippi Jockey Club. Horses were sent for the races from as far away as Kentucky. Local thespians organized a very active dramatic club which they aptly named the "Thespians." Traveling troupes of actors, as well as evangelistic preachers, added to the town's entertainment and enlightenment. Itinerate tradesmen and artists made frequent stops in the town, staying over at the Marshall Inn. In 1842 there was a learned society called the Holly Springs Lyceum.   The Holly Springs Debating Society was functioning in 1843 and proposed a library for the town. Eight years after its incorporation and ten years after the first building was erected, its population was almost 2,000 people. There was the Washington Temperance League, a ten-pin alley, and several gambling houses, six churches, four schools, with another under construction, and a Masonic Hall.

There were fourteen dry goods stores, with Parisian fashions, two shoe stores, with boots from England, and eight produce stores, featuring such delicacies as oranges and bananas from the tropics. There were two taverns, two drug stores, and a full complement of service establishments, including nine doctors' offices, two gunsmiths' shops, and a large cast-iron foundry.[9]

At 15 cents a pound, cotton was king in Mississippi. Thanks to the fertile soil, Marshall County growers cleaned and sold more cotton than did any other Mississippi county.

Augustus Owen Cochran had his work cut out to turn virgin forest into land suitable for growing cotton. His family grew. Frances, his wife, and two sons, Jerome and William Lewis (born January 11, 1834 in Moscow, Tennessee) settled in. The Cochrans

---

[9]During the Civil War, many cities like Huntsville, Alabama, fell silent when all their church bells were dismounted and sent to the Holly Springs foundry to be cast into cannon for the Confederate Army.

still mourned their first born child, Elizabeth.[10] Other children were born to them: Augustus Owen, born March 19, 1838 but died August 17, 1841; Mary Susan, born March 13, 1840; Augustus Owen born November 11, 1842; Lynch Bailey born February 13, 1846. Eugene, and Ann Florence, twins, were born June 15, 1848, but the twins died in 1878 of yellow fever. The last child, James Virgil, was born October 28, 1851.

As the family grew, Jerome continued to be sickly and frail. He probably had recurrent streptococcus infection of his upper respiratory tract. In 1844, at the age of 12, he was old enough to go into the fields with a hoe and help the Negroes with the cotton crop. On the farms, all hands were needed to ensure the success of crops. Chopping cotton in all kinds of weather, he soon began to grow more robust and to thrive. He was then able to take his turn in the fields with the men reclaiming the soil from the forests, plowing, and making crops.

"Breaking up the new ground," as it was called, was back-breaking work. Virgin pines, one hundred feet tall and five feet in diameter, had to be felled by axe and cross-cut saws, all by hand. Then the stumps and the roots and fragments had to be wrenched out by teams of mules and horses -- two to four to a team.[11] Only then could the land be plowed and cultivated, and the crops -- food as well as cotton -- planted.

The site preparation could be done in the late winter and early spring, if it were not too wet. In the early summer the younger children were equipped with hoes and shown how to chop out the less desirable cotton plants in a hill, so that the better plants did not

---

[10]This information was given by S. Vadah Cochran (1918-1995) the great grandson of Jerome's Uncle, Clark Thomas Cochran, five years the junior of Jerome's father. *See* Appendix #3.

[11]Dynamite is used for that purpose today, but Alfred Bernhard Nobel did not begin to produce that substance until 1866.

have to compete with them. Chopping cotton is also backbreaking, hot, sweaty work. In the blistering heat of later summer the crops were laid by, painstakingly picked by hand, then cleaned, using cotton gins.[12]

For the most part, country children experienced little of the wider world. On farms, the only "free time" was on Sunday after church, and after the crops had been laid by. Jerome was reared a Methodist and probably attended church every Sunday with his family, only then seeing something of Holly Springs. One can imagine the shy, reserved Jerome, with an insatiable curiosity, hanging back and taking in all the sights.

When he was old enough, after summer's work was ended, Jerome attended the old field school in his area. When he started school, Jerome immediately became fascinated with learning. He read everything he could get his hands on. His formal schooling was brief, and he apparently did not receive the equivalent of a high school education.

He taught himself, and no person ever had a more demanding or better disciplined or more thorough teacher, and no teacher ever had a more diligent student. Jerome had a "natural indifference to the usual amusements and distraction of youth"... "a very tenacious memory"..."his faculty of acquisition so phenomenal as to excite the surprise of all who knew him." Over the years, he taught himself extensive courses in logic, general science, philosophy, and especially biology, poetry, literature, modern languages, and mathematics.[13] We do not know when Holly Springs got its library, but we are certain that, with it and the several academies and schools in Holly Springs, there were plenty of current books available to Jerome. Even when school was out and he was working long hours beside his father's field hands by day, Jerome continued to read until late into the night or early morning.

---

[12]The Cotton gin was invented by Eli Whitney of Georgia in 1793.

[13]"Dr. Jerome Cochran of Alabama," *Op. cit.,* p 650.

Some mornings the breakfast bell would find him reading or pondering over some puzzling problem.[14]

Jerome Cochran was one of the most learned young men in Marshall County when in 1850, in the nineteenth year of his life (age 18), he left home and became a country school master. He had worked hard on his father's farm. He had survived his childhood illnesses and had gained a certain strength of body and mind, but he was never to be free from debilitating ailments. He left at home his brothers and sisters, ranging in age from 16 to 2. His youngest brother would not be born until October 28, 1851.

This same year, he, who had been reared a Methodist, met a Universalist minister whose preaching made Jerome, with his independent thinking, begin an extensive investigation of all religions that was to last for almost 10 years.

Jerome must have attended the cultural affairs of Holly Springs such as the Debating Club's performances, the Thespians dramatizations, various musical recitals, and the itinerant performers. He must have attended some of the political rallies where he became acquainted with the local and state politicians, their ways and their wiles. He certainly had the opportunities at that time and place. His later life reflected his early polish and his deep knowledge as evidenced by his ability to get legislation passed.

There seems to be abundant evidence that not only a man's mood, disposition, and temperament, but also his opinions, behavior, and even his psychic and moral life are influenced by his physical health. In various endeavors, one may find instances illustrating the influence of physical debility upon the life and character of the individual; and the remarkable thing is, instead of leading to disaster, illness seems often to have benefitted rather than hindered the individual. In Jerome Cochran's case, it seems that because of delicate physical health he turned to the cultivation of the mind. One school of psychology might explain Cochran's genius as an overcompensation for an inferiority complex.

---

[14] *Ibid.*, p. 2.

Jerome enjoyed teaching. It did not pay much, but he was frugal and was able to get along well on his stipend. He even had money to buy books which he used for study. He taught school for six years and made a name for himself as an erudite scholar.

In 1855, at the age of 23, Jerome met Mrs. Sarah Jane Johnson, widow, daughter of Mr. Jared Collins, a wealthy planter of DeSoto County, the county adjacent to Marshall County on the West, and lying on the banks of the Mississippi River. DeSoto County also joined the city limits of Memphis, Tennessee. For Jerome and Sarah Jane, it must have been mutual love at first sight. After a whirlwind courtship, they were married on May 9, 1855. This was Sarah Jane's second marriage. She had married Lewis Johnson on January 3, 1852.[15] Lewis died, date unknown, before she met Jerome.[16]

That same year, 1855, Jerome met Dr. Robert H. Harrison, Professor of Materia Medica and Therapeutics at the Botanic Medical College, Memphis Tennessee. The professor was impressed by Jerome's grasp of the sciences, by his deep understanding of various concepts, and his adeptness at problem solving. Dr. Harrison induced Jerome to enter the study of medicine at his school in Memphis, Tennessee, only thirty-five miles away.

Because he had assumed the new responsibilities of marriage and the prospects of rearing a family -- their first child was due in February of 1856 -- Jerome matriculated in the Memphis Botanic Medical College hoping that the additional education would improve his income. After two courses of lectures -- each lasting six months -- at the Botanic Medical College, Jerome was awarded the M.D. degree in 1857.

It is amazing that although he entered the medical school

---

[15]This information is found in the registry of marriages of DeSoto County, Mississippi.

[16]This assumed. Lewis is not heard from again. Sarah Jane, a Catholic, could not have been buried in a Catholic Cemetery if Lewis had been alive at the time of her marriage to Jerome Cochran.

without any preliminary training -- and with not even a high school diploma -- he graduated number one in his class and was the class valedictorian. It is also incredible that, in his valedictory address, he condemned the botanic system of medical instruction as being untenable in certain areas! Opinionated and self-confident even then, Jerome pulled no punches.

A daughter, Augustine Schamyl, Jerome and Sarah Jane's first child, was born on January 25, 1856, in the midst of Jerome's medical education. Cochran returned to Holly Springs, and he and Sarah Jane settled down in a little white clapboard house with green shutters.[17]

For two years, while Sarah Jane busied herself mothering and planting shrubbery -- especially roses, that she loved so well -- and perhaps, keeping Jerome's books as was the custom of many physicians' wives at the time Jerome practiced medicine. He continued his quest for knowledge, reading medical papers from all over the world. Although he became eminently successful, he grew more and more dissatisfied with his medical training.

At last he could stand it no longer. In 1859, at the age of 27, and with another child on the way, Jerome closed his office and returned to the institutional study of medicine. This time he entered the medical department of the University of Nashville, Tennessee. Here, his diploma from Memphis amounted to less than nothing, but Dr. W. M. Bowling, Professor of Theory and Practice of Medicine, recognized Jerome's genius, and through his influence, Jerome obtained the position of Resident Student in the Hospital of the State of Tennessee.

While at the University of Nashville, Jerome met Dr. Paul Fitzsimons Eve, who performed the first hysterectomy in America, and who had written nearly 600 articles for medical journals. Eve was the first to see the need for a national medical organization.

In 1835, Eve had made a valiant attempt to organize a national

---

[17]Although no longer standing, this house was remembered by a relative, Mr. S. Vadah Cochran.

medical society, hoping that his efforts would be supported by the Philadelphia group. That support was not forthcoming. However the American Medical Association was finally created in 1847 under the leadership of the New York Medical Society. Eve was president of the American Medical Association during the year 1857-1858, the year before Jerome met him. It is he who may have given Jerome his first insight into the proper function of a medical society.

Again in the midst of his medical education, his second child, another daughter, Louisa Ina (nicknamed Ina Lou) was born on January 25, 1860 in Holly Springs. After two winter courses of lectures and one summer course, Dr. Cochran received his second M.D. degree in February of 1861. Here again he was number one in the class, and was elected valedictorian. This class, numbering 154 members, was the largest yet to graduate in the South. The other southern medical schools were also graduating large classes, and good new medical schools, such as the University of Alabama College of Medicine at Mobile, were opening. The South was becoming more and more aware of science and technology. Many educational leaders in the South, like Dr. Josiah Clark Nott of Mobile, were foreseeing a golden age of medicine and the resulting civilization in the South. But the golden age was to be runnelled by scarlet slashes of the blood of civil war.

Peter Bryce, M.D., 1834-1892
—Courtesy of Bryce Hospital,
Tuscaloosa, Alabama

Chapter II

The War Years

-1861-

On April 12, General Pierre Gustaf Toutant Beauregard gave the order to fire, and the guns of Fort Moultry and the Coastal Artillery batteries of Charleston harbor commenced firing on the Union forces in Fort Sumter. The fort soon surrendered. The War Between the States, America's tragic "Iliad," had begun.

Dr. Jerome Cochran had resumed his medical practice in Holly Springs just two months prior to the war's beginning. Dismayed, having to support his family, and naturally wanting to spend time with his wife and two children, he was reluctant to leave for service. In May, Holly Springs formed the Washington Guards for home protection. He volunteered as their surgeon,[1] and kept up his practice. On May 27, however, his 18 year-old brother Augustus Owen enlisted in Corinth. The war moved west in late 1861. News of the war in the East traveled quickly to Holly Springs. Late in 1861, it was evident that the Union army, known as the

____

[1] *Military Annals of Mississippi*, Compiled by J.C. Rietti, of 10th Regiment, Jackson, Mississippi, Washington Guards, Organized at Holly Springs, Mississippi, May 10, 1861, for home protection...Jerome Cochran, Surgeon,

Federal army, was advancing down the Mississsippi River. They also advanced down the Cumberland River past Nashville toward the Mississippi. It was evident that Mississippi would soon be attacked. Dr. Cochran quickly went to join his brother. He entered the army as a contract physician, paid, but without rank.

-1862-

Talk had it that if Fort Henry on the Tennessee River and Fort Donelson on the Cumberland River fell, the Union army would soon come up the Tennessee River toward southern Tennessee and northern Mississippi. Corinth, Mississippi, a major railroad center 20 miles as the crow flies south of Pittsburg Landing, Tennessee would be a most likely target. Corinth lay at the crossroads of the Memphis and Charleston and the Mobile and Ohio railroads. The commanding general of the Confederate forces, Albert Sidney Johnston, had hurried to Corinth to build a force to defend the area.

Cochran helped the troops there while they were staging for the imminent battle of Pittsburg Landing (to be later known as the Battle of Shiloh, for a church that stood in the battlefield.) He found the troops highly motivated. They were cheerful and confident, eager for the fight which they believed would be a lark. General Johnston was a model leader, pleasant, exuding confidence, perhaps a bit too gallant.

April brought torrential rains to the whole area, which muddied fields and made life, in general, miserable.[2] At dawn on April 6, Johnston attacked the Federals camped at Shiloh. The Union army suffered massive losses (10,000 total in two days).[3] At one of the

---

[2]Kate Cumming, *A Journal of the Hospital Life in the Confederate Army of Tennessee*, John P. Morton Co., Louisville, KY, 1866, p. 9.

[3]H.H. Cunningham, *Doctors in Gray: The Confederate Medical Service*, Peter Smith, Gloucester, MA, 1970.

many large buildings, all taken for hospitals in Corinth,[4] Cochran, one of the many surgeons in the area, received both Confederate soldiers and Union prisoners. [5]

On April 7, Grant's army, now joined with that of Don C. Buell, forced the Confederate army to begin a withdrawal to Corinth.

Over the next two months, as the Federals continued to advance, Confederate reinforcements poured into Corinth from all over the South. Among these was a Dr. Anderson of Mobile, arriving April 10 or 11.[6]

Amidst mounting horror, surgeons fought diminishing supplies, soldiers' anguish, and personal exhaustion in trying to save men's lives from wounds of battle and increasingly rampant disease.

Jerome witnessed a horrible difference in the troops coming from Shiloh from those who had gone into the battle. He desperately tried to deal with bandaged arm and leg stumps that were bloody and foul smelling. Amputated arms and legs lay about the hospital yard. Provision had not been made for the disposal of human excrement. He had to leave to the care of nurses, patients with abdominal wounds filled with their own feces, as they awaited slow but certain death. The smell of erysipelas and scarlet fever and the less than "laudable pus" from the pyemias offended his nostrils and those of the most seasoned veteran. Then there was the enigma of gangrene. He was confronted by every surgical catastrophe imaginable. Cochran and the other surgeons worked night and day, usually with very little rest for themselves.[7] A number of injuries included scrotal wounds. . . the end of young mens' dreams for the girl back home.

As a contract physician, Cochran went where needed. In

---

[4]Kate Cumming, *op.cit.*,p.9

[5]*Ibid.* p. 12

[6]*Ibid. p. 12*

[7]*Ibid.* p. 18, 31.

probable anguish, he commended his brother's safety to God, and traveled 70 miles due south by rail with a trainload of wounded, both Confederate and Federal, to the hospital at Okalona.[8] It is not known when he sent for his family, or if he actually managed to take them with him.

Okalona boasted a large general hospital. The hospital had made hasty additions by building many well-constructed sheds that could each house 15-20 wounded.[9] Thus expanded to approximately three thousand beds, it was the largest Confederate hospital outside of Richmond, Virginia. It became the principal treatment center for the Confederate casualties in the West.

At that time, he requested the commission of Surgeon in the army, as he had his family to provide for. A Surgeon was afforded the rank of Major and a pay range of $1,944 -$2,400 per year. He was recommended for that position by the Board of Medical Examiners stationed at Mobile. In response to this application, the Surgeon General of the Confederate Army, Dr. Samuel Preston Moore, sent him the commission of Assistant Surgeon -- a rank of Captain with a pay range of $1,320 - $1,800 per year.[10]

Perhaps his Scottish heritage with its stubborn, opinionated fierceness came to the fore. Perhaps he knew himself to be more capable than the lower rank of Captain. Or he may have simply been insulted at what he could assume was a slight; because Cochran declined the commission of Assistant Surgeon. He instead remained as a contract physician. The requested commission to the full rank of Surgeon was promptly returned to him.[11]

---

[8]"Doctor Jerome Cochran of Alabama," *Op. cit.* p. 4.

[9]*Ibid,* p. 31

[10]Annual salaries calculated on the basis of monthly salary rates listed in H.H. Cunningham,*op. cit.*, p.22.

[11]"Dr. Jerome Cochran of Alabama," *op. cit.* p.4.

Soon the infectious diseases began ravaging the weakened, wounded warriors. Measles became a virulent killer. Typhoid fever became epidemic. Malarial fever began to exacerbate. Typhus moved in. Sniffles became pneumonia. Cochran and the others, already tired, now had to prevent the spread of these diseases to the townspeople.

During this time, little Holly Springs was plagued by raids from both armies. The Yankees would come in and rob and steal. Then, of course, the Rebs would have to come in and chase them out. The Rebs would requisition horses, grain, food, etc., and pay with Confederate money. The people suffered at the hands of their enemies and their saviors alike. Jerome was thankful he had his wife and girls with him, and prayed constantly for the safety of the rest of his family.

The account of Confederate General Earle Van Dorn's raid on Holly Springs in late 1862, as told by J.G. Deupree, First Miss. Cavalry, C.S.A., sometime Professor of Pedagogy, University of Mississippi, is a classic.[12]

Dr. Cochran remained on duty at Okalona until after the Union Troops had taken Corinth in a second battle late in 1862. After this, the large hospital at Okolona was dismantled and its materials and personnel were shipped over 100 miles further south to Meridian, and to Marion Station, a small railroad town five miles north of Meridian. He brought his family and remained stationed at a hospital in Marion Station.

-1863-

Early that summer, Cochran was in a railroad accident. He jumped from a train that was derailing, badly contusing his ankles. This necessitated a prolonged use of crutches. However, he

---

[12]"Confederate General Earle Van Dorn'a raid on Holly Springs in 1862" As told by J.G. Deupree, First MS Cavalry, C.S.A., *Holly Springs Mississippi to the Year 1878,* William Baskerville Hamilton,The Marshall County Historical Society, Publisher, Holly Springs Mississippi, pp. 35-40.

continued to work, even on crutches.[13]

Sherman, who had succeeded Grant (who had been called to Washington to become the overall commander of the Union Forces), advanced on Meridian after the fall of Vicksburg, July 4. As Sherman approached, all haste was made to dismantle the hospitals and ship them and their equipment to safer areas. Most of the doctors left with wounded on early trains. Still on crutches, Cochran remained at his post and supervised loading the precious medical and surgical supplies until the last car was loaded and attached to the last engine. He had no idea where he would be stationed, or under what conditions. He was forced to leave his family in the relative safety of Marion Station. Besides, Sarah Jane was pregnant again. He gave the order to pull out and climbed aboard. At 9:00 P.M. on Saturday night, he passed through Meridian. Sherman marched into that city at about 7:00 A.M. Sunday morning. Dr. Cochran had saved the Confederacy thousands of dollars worth of equipment.[14]

When Jerome Cochran entered military service in 1861, troops were fresh and healthy. By the time he went on duty at Okolona Hospital in 1862, medical and hygienic conditions were at their lowest possible level. By the time of "First Corinthians," as the first battle for Corinth was called, twenty thousand men in General Beauregard's army were hospitalized and several thousand more, though answering roll call, were really unfit for duty. Conditions were not much better in the Union Army. Causes of disease were numerous and complex: fatigue and continuous exposure to the unpredictable elements; bad and insufficient food, salt meat, lack of fresh fruit and vegetables; ragged and unlaundered clothing, lack of personal cleanliness; poor shelter with crowding and lack of ventilation; and infected tents, hospitals and camps. Troops were

---

[13]"Doctor Jerome Cochran of Alabama," *op. cit.* p. 5.

[14]Ibid., p.5.

inducted without proper examinations and many were already sick upon entering the camps. In 1863, a directive stated: "When a conscript is found equal to, or in the performance of the active duties of the various occupations of civil life, he is able to discharge the duties of a soldier." Some of the troops would have come down with illness anyway, but a "bad cold" in a warm home quickly became pneumonia in a man sleeping on wet ground with the atmospheric temperature hovering around the freezing point.

[The conscription act of 1864 requiring military service of all men between the ages of 17 and 50, brought into the service many men who were too old to be of much real value. It soon became apparent that men over 40 could not easily make the transition from civilian to soldier without suffering increased incidence of disease.][15]

It came as a surprise that city boys adapted faster to military camp life than did their country cousins. Dr. Paul Fitzsimons Eve stated, "at the organization of the army, one town regiment was more efficient than two or even three from the country." Many of the country boys had never been vaccinated against smallpox, and had not had the infantile diseases so prevalent in camp. Most enlisted men had no idea of personal hygiene. Some men went for six months at a time without taking a bath. Officers were better about their personal hygiene than were the enlisted men, and they suffered less from disease. Regimental surgeons were responsible for camp sanitation, which included learning about diseases common to the locality and the means of combatting them, insisting on strict personal cleanliness, seeing that the water was pure, seeing that premises were policed, offal burned or buried away from camp, and policing the grounds where animals were kept.[16]

When Jerome Cochran departed on the last train out of Meridian, Mississippi, he took with him about $100,000 worth of medicines

---

[15]H. H. Cunningham, *op, cit.*, pp. 163-65.

[16]*Ibid.* pp. 166-181.

and equipment. These were the remnants of a hospital that he had made quite clean and efficient. These medicines had become very scarce due to the tightening of the Federal naval blockade. The matériel was routed through Mobile, Alabama to the medical purveyor at Montgomery, and Cochran was ordered to set up a military hospital in Tuscaloosa.

He rented the Indian Queen Hotel. This old hotel was the most nearly adequate building. He had it refurbished and cleaned up and made ready for occupancy. At this point he was ordered to turn the project over to Dr. R. N. Anderson. Cochran was ordered to Gainesville, Alabama in the capacity of Surgeon of that post.

Righteously indignant, and with nerves frayed by his recent travails and by the turn the war was taking, he wrote an exceedingly critical letter to the Medical Director of the department, Dr. Preston B. Scott of Louisville. This display of temper led to his being detailed for the examination of conscripts in north Alabama. As the ranking medical officer, he was President of the Board, and although he made his headquarters in Tuscaloosa, his field of duty extended over Tuscaloosa, Fayette, Jefferson, Marion, Blount, and Walker Counties.[17]

Records show that on November 9, in Marion Station, Mississippi, Sarah Jane gave birth to their first son. We do not know whether Cochran was able to attend the birth. Probably not. They named their son Jerome Bowling (for Cochran's mentor at the University of Nashville's College of Medicine). As soon as she was able to travel, she and the children joined Jerome in Tuscaloosa.

Dr. Cochran was notified that his brother, Augustus Owen, had been captured at Knoxville, Tennessee on November 29 and taken to Louisville, Kentucky, then to Rock Island, Illinois.[18] Imagine his dread, then his feeling of helplessness at being unable to aid Augustus.

---

[17]"Doctor Jerome Cochran of Alabama"*op.cit.*, pp. 5-6.

[18]*See* Appendix #2 *Genealogy* by Mary Gregg.

-1864-

Dr. Cochran, his wife, Sarah Jane, and the children, 8 year old Augustine, 4 year old Ina Lou, and 2 month old Jerome Bowling, were to remain in Tuscaloosa until a year after the war ended. During the hostilities, Cochran became interested in the study of mental diseases at the State Insane Hospital. He had met Dr. Peter Bryce, the hospital's superintendent and a man ahead of his time in the humane treatment of the insane. The two became fast friends for life.[19]

The influence this man's methods had on Cochran prompt a brief biographical sketch of Dr. Bryce.

Peter Bryce was born in Columbia, South Carolina in 1834. He graduated from the Medical College of the University of New York in 1859 and served as assistant physician at the Hospital for the Insane of New Jersey and the State Hospital for the Insane at Columbia, South Carolina. He visited the hospitals for the insane in Europe and was recommended by Miss Dorothea Dix, the great apostle of care for the insane. Miss Dix had visited Alabama on two occasions and urged the founding of the State Hospital for the Insane. In offering Dr. Bryce the position of superintendent of the institution, the board of directors specified that he must be married. With the position and its assured income of $2,000 annually plus rent and household expenses Dr. Bryce needed to wait no longer. He brought his bride, the former Marie Ellen Clarkson of Columbia, South Carolina, and the two commenced an administration that was to shed great luster on that institution and considerable credit on the Bryces, husband and wife.

The Bryces never had any children. All the patients in the hospital were their brood. Mrs. Bryce was a talented and well educated woman. She devoted her life to the aid and care of the hospital patients. She exerted a profound effect on the lives of the patients of the hospital, giving musical programs and providing

---

[19]"Doctor Jerome Cochran of Alabama," *Op. cit.*, p. 6.

entertainment, as well as conducting religious services. At a time when little was known about the mentally ill, thirty years before Sigmund Freud and Adolph Meyers, Peter Bryce advanced his own principles of management. These principles he insisted should be started as early as possible: 1) Tender loving care. 2) Occupational therapy and 3) Non-restraint. Dr. Bryce never departed from these three principles, and the great doctors who have succeeded him at that post have rigidly followed his precepts.[20]

Cochran very quickly saw the genius of Bryce. He saw not only the personal magnetism that brought about cures in its own right, but he quickly understood the organization of the great hospital. It was organized to bring about the greatest good for the greatest number of patients. They were categorized and segregated according to the best descriptive diagnoses he could give them. One group of patients had been called General Paralysis. Bryce renamed the condition "General Paresis." In 1861 it was not known that the condition was due to advanced Syphilis. Bryce was the most loving and the most friendly person one could encounter; however, there were a few things that he simply would not tolerate: discourteous treatment, impolite language to a patient, and failure to keep the patients clean, neatly dressed, and properly attended at all times. He devised a system of rules and regulations for the employees toward the patients. Nurses and employees who would not comply with his rules were subject to fines of not less than twenty five cents. To show how firmly he enforced these fines, the first year netted $500. These rules were kept in effect during the entire administrarion of Dr. Peter Bryce. He was outspoken in his views on alcoholism, tobacco and opium, anticipating the present views on the morbid and mortal effects of these poisons by seven score years. These views were later recorded in his annual reports on the Alabama Insane Hospital to the Medical Association of the State of Alabama.

---

[20]Howard L.Holley, *A History of Medicine in Alabama*, The University of Alabama Press, University of Alabama, 1982, pp. 313-320.

Cochran must have been in Tuscaloosa on the nights of April 3-4, 1864, when Brigadier General John T. Croxton of the Union Army led his 1500 mounted and heavily armed raiders into Tuscaloosa. Resisted by a handful of students and old men and women, Croxton, at the time when the war was as good as over, burned the University of Alabama with its excellent library. How the AIH escaped the fiery fate of the University, one will never know. It must have been a miracle or, most likely, an oversight on the part of Croxton. There were still books at AIH, and Jerome continued his studies with Dr. Bryce.

Also, during this time in Tuscaloosa, Cochran began again to give thought to religion. He had been reared in the Methodist Church as had all his family and friends, and until age eighteen, he never gave thought to any other persuasion. He naturally looked on the Protestant Reformation as one of the most glorious revolutions in the entire history of humankind and a giant step toward the liberation of the oppressed serfs of the feudal ages and a lifting of the suppression of truth, practiced by the medieval church. He never thought of the Roman Catholic Church as a force of evil. He simply did not think of it.

During the war, he had seen members of many religious denominations fatally ill or dying. Most of them seemed to die easier after they had made their peace with their God. Many times, Cochran probably recalled the Universalist Minister who showed that it was quite possible to say something in favor of a very different set of doctrines than those he held so firmly. Once aroused to the deep consideration of the true meaning of religion, and once free to give independent thought to the subject, he more than likely explored the whole of religious endeavors, their faiths and their obligations, to their very roots. Over ten years, he read everything he could find on the subject. Available were the standard works of some of the great Protestant writers. He read Rousseau, Voltaire, and the other great French free thinkers. He read the German Philosophers of the day, the humanists, and the English Divines. Finally he would have considered modern scientific materialism.

During the war, he became confused and drifted into a feeling of no belief of any kind. He was caught in a web of deep skepticism, in which he questioned, not only religion but also philosophy and ethics. He suffered as only a man of genius can. Saint Thomas of Aquinas seems to have given him some glimpses of metaphysical certitude.

Now that he seemed settled in Tuscaloosa, with the war going so badly, he renewed his search. Although the University of Alabama had been burned to the ground, there were still many good private libraries in Tuscaloosa, and Dr. Cochran was able to find books on Christian polemics. Slowly, in the months following the burning of the University library, the reasoning and the picture came into focus, and he returned to the realm of Christian ethics. After much consideration, he approached Father McConough, pastor of St. John the Baptist Catholic Church. Finding his answers, he took instructions. He joined the Roman Catholic Church and was baptized into that faith on September 14, 1864.[21] It seems remarkable to some people that Cochran was able to reconcile in his own mind his religious tenets with the facts of contemporary science, the philosophy of evolution, or Darwinism.[22] Today, since the Roman Catholic Church accepts some theories of evolution and, recently, has stated that the "big bang" is not incompatible with the Holy Scriptures,[23] it seems foolish to consider science and religion as incompatible. Certainly, the tremendous mind of Jerome Cochran was able to see through the puzzle.

---

[21]See Appendix #4, Copy of baptismal records from St. John the Baptist Catholic Church in Tuscaloosa, Alabama.

[22]"Doctor Jerome Cochran of Alabama," *op..cit.*, pp. 23-24.

[23] Stephen Hawking, *A brief History of Time,* A Bantam Book, April 1988, p. 46-47.

Jerome and Sarah Jane had Augustine and Jerome Bowling baptized on Christmas day. Ina Lou must have been ill for baptismal records show her baptism delayed until January 14, 1865.

-1865-

April 9, Lee surrendered to Grant at Appomattox.

April 14, Lincoln was assassinated.

May 4, Confederate forces in Alabama and Mississippi surrendered.

May 26, the last Confederate troops surrendered.

June 18, Augustus Owen was released from Rock Island prison. At the age of 22, he was said to be 5'9" tall, of dark complexion, with brown hair and blue eyes.[24] As we have no full description of Dr. Jerome Cochran, we can presume a family resemblance. We do know that he had "A large head, a thoughtful and somewhat saddened brow, a firm mouth, a quiet, dark gray eye, and a complexion rendered sallow by ill-health and sedentary habits, give ordinarily an air of stoical apathy to his well-formed, intellectual, and rather attractive face."[25] Of Sarah Jane and the children, we have no description, save that of Jerome Bowling's obituary, a picture which shows a remarkable resemblance to his father, beard and mustache included.[26]

Cochran had no reason to return to Marshall County, Mississippi, after the war. He was no longer a farmer, and the little city, Holly Springs, had been virtually wiped out during the war. Because of his change in church affiliation, he probably sought other people of similar religious views and perhaps this is the reason he moved to Mobile. Or perhaps the old family urge to seek new territory was upon him.

He moved his family to Mobile, Alabama and hung out his

---

[24] *Genealogy* by Mary Gregg

[25] "Doctor Jerome Cochran of Alabama," *op. cit.*, pp. 24-25.

[26] See appendix # II c, Obituary of Jerome Bowling Cochran.

shingle where his farsightedness and tenacity were to catapult him to the forefront of the medical profession.

Chapter III

Mobile — The Beginning

1865-1868

At age 33, Jerome and his little family arrived in Mobile in late June, 1865, probably without funds and few acquaintances. The city was much larger than any they had lived in previously. Undaunted, Cochran moved his family into the house on the corner of Main and Lawn Streets. He opened his office and hung out his shingle on the corner of Madison Avenue and Conception Street. [1] Here he awaited his first patient.

In a short span of time he built up a thriving and appreciative practice. He continued to practice successfully for the next five years, during which time he became ranked as one of the most successful practitioners in the State of Alabama.

Some of Cochran's case reports give insight into his practice and incidentally, his sense of humor,[2] and, as such, are worth quoting.

The first is a case of removal of an ovarian cyst. He describes

---

[1] Mobile County Directory.

[2] Jerome Cochran, "Supplementary Report on Ovariotomy, Haematocele and Vaginismus", *Transactions of MASA*, 1871, p 401.

his careful preoperative diagnosis, then his meticulous surgical technique and the ligation of each artery individually, using Sims' silver wire ligature.[3] Then he makes this statement:

"In the preparation and after-treatment of the case I ventured to depart from the ordinary course. I took as my guiding principle this: To disturb as little as possible the habital state and natural operation of my patient's system. Finding the bowels open every morning, I could not understand what advantage was to be gained from the customary purgatives, and therefore I omitted them. To be sure, however, that the bowels were well open, I ordered an enema a few hours before the operation. Neither could I understand why opium should be given after the operation, as a matter of course, or as prophylactic of troubles that might never make their appearance. Accordingly I determined not to give it unless symptoms should supervene clearly demanding it. No such symptoms being developed, she took no opium. "

Another of Cochran's early Mobile cases was a mulatto girl aged seventeen, named Frances, whom he began treating in the fall of 1865. She was afflicted with intermittent, painful hematuria. She had been treated with "tincture of the chloride of iron, tincture of belladonna, and a morning dose of quinine. She was chronically ill. She was physically normal except for small breasts. She was 'an utter stranger to the sexual passion.' She menstruated regularly. She had constant pelvic pains which were much worse during menstruation.

"At age eighteen she began to have 'fits'. She would grow cold, comatose, insensible, unconscious, and she convulsed. Atropine seemed to help some of the symptoms and as Cochran describes it:

"... In the meantime, the year 1867 was added to the great sum of time past, and the spring of 1868 was scattering over the nations the various influences of that delightful season.

"In Spring a young man's fancy lightly turns
        To thoughts of love."

---

[3]James Marion Sims, an Alabamian, the Father of Gynecological Surgery.

"And so it happened that a young man named John took a notion that he wanted Fanny for a wife. Doubtless John had never so much as heard of Herrick, much less of certain verses of his, which are of such exquisite beauty that I cannot forbear introducing them here namely:

'Gather ye rosebuds while ye may,
    Old Time is still a flying;
And this same flower that blooms to-day,
    To-morrow may be dying.'

"...So the marriage was celebrated; and everybody who was cognizant of the happy event had at least the opportunity to exclaim Miltonically, 'Hail wedded love! perpetual fountain of domestic sweets!' etc.

"It would have been barbarous to disturb the honeymoon with pills and potions, and I discontinued my professional visits, and heard but little of John and Fanny for several weeks; when one day John came into my office with a face in which perplexity and dismay were most legibly written and requested I should go and see his wife. I found her in a bad way generally.

"She had had some of her old fits again, and her pelvic pains had ungraciously returned, and worst of all, John's embraces gave her so much pain that she had lost faith in Milton's 'domestic sweets.' . . . I made another examination, from which I learned nothing, except the fact of the hyperesthesia--the vaginismus."

Cochran tried local palliative treatments for one month with no benefit. "...Affairs were getting desperate. John's face was a study for a physiognomist, and Fanny had got to regard her husband with perfect terror, and vowed that he should never touch her again. Cochran resorted to surgery, the Sims' Operation: "...we removed the remains of the hymen and cut through the sphincter vaginae muscle on each side, about half an inch from the commissure, and extended the incision to the raphe, making each incision two inches in length. The operation was followed by several weeks of wearing a vaginal dilator two to three hours a day. The incisions healed without a scar and "... On the 19th day of June, one month and two days after the operation, I was able to restore Fanny to the arms of her husband, with the assurance that his embraces would no longer meet with any obstacle.... Not only was the vaginismus relieved, but my patient never had any more pelvic neuralgia, never had any more paroxysms of that terrible epilepsy, never had any more hysterical trouble of any sort. She is emphatically a well woman. Her breasts have swelled up to a respectable size; the sexual appetite has been developed, and, as she expressed it, she is now like other folks."[4]

Being a man of "untiring industry" of "intellectually most imposing proportions; matchless memory, large powers of analysis, comparison and reflection, a self control which is never disturbed, and a self-reliance based upon a consciousness of strength..."[5] Jerome must have set out to meet, and become associated with, his peers in Mobile.

Those peers whom he found were exceptional: Dr. Josiah C. Nott, Dr. William Henry Anderson, Dr. George Ketchum, Dr. J.L. Gilmore, Dr. James F. Heustis, and Dr. F.A. Ross, among others. He captured their attention, especially in 1866 when he read a paper before the Mobile Medical Society on the origin of malarial poison.

On April 10, 1867, Dr. Cochran's fourth child, a girl, Mary Fooshea was born. In that same year he published a scientific paper: "The Administration of Chloroform by Deglutition." Life was, indeed, good.

Cochran passionately believed in bettering the health of the people of Alabama, the United States, and, obliquely, the world. He realized the need for a high standard in the practice of medicine. For physicians, he believed in custom, rules, and a strict code of

---

[4] Jerome Cochran, "Ovariotomy...." *op. cit.*, pp. 401-412.

[5] "Doctor Jerome Cochran of Alabama," *op. cit.* pp. 23-24.

ethics, and he advocated ongoing education through participation in an association and discussion of cases. With his fertile brain, and unselfish work, he threw himself into the process of bringing his beliefs to reality.

He was a very private man even in his service to his profession, and left only his professional papers by which we may know the workings of his mind. Of the man himself, we have only the words of his contemporaries to describe him.

William Henry Anderson, M. D.
—Courtesy of the Erik Overbey Collection,
University of South Alabama Archives

George Augustus Ketchum, M.D., 1825-1906
—Courtesy of the Erik Overbey Collection,
University of South Alabama Archives

James Fountain Heustis, M.D., 1829-1891
—Courtesy of the Erik Overbey Collection,
University of South Alabama, Archives

Chapter IV

The Professor

1868-1877

An old adage has it that "if one wants to really learn a subject, he should teach it."   Nature had endowed Jerome with the capacities of a great scholar.   He read and retained a vast amount of information.   This, plus "a fine command of language, a chaste and luminous style, aptness for philosophical speculation, large powers of analysis comparison and reflection, a self-control which is never disturbed, and a self-reliance based on a consciousness of strength, give him an absolute command of his resources, and render him at once an able writer, an instructive and interesting talker, and a consummate master of debate." [1]

Dr. Jerome Cochran had been in Mobile for three years and had established himself as one of Alabama's most knowledgeable and most inventive practitioners.   He continued to study everything he could get his hands on, the practice he began in his teens.   Among the subjects he chose was chemistry.   In 1868 he was elected Professor of Chemistry of the Medical College of Alabama in Mobile.

---

[1] "Doctor Jerome Cochran of Alabama," *op. cit.*, p. 25.

The Medical College was just being restarted after the break caused by the war, a break lengthened by one other extremely unpleasant determinant:

In the war, Union General Oliver O. Howard's command, the Eleventh U.S. Army Corps, was annihilated by Stonewall Jackson's Confederate Corps in Jackson's famous flanking maneuver at the Battle of Chancellorsville. Five Alabama regiments led this attack. After the war, this same General Howard appeared in Mobile, Alabama, as the chief agent of the Freedmen's Bureau. With the region beaten to its knees, General Howard boldly confronted aging Dr. Josiah Clark Nott demanding, as housing for his wards, the Medical College Building for which Dr. Nott had worked so hard. Dr. Nott, controlling his temper as well as he could, replied, "I'd rather see it burn."[2] He had already seen the University of Alabama in Tuscaloosa burned. He knew that LaGrange Academy had been burned to the ground, never to recover to its former grandeur, as were so many other Alabama institutions. But this beautiful building, so admirably suited and furnished as an institution for relieving human misery, the medical school was spared because General Howard wanted it for his wards. The medical specimens and models that Dr. Nott had bought in France before the war were vandalized and mostly destroyed.[3]

It wasn't until 1868, when the corrupt Freedmen's Bureau was losing power, and when the "Carpetbaggers" had lost some of their hold on the State, that the medical school building was returned to the University and classes could be resumed. Although cleaning and refurbishing was in order, it could not be fully done for lack of funds. The reconstruction legislature had repealed the law that gave the Medical School its only state revenue. A few of the valuable specimens that Dr. Nott had purchased at a prewar cost of $70,000,

---

[2] C. Loring Brace, Ph.D.,*Bull. N.Y. Acad. Med.*Vol.50, No.4, April 1974, p. 523.

[3]Today, a few of the Papier Maché Models have been restored and can be viewed in the Heustis-Eichold Museum in Mobile.

could be reclaimed, but most were damaged beyond repair. Drs. William H. Anderson, George A. Ketchum and James F. Heustis were the only ones left from the original faculty that had last taught there in 1861. Dr. Josiah Clark Nott, in failing health had moved to New York. Dr. Nott would return to Mobile, the site of his most useful labors, only to die. In 1868, however, he was still interested in the Medical College of Alabama, and donated money for a student prize.

Dr. William Anderson resumed his position from pre-war years as Dean. Dr. George Augustus Ketchum resumed his pre-war chair as Professor of Theory and Practice of Medicine. Having known Dr. Cochran during the war, knowing his grasp of basic sciences, and having heard a paper on malaria read by Cochran to the Mobile Medical Society in 1866, Anderson spoke to his faculty about Jerome. Dr. Jerome Cochran, subsequently elected professor of Chemistry, took the pre-war place of Dr. J.W. Mallet, one of the leading chemists of the South, who had gone to the University of Virginia after the war.

Besides Cochran, other new faculty members were: Drs. J.T. Gilmore in Surgery, E.P. Gaines in Clinical Medicine, Robinson Miller, and then after the yellow fever outbreak of 1870, Goronwy Owen in Obstetrics, and E.H. Fournier in Materia Medica and Therapeutics. All in all, this was a very fine group of doctors.

In order to realize what drew the scholarly, learned Jerome to accept a professorship, one must appreciate the atmosphere of professionalism that emanated from the physicians who resumed positions at the college. It is prudent here to give brief biographies of Anderson, Ketchum (to become Cochran's most long-standing and best friend), and Heustis, (one of the most prominent anatomists and surgeons in the South, and a contemporary of Cochran in the medical college).

William Henry Anderson[4] (1820-1887) was a very well-educated man. He graduated from William and Mary College. Then, as was customary in those days, he took a course of private lessons in medicine. He matriculated in the University of Virginia and, after one year of the study of medicine at that institution, obtained an M.D. degree in 1842. He tried his hand at the private practice of medicine for one year. But feeling his inadequacies, he became a resident at the Baltimore Almshouse Hospital. In 1844, still dissatisfied, Anderson attended a course of lectures in Philadelphia. In 1845, at the University of New York, he took a year-long lecture course, visiting Bellevue Hospital daily with a private tutor. In 1846, Anderson was off to Europe, visiting London, Edinburgh, Berlin, and Paris. In Paris he took an eight- month course under the famous physiologist, Claude Bernard (1813-1878). 1846 found Anderson settled in Mobile, practicing there until his death in 1887.

Dr. Anderson was elected dean of the Medical College of Alabama at Mobile when it first opened its doors on November 14, 1859. After an auspicious beginning, the Medical College closed in 1861 because all the students and professors joined the Confederate Army.

Anderson entered the Confederate army with the rank of surgeon of the 21st Alabama Regiment, which was mustered into service in Mobile on October 13, 1861. In January 1862, he was appointed medical purveyor of the district that included Alabama. After the war, Anderson returned to Mobile, and in 1868, when the Medical College of Alabama reopened, he resumed his duties as Dean.

It is likely that Anderson and Cochran had met during the war. They certainly became friends, and it was probably Anderson, along with Ketchum, who was instrumental in getting Cochran to accept the position of Professor of Chemistry at the Medical School.

The American Civil War seems to have impressed all the doctors who endured it, with a sense of need for public health. Dr. Lafayette Guild, who had been the chief medical officer for Lee's

---

[4]Howard Holley, M.D., *A History of Medicine in Alabama,*The University of Alabama Press, University of Alabama, 1982, pp. 81-89.

Army of Northern Virginia, served as quarantine officer after the war. Dr. Hunter McGuire, the chief medical officer of Stonewall Jackson's Corps, went into public health late in his career. Dr. William H. Anderson was very much interested in public health and, as dean of the Medical School, he was instrumental in installing a chair for Public Hygiene and Medical Jurisprudence in 1874, and in persuading Dr. Cochran to accept it.

Anderson was not only a well-educated doctor, he had somewhat of a literary flare. His poem to Dr. Nott on the occasion of that man's 60th birthday is published in the 1877 Transactions. During this same time, a compilation of brief biographies of notable men of the South began. In this book, there is a simple, clear, and concise biography titled: "Doctor Jerome Cochran of Alabama." This is the source of most subsequent biographical essays on Dr. Cochran. At the end of this biography is a statement:

"This biographical sketch, as far as it goes, is authentic and authoritative. The dates and facts have been verified by Dr. Cochran himself. It has been prepared chiefly by a distinguished lawyer of Mobile; but the section entitled 'Characteristics' was contributed by an eminent physician of Montgomery."

It is believed by this author [Dr. Morris] after studying the life and work of Dr. Anderson, that it was he, as Dean of the medical college, as friend of Dr. Cochran, as an accomplished writer himself, who was actually asked to edit the work of the two individuals cited in the above credit. That he did not credit himself would have been typical of Dr. Anderson. One of the main reasons we [both authors] feel this would have ultimately been the work of Dr. Anderson is the belief that the distinguished lawyer would most likely not have put any medical paper into the sketch. We believe that Dr. Anderson corroborated all historical facts with Dr. Cochran. Then, to further exemplify the brilliance of his protegé, he added the "extract from a curious discussion of 'The Mystery of Reproduction' abstracted from his [Dr, Cochran's] paper on the 'White Blood

Corpuscle' published in 1874"[5] in the Transactions of MASA.

Dr. George Augustus Ketchum (1825-1906)[6] became Jerome Cochran's closest friend, and next to Cochran, he was probably the one most responsible for the early prosperity of the newly reorganized Medical Association of the State of Alabama. Ketchum was a leader in the Medical Profession of Alabama for sixty years, Professor of Medicine, Dean of the Medical College of Alabama, and one of the founders of the Medical Association of the State of Alabama. Like most of Alabama's early doctors, George Ketchum was born in another state and immigrated to Alabama. George was born in Georgia in a family of Welsh origin. The fifth son, George was born April 6, 1825. In 1835, George's family moved to Mobile, Alabama, and young George received his early education from private tutors. His father had some severe business reverses and young George, who was preparing himself to enter Princeton College, was obliged to accept the position of assistant teacher in the female seminary, Livingston, Alabama. He was only sixteen years old at the time. In 1842, George read medicine under Dr. Frank Armstrong Ross of Mobile, and was a resident medical student in the City Hospital for two years. In 1844-45, he took a course of medical lectures in the South Carolina Medical College at Charleston. In 1845, he became an intern in the old Blockley Alms House in Philadelphia. In October 1845, he entered the Medical Department of the University of Pennsylvania where he was awarded the M. D. degree in the spring of 1846. He commenced the practice of medicine in Mobile in May of the same year.

On December 2, 1847, the Medical Association of the State of Alabama was formed, and Dr. Ketchum was elected secretary.

In 1848, Ketchum was elected Physician to the City Hospital of Mobile, and during the same year, he joined with Drs. Nott, Heustis, and Anderson in establishing a private infirmary for the

---

[5]*Ibid.* p.28

[6]Emmett Carmichael, "George Augustus Ketchum: Teacher -Administrator- Physician," *Alabama. Journal of Medical Science Vol. 5, No. 4*, 1968, pp. 511-514.

accommodation of sick Negroes. The Infirmary was a pecuniary success. Encouraged by their successful organization of the Infirmary, these men, along with Dr. Frank Armstrong Ross, Ketchum's preceptor, joined in the project of founding the Medical College of Alabama at Mobile. In a rented building, the Medical College of Alabama opened in 1859 with the most lavish museum of anatomical and pathological models in existence. The building did not house the exhibits properly, and the committee appointed Dr. Nott to work with an architect to design a building more suited for medical education. Dr. Nott worked diligently, and the new building was available for the term of 1860-61.[7]

Gifted with oratorical powers of the highest order, Dr. Ketchum was, at various times before, during, and after the Civil War, a member of the City Council of Mobile. In this capacity, in 1865, he was one of the deputation which surrendered the City of Mobile to General Gordon Granger.

In 1868, Dr. Ketchum was active in the reorganization of MASA. He was honored by being elected the Annual Orator for 1870 and again in 1875. In 1873, Dr. Ketchum was elected president of MASA, and presided during the first year of the new constitution and bylaws.

After the reopening of the Medical College in 1868, and with his oratory being of such high quality, Ketchum's lectures to his medical students were masterpieces. They not only stressed the need and importance of a store of medical knowledge and skills, but also the cultivation of that spirit and feeling which alone harmonizes with the objects, interests, and true aim of the science of medicine. He suggested that the true professional spirit looks beyond selfish aims and personal profit to the respectability, honor, dignity, and humanity of a calling. Dr. Ketchum served as professor of the Theory and Practice of Medicine, a position he held until about a year before his death in 1906. Due to ill health, Dr. Anderson resigned as dean in 1884 and Dr. Ketchum became the second Dean

---

[7]The building stands today with only a few modifications.

of the Medical College; a position he held until his death.

Dr. Ketchum was elected President of the Board of Health in Mobile in 1871, and was reelected annually until his death. Remembering the epidemics of typhoid fever spawned by the conflict, Ketchum made every effort to obtain an adequate supply of good water for Mobile. His efforts were blocked for about twenty years by the improvident reconstruction government, then his persistent efforts paid off and the city did obtain an abundant supply of pure water. In recognition of his efforts in this regard, a bronze fountain was erected in Bienville Square, Mobile.

Dr. James Fountain Heustis[8] (1829-1891), the son of Jabez Wiggins Heustis, graduated from the Medical Department of the University of Louisiana in 1848. He was an assistant surgeon (with the rank of captain) in the United States Army from 1850 to 1857. He settled in Mobile and became one of that city's outstanding surgeons. He became the first Professor of Anatomy at the newly organized medical college at Mobile.

Dr. Heustis, with his military experience, entered the Confederate Army Medical Department and served there as medical director of the hospitals in the Department of the Gulf with headquarters in Mobile.

After the war, Heustis returned to Mobile and, in 1868 resumed his position as professor of anatomy. He was still one of the most outstanding surgeons in that city. In 1881, Heustis wrote in the *Transactions of MASA* of Lord Lister's antiseptic method: "while recognizing its great value in operations, I cannot say that I see its special need in oöphorectomy, though statistics show that the mortality from this operation is reduced to minimum." Heustis thought that ordinary cleanliness and the use of silver wire sutures in closing the peritoneal surface were enough.

On a later occasion, he showed more emphasis in his praise of the Lister technique as he wrote that "Of all the recent advances of surgery, Lister's antiseptic system maintains the first place, and the wonderful reputation made for it by him has spread to every part of

---

[8]Howard Holley, M. D. *op. cit.* pp. 84,88,132,155,157.

the world, and has been added to by such brilliant results everywhere, there can be no doubt of its complete success, and of its deserving all its claims."

In 1881, Heustis reported on a series of the surgical cases that he had done. Among these cases, he described the removal of a large ovarian cyst from a young female, using aseptic precautions. He was honest enough to report a cesarian section on a fourteen-year-old female with an infantile pelvis. The mother and infant succumbed, which he thought was due, at least in part, to the fact that the surgery had been too-long delayed in order to allow for an attempted normal delivery. Likewise, he reported successful surgical repair of a congenitally absent vagina in a sixteen year old female. He apparently rebuilt a vaginal canal and maintained its patency with repeated dilatations. He used dilute carbolic acid solution to irrigate the vagina routinely. Dr. Heustis also reported on the closure of urethrovaginal, vesicovaginal, and vesicouterovaginal fistulas using his own modification of the Sims-Bozeman techniques.

Jerome Cochran enjoyed teaching. In his early twenties he had gained recognition for his amazing depth of knowledge and the ability to pass that knowledge on. It follows, then, that he was well suited to teaching in the Medical College, and passionately meticulous regarding accurate detail.

As a Professor, Dr. Cochran attracted a fair following of private students. According to the custom of the time, he taught them in his office. In 1870 one of the subjects included the methods and theories he had evolved regarding cerebro-spinal fever. These theories clashed with the teaching of one of the other clinical professors, and Cochran was criticized for this. Cochran immediately tendered his resignation, but was finally persuaded to withdraw it. To the credit of that clinical professor, a year later he admitted publicly in a meeting of the Mobile Medical Society, that he was wrong about the nature of cerebro-spinal fever and Dr.

Cochran was right. [9]

In 1869 and 1870 Cochran attended the meetings of the American Medical Association. Based on the 1869 subject of medical education discussed by the AMA, Dr. Cochran's fertile mind gripped the ideal of a betterment of medical education for the physicians of Alabama. He wrote and introduced at the 1870 Medical Association of the State of Alabama session[10] "a series of resolutions and made an address on this *questio vexata* of medical education, in which, and reviewing our present college system in the strongest words that I was able to command, I made a proposition in the name and on behalf of the faculty of the college to give up the privilege of examining our own students for the degree of doctor of medicine, to then forego for the benefit of the profession the privilege, so dear to each medical school, of conferring diplomas carrying with them, by laws of the land, the right to practice medicine and collect fees, to now place the whole matter of admission into the profession and thus the enjoyment of professional honors and privileges in the handling of the profession itself, under the special direction of a board of censors, to be appointed for the purpose by this Association."[11]

Cochran was looked upon "as a dreamer, better fitted to live in Utopia than in this common-place world where the almighty dollar is so devoutly worshipped, and where the most approved principle of action seems to be that every man should take care of himself or." He continued, "What sort of reception did it [his proposition] meet at the hands of this body, Mr. President? It seemed to fall still-born. No man thought it worth while to waste upon it a single word of sympathy. It did not even provoke so much notice as to be honored with a breath of reprobation."[12]

---

[9]"Doctor. Jerome Cochran of Alabama,"*op.cit.*,p. 7.

[10]*Transactions of MASA*, 1871, p. 16.

[11]*Ibid.*, p.58

[12]*Ibid.*, p. 59.

Yet Cochran felt that "although it met with some opposition, it evidently has friends who are resolved that it shall have a fair showing..."[13]   For, as a result of considering Dr. Cochran's proposal, he was able to report later that, in August, the faculty decided to abolish fees for lectures in the medical college.

This aroused the apparent ire of some members of the Medical Association. They worked hard to negate this practice.

At the 1871 session, after having attended the 1870 AMA meeting and gaining further insight into the topic of medical education, Dr. Cochran again addressed the topic, this time by incorporating it in his draft for a new constitution. Cochran gave an impassioned speech to the Association at the 1871 session in support of the faculty's position, and outlining the reasoning behind this decision. He cried out "Shall we say to the young men, 'you can have no help from us in working out a glorious future?' Shall we bid them labor with their hands that their brain may thrive and add to the toils of a student's life in the constant harrassing care for wages and means wherewith to pay for tuition? Particularly does this aspect of the question have force in all of the Southern States. Our people are impoverished, our young men — many of them — would feel the burden of every additional hundred dollars which an education would cost them. ...I am glad, gentlemen, glad that these professional brethren, the faculty of the Alabama Medical College, have had the large heartedness to say to these young men, 'come to us, we will extend a helping hand -- we will, as much as in us lies, lift the burthen from your shoulders while you give every energy of mind and body to the tasks of student life -- only asking of you in return that you so use these advantages that we may feel proud of you as graduates and members of our loved profession.'[14] Cochran decried the national trend that "the price charged for lectures should be made the criterion of merit in our colleges." He justified the

---

[13]*Ibid.*, p. 59.

[14]*Ibid.*, p. 59.

right to offer free medical education by reminding the Association that "...in 1869 a resolution [by the American Medical Association at their annual meeting] was passed fixing the minimum price of lectures at $120. But in 1870 a motion to fix the price for tuition failed, and was laid on the table [i.e. tabled; put off; not acted upon.]" Cochran concluded that "The American Medical Association, therefore, stands today uncommitted to any theory for the advancement of medical education. The action of 1870 rescinds that of 1869."

Cochran further stated, in this 1871 address, "And I dare to say, Mr. President, in the face of men and angels, that she [the college] did right, and I am willing, nay I am proud, to shoulder my share of the responsibility. Not that I would not like to be paid for teaching. I would like it exceedingly well, but, under the circumstances, that is simply impossible, and so -- not that I love Caesar less, but that I love Rome more -- I make a virtue of necessity, and accept the situation. And I do this, sir, with all the better grace, because I know that the sun shines on the other side of the cloud, and that in some way future good will be brought out of this present evil."[15]

He ended his plea in this manner, "The conclusion then, of the whole matter is this: the faculty of the Medical College of Alabama, in establishing a system of free medical lectures, have violated no rule of medical ethics, either express or implied; have not even violated any ancient and established custom of the profession; have done nothing to lower the standard of professional qualifications; have done nothing to flood the land with incompetent doctors; in a word, have done nothing which they did not have the perfect right to do." "...as the Faculty work for the honor of teaching, we may well trust them to make it honorable".[16]

In 1873, the faculty attempted to take the City Hospital from the control of the Sisters of Charity, who held it under a lease from the city. Cochran opposed this move because he believed it to be

---

[15] *Ibid.*, p. 56

[16] *Ibid.* p.66

unwise and unjust to the Order. He believed the move would be disastrous. He stated his views, and seeing that he could make no headway with the faculty, he peremptorily resigned from the chairmanship of the Chemistry Department. Sure enough, the removal of the Sisters of Charity was a disaster.

The faculty did not want to lose a professor of Cochran's caliber. He was persuaded to return before the beginning of the following term to a chair that they had created especially for him, the chair of Public Hygiene and Medical Jurisprudence.[17]

Cochran firmly believed that the way to improve the practice of medicine among the doctors of his day was through a strong organization that would tighten the institutions of medical learning, compel the study of diseases and their effects on people and control, and eventually eradicate the false medical doctrines. To this end he worked tirelessly

In 1875 Cochran said this about medical education:[18]
"There has never been before the Medical Association of the State of Alabama, a subject of greater and of more lasting importance than that now under discussion, the subject, namely, of elevating the standard of professional qualifications. As you are aware, Sir, it was mainly with this object in view that the American Medical Association was originally organized; and since its organization, I think I may safely say, that no subject which engages the attention of medical men, has received from that august body more attention than this. ...This matter of medical education has also been a constant theme of resolutions and discussions in all of our State Medical Associations...and for the last twenty years the pages of medical periodicals have literally bristled with articles upon it.

"Now, Mr. President, what has all this almost endless discussion accomplished? Alas, that I should have it to say, for all practical

---

[17]"Doctor. Jerome Cochran of Alabama," *op. cit.*, p. 7.

[18]Dr. Cochran's Address on Medical Education, *Transactions of MASA*, 1875, pp. 171-178.

purposes just nothing at all.

"Everybody blamed the Medical Colleges: ...The rapid multiplication of these institutions and the anxiety of their professors to attract large classes have caused them to be conducted on principles of ordinary commercial competition, the object in view being not to secure the highest standard of professional qualification, but the largest number of students. As was to have been expected under such circumstances, the qualifications for graduation have been deplorably lowered, and ignorant and incompetent men by the thousand have been thrown into the ranks of the profession. ...They have received students without proper qualifications for commencing the study of medicine, and they have conferred diplomas upon men incompetent to commence the practice of medicine. They have done this. They have sinned and they must suffer the penalty. But in spite of all this I undertake to say that the profession at large -- that same profession which has raised such clamor of virtuous indignation against the colleges, are blamable to a far greater extent than the colleges themselves.

"They are more to be blamed because they have had the power to control the evil of which they complain, and they have failed to exercise it. ...If the colleges graduate incompetent men, let the profession resolutely refuse to receive them into its ranks, refuse them admission into all medical societies, refuse them consultations, refuse them, in a word, all professional recognition. Do this truthfully and earnestly, and the profession can mold the qualifications of its members just exactly according to their own wishes. And not only this, but they can also control the colleges. They have only to refuse to recognize those colleges which bring dishonor on the degree of Doctor of Medicine, by awarding it to unworthy aspirants; having only to keep their students away from such institutions, leaving their halls and coffers empty to accomplish either their conversion to better habits or their destruction. ...[This] requires that every District Medical Society shall appoint annually a Board of Censors, whose duty it shall be,
1st, To register the names of all the physicians of their respective districts who are recognized to be of good standing at the time the

registration is made, the status of these not to be changed.

2nd, To examine all persons who propose commencing the study of medicine, to determine if they are properly qualified for such an undertaking.

3rd, To examine all persons who propose to commence the practice of medicine in their respective districts to determine their professional competence.

"...the remedy in question is just where it ought to be, in the hands of the medical profession itself. If it is not effectually used it is the fault of the profession -- certainly not the fault of the colleges. ...The conclusion of the whole matter may be stated in a few brief words:

1st, The standard of qualifications for admission into the medical profession is too low; and there is urgent need that something shall be done to secure greater efficiency.

2nd, The colleges are bound hand and foot and are powerless to bring about the desired reformation.

3rd, It is futile to expect assistance from the State; that being under control of men who do not even understand that any reformation is needed.

4th, The medical profession, as such, has the power to regulate the standard of qualifications according to its wishes, can control the matter absolutely."

Dr Cochran recognized the inadequacies in American medical education. He spelled them out to the profession, and offered his solution forty years before the Flexner Commission, with the help of the Carnegie Foundation and some real support by the American Medical Association, applied the final solution in 1910.

In the Alabama Medical College, Dr. Cochran held this position of chair of Public Hygiene and Medical Jurisprudence until 1877 when, due to so many other pressing commitments, he tendered his final resignation. He never taught in the college again after 1877.

The Old Medical College of Alabama, Founded by Doctor.
Josiah Clark Nott and his Group in 1859.

—Courtesy of the
Erik Overbey Collection, University of South Alabama Archives

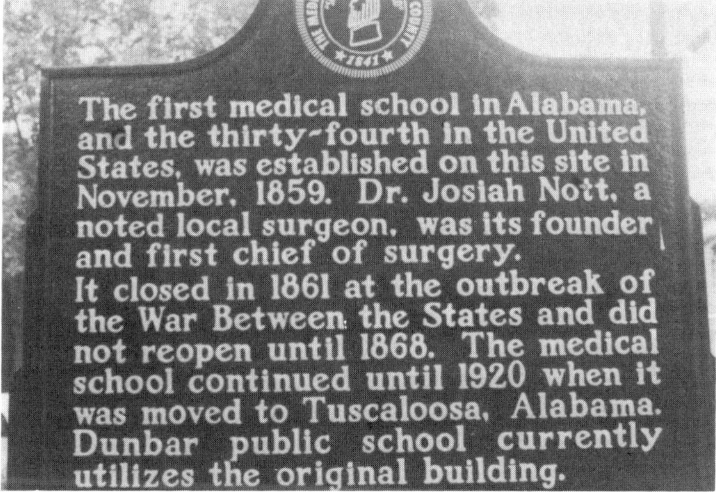

The Medical School Building in 1993. The roof was blown off by a hurricane in 1916. Only the lower two floors could be salvaged.

The Chemistry Laboratory where Dr. Cochran taught
—Courtesy of the Erik Overbey Collection, University of
South Alabama Archives

The Microscopy Laboratory. We do not know that Dr. Cochran ever used a microscope, but he wrote fluently about microscopic organisms.
—Courtesy of The Erik Overbey Collection, University of South Alabama Archives.

Chapter V

Aspirations Compound

The tapestry of life begins in youth with the exposure to the various threads of careers that are possible. The warp thread is the basic direction followed according to the nature of the man. Dr. Jerome, with his sturdy, opinionated, and stubborn ancestry, his sickly childhood that taught him stoicism, his soon-exposed insatiable appetite for learning, his budding genius, and his innate honesty and compassion, combined in God's design to form tough, unbreakable cords that would become the basis of his life.

The weft threads are those activities that are woven through the warp threads and set the tone for the finished product of one's life work. The complexity of the pattern depends upon how many pursuits are afforded, and how skillful and persistent the person is in completing any of the pursuits he has chosen for his life's aspirations.

During the years of his professorship, much else was happening in Dr. Cochran's life.

-1868-

Early in 1868, physicians around the state began to answer a call from the Selma Medical Society to reorganize the state Medical Association.   Cochran embroiled himself with great enthusiasm. On March 3rd and 4th, 20 state physicians from five counties met in Selma. Only six of these had been antebellum members: Drs .H. Backus, C. J. Clark, A. G. Mabry, A. J. Reese, W. P. Reese, and F. A. Ross. The new members were: Drs. B. H. Riggs, Charles F. Force, John A. McKinnon, G. W. Kyser, and L. E. Locke of Dallas County; Drs. Thomas C. Osborn, F. M. Peterson, and Jacob Huggins of Hale County; Drs. R. F. Michel, W. C. Jackson, and H. S. Howard of Montgomery County; Drs. J. L. Gilmore and Jerome Cochran of Mobile County, and Dr. E. D. McDaniel of Wilcox County. The organization began with the chair given to F.A. Ross of Mobile, with Cochran, a newcomer, elected as secretary. The initiation fee was $1, and thereafter, membership was $5 a year to help defray expenses. The only medical paper read at this meeting was one by Henry Backus, on the "Unity of Disease."[1] Dr. Cochran was also placed on the committee to revise the constitution and by-laws of the Association, as well as on a committee to report on licensing of doctors. His work on these committees was to continue for years.

On June 25, 1868, Alabama was readmitted to the Union. That same year the corruption in the state government came under some semblance of control.

In 1868, life for Dr. Cochran and his family must have been exciting and satisfying. The war was behind them. Jerome and Sarah Jane, with their four children, had settled in, and Mobile was now truly home. Jerome, himself, was 36; Sarah Jane (her birthday was just one week after Jerome's, on December 11) was 34; the four children were growing: Augustine Schamyl at 12, Ina Lou at eight,

---

[1] Jerome Cochran, "The Medical Profession," *Memorial Record of Alabama,* Vol. II, Brant & Fuller, Madison, WS. 1893, p. 121.

Jerome Bowling at four, and Mary Fooshea at one year of age.

Dr. Cochran's practice was well established, for he was recognized as a brilliant diagnostician and practitioner by his patients and by his peers. He began his professorship and was proud to be contributing so much to his city and his profession. But joy and tragedy were to strike the very next year.

-1869-

The second session of the Medical Association was held in Mobile on March 2 - 4. Work continued in the organization of the Association. Cochran, with his insatiable appetite for reading, kept up with the happenings in the world of medicine. And with his tenacious memory,[2] he was able to quote these writings to aid him in discussions or debates with his colleagues.

In this year he attended the annual meeting of the American Medical Association in New Orleans. One of the topics was about standardizing the charges to attend medical school, something that greatly interested Cochran as he was on the faculty of the Medical College of Alabama at the time. [*see* Chapter IV.]

Dr. Cochran's practice continued to prosper, but it had its ups and downs as do all doctors' practices. He had one case on the 19th day of July in which, assisted by several professional friends, he excised an ovarian cyst, and the patient recovered well.

On the other hand, he was reconsulted by a woman whom, in 1866, he had diagnosed with a cystic ovarian tumor, and advised surgical interference. She refused, but, because she finally could stand no more, in September of 1869 she agreed to "brave the dangers of the operation." Cochran wrote that the prognosis now "could not be very favorable" He operated on the 13th of October, assisted by several medical friends, among whom was Dr. Gilmore. The tumor was found lying in the right side extending from the floor of the pelvis up to the liver, with attachments to the omentum; to the large and small bowels at several points; to the fundus uteri; and to

---

[2]"Doctor Jerome Cochran of Alabama," *op.cit.* p.2.

attachments to the omentum; to the large and small bowels at several points; to the fundus uteri; and to the walls of the abdominal cavity. It took a long time to ligate all the bleeding surfaces. The patient did well until the next night when she began to experience restlessness, fever and thirst. She was allowed ice water and pounded ice, brandy, morphine and beef tea. At two o'clock the next day she began to vomit. Dr. Cochran realized that she was suffering from a large bleed in to the abdominal cavity. Her surgery on the 13th had lasted one and one half hours, under an anesthesia of chloroform.[3]   Her system suffered shock after shock, and she died on the 16th of October.[4]

Through the genealogical charts, and his various writings in which can be found nuggets of his belief in strong families, we deduce that Jerome was a constant of his beloved Sarah Jane, a loving father to his children; and, from S. Vadah Cochran Jr. (1918-1995), we know he kept close ties with his family, following long-standing clan ways. In 1869 another son, their fifth child, Edmund Collins Cochran, was born amidst joy.

That same year, Augustine Schamyl, died at the age of 13. The Cochrans probably bought the grave site then, and she was the first to be interred at the family plot on the hill at the Catholic Cemetery in Mobile, in Section A, lot 50. There is no record of what caused her death.

Mourning a child robs one of peace. In a close family such as the Cochrans, parents and children alike mourn. And as the pieces of shattered life are put back together, families either grow in God, or are torn asunder. It appears the Cochrans grew in God. Certainly they had an "angel in heaven" to whom they could pray. Jerome was no stranger to death in families. After all, his own parents had mourned the death of his elder sister who died just before he was

---

[3] Apparently, there was never a question of reopening her and repairing the bleeder.

[4] Jerome Cochran, Supplementary Report To the Medical Association, "Ovariotomy, Haematocele and Vaginismus", *Transactions of MASA*, pp.401-406.

born; and when he was seven, he was old enough to remember the birth and death of a brother, Augustus Owen, who lived from 1838 to 1841.

Being an innately compassionate man, it is presumed he gave his family love and support through this agonizing time. His work with the Medical Association and his teaching at the Medical College allowed him to submerge his own grief by immersing himself in service. Though he continued to teach in the Medical College until 1877, his own health was soon to limit the arduous hours and physical pushing of his patient care practice.

-1870-

In February, in his capacity as Professor in the Medical College of Alabama, Cochran was invited to give an address before the Alumni Association of his medical school alma mater, The University of Nashville. He spoke: "On the Principles of Organization, and the Evolution of Organic Forms." The trip was made during exceedingly cold weather. He contracted a very painful disease which first affected his bones and joints and was regarded as rheumatism, then it affected the alimentary canal, then it assumed more of a neuralgic character. This disease hampered his active work, causing pain and disability for several years. He never completely recovered from it. The disease was never adequately diagnosed because Cochran refused to give in to his disability and be treated by a colleague.[5]

Ill, he nevertheless pushed himself. The annual meeting of the Medical Association was held in Montgomery, March 15 -17. Cochran, in his capacity as Secretary, attended. He also read his paper on Ovariotomy, Haematocele and Vaginismus.

Still pushing, Cochran attended the annual meeting of the American Medical Association in Washington. Again, the subject of medical education was discussed. He "listened attentively....It seemed strange to me, in listening thereto, that the price charged for

---

[5]"Doctor. Jerome Cochran of Alabama", *op. cit.*, pp. 6, 26.

lectures should be made the criterion of merit in our colleges."[6] It was after discussion of this report, about the beginning of the summer, that the professors of the Medical College of Alabama "determined to make the lectures free."[7]

1870 appears to have been a very bad year for epidemics. Malaria and pulmonary consumption were ever-present. Typho-malarial fever, also known as malarial fever and typhoid fever moved from north Alabama to south Alabama. Diphtheria was also noted sporadically. Yellow fever was a scourge. Dr. George A. Ketchum went so far as to say: "1870...might aptly be termed the epidemic year. The terrible work of desolation which disease and death have accomplished during the past twelve months in our midst, will long be remembered as adding another to the dark days of mourning, when our fair city, clad in sackcloth and ashes like Rachael contemplating her offspring, refused to be comforted. Death has stalked through her streets, and entering the mansion of the rich and the hovel of the poor, has, alike from each, demanded his victim. Among those who had been appointed to meet him and do battle at every point, and dispute his progress at every step, he remorselessly exacted victim after victim, and our profession has paid the tribute to his demand of seven valuable lives. McCleskey first, then in quick succession Burke, Toxey, I. W. Anderson, Herndon and Coale followed; and now but recently another, who could illy[sic.] be spared from the high duties that his position imposed upon him, has been called away, and we find the chair which Dr. Robinson Miller filled, whenever work was to be done to advance the best interests of our noble profession, vacant for ever more."[8]

---

[6]Address of Dr. Jerome Cochran to the MASA, *Transactions of MASA, 1871*, p. 56.

[7]*Ibid*, p. 57.

[8]George A. Ketchum, "Diseases of Mobile for the Year 1870, " *Transactions of MASA, 1871*, p. 56.

God was not finished calling the Cochran children home. On April 10, Mary Fooshea died at the loving age of three, the age when baby language begins to allow insight into the wondrous thought processes of the child. Once again anguish filled their lives. Another grave, another angel. There is no record of the cause of her death. Was it one of the epidemic diseases? Was it yellow fever? If so, her name does not appear on Dr. Cochran's list of the dead from this dread disease.

What caused Cochran to launch a personal and aggressive search for the prevention and treatment of yellow fever? For during this same time he also began a lifelong mission to assure provision of adequate public health, not only to those of his city and his state, but, eventually, to his country.

A career grows in the application of Self. What "sight" causes the taking up of multiple tasks -- the intricate pulling of all the threads in a weave sometimes haphazard, sometimes forced, sometimes hauled with deliberation? From whence comes the determination to keep on pulling? From what palette in the psyche does the color come? In Cochran's case, did the "sight" arise from the agony of loss, the brilliance of a far-seeing mind, or the dedication and selflessness of a true physician? Perhaps it was an unconscious combination of all three. And genius holds inherent its own frenetic colors that bleed into the threads in hand. Sometimes the weaver does not realize the potential enormity of the finished tapestry, but is only caught up in the pulling of the threads. Such began the multiple-threaded career of Dr. Cochran -- in the application of Self.

In August, Cochran received a letter from Dr. Frank A. Ross, President of the Medical Association of the State of Alabama.[9] In it, Ross, wrote regarding "devising some method by which our profession in this State can be roused to a proper appreciation of our position and necessities and the vital importance of a general and combined effort being made to accomplish the great ends which we

------

[9]Letter from Dr. Ross to Dr. Cochran, *Transactions of MASA, 1871*, p.14.

should all have in view," he stated, "I have been so favorably impressed with the plans which you have originated and expressed to me, that I desire to entreat you to put them in some form, by which we can reach our brethren throughout the State. By doing so, you will confer a favor upon the profession in general, and, in particular, upon your friend."

Dr. Cochran replied immediately that he had already prepared, "and herewith respectfully submitted for your consideration..."[10] a circular to be sent that month to all physicians in the state. With uncanny genius and vision, he had written detailed bylaws for the Association, as well as a treatise urging a proper organization of physicians as good influence over public opinion and State legislation as well as over the advancement of medical science and medical art.

In this circular, Cochran requested names and addresses of all physicians in the state, and asked that these physicians inform him of the conditions in the county in which they practiced. He lamented the poor "means of intercommunication between the different sections not always to be most expeditious or convenient."[11] He hoped that "with the multiplication of railroads, and the improvements contemplated in our river navigation these difficulties will gradually become of less magnitude, but in the nature of things they must always continue to be of very embarrassing dimensions." In this circular, Cochran vividly expressed his firm belief that "...it is not to be expected that any great enterprise can be conducted without labor and expense and personal self-sacrifice."[12]

Ill and in mourning, he continued his teaching at the Medical College. Cochran still continued in his position as secretary of the State Medical Association, as well as the committee work for the

---

[10]Letter from Dr. Cochran to Dr. Ross, *Transactions, 1871*, pp.14-15.

[11]Circular Address by Cochran to MASA, *Transactions, 1871*, p. 18.

[12]*Ibid.*, p.18.

organization, detailed and time-consuming because of his precise attention to detail.

He began his fight for public health at the local level by writing a series of articles which were then published in the Mobile Register in December, 1870 and January, 1871 entitled "The Origin and Prevention of Endemic and Epidemic Diseases of Mobile."[13]

He continued working tirelessly on the committee for licensing physicians. His fertile brain devised detailed and comprehensive ideas, and he tucked this project in with all the rest.

-1871-

In March, at the Mobile meeting of the Medical Association of Alabama, he gave the address. He spoke "On Medical Education and the Degradation of the Professions by the Medical Colleges." [14] He also presented his bylaws for the Association in the form of a new Constitution to be printed, distributed, studied, and brought to the 1872 Association meeting for consideration. Though for the most part unable to be an up-and-about practicing physician caring for patients, he was letting no time go wasted.

Since his medical school days, Jerome Cochran had taken a great deal of interest in the causes and prevention of diseases. As early as 1866, he had read a paper before the Mobile Medical Society on the origin of the malarial poison. In 1869 he published a letter on the malarial influences at work in the suburbs of Mobile. When, during the months of December, 1870 and January, 1871, he published a series of articles on the public health, he captured the attention of the residents of Mobile, and the U.S. Government as well. In these articles he discussed, at some length, the natural history of yellow fever. He also explained the various sanitary measures necessary to improve the health of the city. Somewhat later, in the same newspaper, he published a few notes on the

---

[13]Jerome Cochran, "Endemic and Epidemic Diseases of Mobile," *Transactions of MASA.*March ,1871, pp. 225-263.

[14]"Doctor Jerome Cochran of Alabama," *op. cit.*, p. 26.

influence of underground drainage in the diminution of the death rate from pulmonary diseases. In March of 1871, he combined these writings, and after careful editing and with the addition of much new material, submitted them to the Medical Association of the State of Alabama for publication in their *Transactions*, with this statement:

"If the doctrines which I advocate as to the production and prevention of diseases are true, it is hardly possible to estimate at too high a rate their importance to the medical profession and to the people of the State; and it has therefore seemed to me to be eminently proper that they should be brought before the State Association for discussion. If they receive the endorsement of the association, they become invested with so much authority that they become at once the basis of all future sanitary legislation in the State of Alabama, and I shall be able, and I hope without unmanly vanity, to feel that I have some little claim to the gratitude of my fellow men."[15]

The following excerpts are taken from the above presentation of his paper to the Medical Association. They show the depth of his study, the vastness of his interest and knowledge, and the vision of his genius.

Dr. Cochran obviously believed there were few questions of more immediate importance to men and women than those relating to health and disease. In actuality, this belief was the final *raison d'etre* of the public health specialist. Cochran also believed that the health of the citizens should be precious, not only to the citizens but to the community in which they live. Good health means the ability to work, and hence it means also comfortable support of happy families, and the prosperous growth and development of cities and states.

Of PUBLIC HEALTH Cochran wrote: "It makes all the

------

[15]Jerome Cochran, "Endemic and Epidemic Diseases of Mobile," *Transactions of MASA 1871* p.225.

difference between living under our own vine and fig tree with none to molest us or to make us afraid, and of dragging out miserable existences in hospitals or pauper asylums. Hence the care of the sick and the removal of the cause of disease are placed, both by Christian philanthropy, and by modern unchristian political economy, among the recognized duties of all civilized communities.

"These are commonplace truisms which everybody, in a general way, is willing to admit; but only those can give it adequate appreciation who have witnessed the ravages of some desolating pestilence in the crowded population of a great city -- such a visitation, for example as the city of Mobile has recently suffered from yellow fever.

"It is because I desire to take advantage of the opportunity which may be presumed to exist, while the dreadful lessons of the late [yellow fever] epidemic are fresh in the minds of all our citizens, professional as well as unprofessional, that I select the present time to make such suggestions as to the preservation of the public health which have been in my mind for several years but which have not been presented to the public before, because I had no reason to believe that they would receive the attention which their importance demands."

To MASA's assembled physicians, Cochran drew on his vast knowledge of current and recent events, and spoke of the great work going on in public health. Research was progressing all over the civilized world by distinguished physicians, also by intelligent men not members of the medical profession. Public health had become the subject of legislation for some of the most civilized governments in the world.

Cochran quoted the following passage from Mr. Thomas Huxley (1825-1895) a famous London surgeon and zoologist and writer.: "We have learned that pestilences will only take up their abode among those who have prepared unswept and ungarnished residences for them. Their cities must have narrow unwatered streets, foul with accumulated garbage. Their houses must be ill-drained, ill-lighted, ill-ventilated. Their subjects must be ill-washed, ill-fed, ill-clothed. The London of 1665 was such a city.

The cities of the East, where plague has an enduring dwelling, are such cities. We in later times have learned somewhat of nature, and partly to obey her. Because of this partial improvement of our natural knowledge, and of that fractional obedience we have no plague; because of that knowledge is still very imperfect, and that obedience yet incomplete, typhus is our companion, and cholera our visitor.

"But it is not presumptuous to express the belief that when our knowledge is more complete and our obedience the expression of our knowledge, London will count her centuries of freedom from typhus and cholera, as she now gratefully reckons her two hundred years of disappearance of the plague, which swooped upon her thrice in the first half of the seventeenth century."

According to Cochran, compared to other American cities, Mobile was a healthy city. The annual percentage of deaths to the whole population was about twice as great in New York City as in Mobile. He felt that if there were no yellow fever, Mobile would be the healthiest city in America. He added that Mobile did have endemic diseases, such as the malarial fevers, and notably pulmonary phthisis, and he believed these could be eradicated.

Of MALARIA Cochran believed, and the other physicians of Mobile bore him out, that the malarial fevers accounted for more than half of the sickness in Mobile. To that source he traced intermittent, remittent and congestive fevers; neuralgias; dysenteries and bilious colics; together with many other visceral and cachectic troubles. He dogmatically asserted that "ought not to be so, because of all the diseases flesh is heir to, those produced by malaria are easiest to prevent by the removal of the efficient cause."

It is true that he did not know what malaria's etiological agent looked like. He only knew it from observation of effects on the unfortunate persons afflicted. He wrote of the malarial agent: "It cannot be weighed or measured. It evades the most jealous scrutiny of the microscope. But that it is a real thing, powerful for evil, the prolific cause of many diverse maladies, in the light of abundant and painful experience we know the deadly effects beyond doubt and only too well. We know the circumstances under which the poison is generated, the laws which regulate its transportation, its barriers which obstruct its pestilential progress, and what is of more importance, we know the certain means of accomplishing its destruction."

Based on information gleaned from his wide reading, Cochran recalled to the Association the origin of the name, malaria: a miasma or bad air coming from water and decaying vegetation. He told of the plain in Spain where there were no trees or other vegetation. There was ample water just below the surface of the soil and troops of the Royal Infantry could obtain drinking water by digging shallow springs. Many of the troops came down with malaria. He compared this to a region near New Orleans where there were swamps, decaying vegetation, and all the conditions favoring malaria. Yet, no malarial diseases were found there. He put forth his conclusion that the only requisites for malaria to thrive must be: confined warm water in a region infested by malaria. He purported that to control malaria, all standing water on the surface and below the surface of the soil in malarial regions must be drained. Cochran believed that if the authorities of Mobile would do this, they would be rid of half of the diseases which afflicted its inhabitants.

As for YELLOW FEVER, Cochran realized that "of all the diseases known to the people, that which is most dreaded, and which interferes most seriously with the commerce of the city, and the activities of its people, is yellow fever." He said: "The annual endemics of malarial diseases which afflict so severely our suburban population can be utterly abolished and destroyed....Of the possibility of banishing yellow fever from our borders for all time to come, I cannot speak so confidently. But I believe this also can be done. I believe it with a firm, unwavering faith, which is the result of a careful study of almost all that has been written or spoken on the subject."

He named all the ways yellow fever may be transported from place to place: "over wide spaces of land and sea by ships and railway cars, in clothing, and bedding, and various merchandise. Yellow fever poison thus carried from infected places under circumstances of a congenial character, inaugurate epidemics in localities ordinarily exempt from its ravages." Cochran believed yellow fever was not indigenous or endemic to the city of Mobile, but was always brought in by ships principally from Havana or trains from New Orleans.

"Therefore, the deadly disease, from which Mobile suffers so much in the loss of the precious lives of the citizens, and the loss of wealth, which is also precious in its way, could, by proper sanitary regulation, be kept permanently away from the city."

Cochran gave a very lucid explanation of THE NATURE OF THE YELLOW FEVER POISON AND THE MODE OF DISSEMINATION:

He believed the poison of yellow fever to be specific, causing only yellow fever and no other disease. He believed it to be organic, " -- composed of living germs in innumerable number --living organisms of inconceivable minuteness, which eat, and drink and multiply their generations under the sun just as other living creatures do with which we happen to be more familiar."

". . . Extremely minute organisms, have hitherto, for the most part, eluded the most jealous scrutiny of our most powerful microscopes."

Cochran reported that much recent attention had been focused on the theory of germs as the causative factors of all contagious diseases.

Cochran concluded that:

1. Yellow fever poison is composed of living organisms endowed with the faculty of reproducing their kind.

2. That reproduction is "primarily manifested in the bodies of human beings," where the poisonous organisms find their "fittest pabulum."

3. That reproduction and survival is "manifested secondarily in some other situation" whereby the germ is properly nourished. He believed this secondary habitat to be "the air we breathe."

While Cochran believed and explained the disease to be airborne and contracted by the respiratory route, he, nevertheless, saw the transportation from place to place as slightly more difficult to explain. He did not fully subscribe to Nott's earlier belief that it was the mosquito that carried the disease, because mosquitoes were a bane of existence, and to his knowledge, bites did not result in wholesale death by yellow fever. He felt that "...it can certainly be carried in the bodies of those afflicted with the disease, and in the bodies of those not yet sick. It can also be carried in ships and railroad cars, in the shape of fomites, clothing and certain merchandise. But there is another mode of dissemination about which our knowledge is not so definite, namely, its diffusion through the air and its transportation by means of atmospheric currents. That it can, in this way, be transported for short distances, as from one room of a house to another, or possibly from one side of a street to the other, is not to be doubted....I believe that, in the propagation of epidemics the atmospheric dissemination of the poison is of quite subordinate importance, and efficient only for short distances, and that when the poison passes over wide intervals of space, whether of sea or land, it is carried by some agency or human travel by ships or cars, in clothing or merchandise of some form of fomites, or in human bodies."

Cochran told the members of MASA that he had been asked whether there were any medical means to prevent future epidemics, and that inquiry had prompted his newspaper articles.

Cochran emphatically believed that it was quite within the power of the people of Mobile by the wise employment of appropriate measures of prophylaxis to prevent yellow fever for the most part from making its appearance at all; and that when it did come, they could limit its propagation so as to keep it from assuming the formidable proportions of an epidemic. He stated, "This is a consummation most devoutly to be wished.[16]   He outlined his measures of protection.

1. Prevent importation of the disease.

2. "Modify the telluric and atmospheric conditions of the city that

---

[16]This is a term he frequently used.

the organic germs of the fever poison, even after its importation, would not find an environment favorable to their development and multiplication, and so would fail in their malignant mission to generate pestilences."
3. Restrict disease to the smallest possible area and the fewest possible persons.

Cochran understood that absolute quarantine was impracticable. He suggested a modified quarantine that should be applied: "During epidemic seasons no person sick of the fever should be allowed to approach the city; no well person should be allowed to come in until his clothing and baggage had been disinfected; no ship should be allowed to come near the city until she had been purified from stem to stern; no cargo should be landed until it was accounted above suspicion."

He recommended disinfecting infected houses, ships and railway cars with chlorine gas because of its affinity for organic matter. He realized that in spite of all these measures, yellow fever would still occasionally appear among them. Then it would be imperative to limit the disease, its area, the number of persons and obstruct its progress with barriers. He proposed isolation and disinfection. By isolation, he meant "the separation of the sick and the well by the most forceful methods, even if they seem inhumane at times. People fled yellow fever areas. He proposed barricading the streets of infected neighborhoods and marking the houses. Dr. Cochran recommended sulfur candles or chlorine gas to disinfect affected houses.

In his discussion of PULMONARY CONSUMPTION, Cochran said: "Of all the physical diseases which flesh is heir to consumption, as the popular name, is that which inflicts upon civilized communities the largest amount of suffering and claims the largest rate of human lives. So dreadful have been its ravages that, in the language of another, 'it has been regarded as a special mode sent by providence to reduce a redundant population, as feeble trees in a forest are crowded out of existence by their more vigorous neighbors.'" Cochran disagreed that the disease was evenly distributed across areas and peoples. He stressed that by using vital statistics to study disease, we might find a way to avoid it.

Cochran's observations on tuberculosis are somewhat applicable today, with the introduction of antibiotic resistant strains of the organism, and the threat of epidemic especially among immune compromised persons. We seem to be confronted with the same problems that he had in 1870:

"Of the removable causes of consumption, there are two which have been so fully established by large statistical returns as to admit of no reasonable doubt:

1. The respiration of foul air by overcrowding and by defective ventilation. He stressed the reversal of disease by designing buildings with adequate ventilation.

2. Another very potent agent in the production of consumption is soil moisture. He gave examples from England that when underground drainage was established, cases dropped 15-41%.

Dr. Cochran believed that, even though he didn't know the answer to the problem of prophylaxis of consumption, the measures he had suggested would "rob the destroyer of one fourth to one third of his victims."

He had definite and dogmatic views on SANITARY SUPERVISION: "It may be true, according to the prevailing political theories, that knowledge of public affairs and ability to make laws comes, like Dogberry's reading and writing, by nature. But it is very certain that knowledge of medicine comes only as the reward of long and hard study -- only to those who scorn delight and love laborious days. Hence, in our schemes of sanitary improvement it becomes necessary to invoke the aid of medical science in the persons of its legitimate expounders -- regular well executed[sic] physicians.

"The carrying into practical operation of any sanitary system necessarily involves many problems, which require for their solution some knowledge of terrestrial mechanics and engineering; and, as knowledge of this sort is not learned in Dogberry's school any more than knowledge of medicine, we cannot dispense with the assistance of competent engineers. Cochran stressed "in the most emphatic choice of words" the need for a competent city engineer, searching elsewhere if a competent local man was not to be found.

Cochran then outlined the most pressing needs to be addressed by a city engineer:

1. An efficient drainage system, covering the city and its surrounding area, to prevent stagnation.

2. To secure an adequate supply of water "so that all filth might be washed away." He wanted baths in households, fountains in neighborhoods "so that every house would have the means of deluging itself with water, making destructive fires romantic impossibilities, and fire engines things of ornament rather than of use. "

3. To grade and pave streets in order to improve transportation and "prolong the lives of our horses." It would also eliminate clouds of dust.

Of one thing Cochran was most dogmatic: "all efforts toward sanitary improvement must be under the general direction of physicians -- medical experts; for the simple reason that nobody else can presume to have the requisite knowledge of diseases and their causes, and of available measures of prophylaxis. Therefore, it is necessary to inquire into the best organization of the Department of Health in our city government." But he cautioned against dumping waste into rivers or the seas. He strongly recommended the use of pumping stations which would separate the filth from the water and decontaminate it before allowing the cleaned water back into the system.

Cochran felt that the Chapter XIV and XV of Mobile's code of Ordinances, providing for quarantine and for hospital accommodation for the sick poor, was outdated, and should be thoroughly revised and extended considerably.

Regarding a BOARD OF HEALTH, Cochran recommended that it should consist exclusively of physicians of experience and proven ability. They should have general supervision over all matters relating to the health of the city, over quarantine and the establishment and management of pest-houses and public hospitals, over the streets and yards of the city; over public and private schools, jails, guardhouses, poor-houses and asylums; in a word, every interest of the city in which considerations of the public health are involved. Since the Board of Health would be essentially a deliberative body, Cochran wrote that it "would require an executive officer to provide them with information on which they should act, and it will require a secretary to keep records of their proceedings and attend to its correspondence. Under authority of the Board of Health, the Health Officer should be charged with the sanitary supervision and inspection of the entire city and its dependencies. For the vigor and prudent discharge of the duties of this position, a high order of ability is requisite; and as the consumption of time would be large, the compensation allowed ought to be liberal. The permanent executive officers of the Board of Health -- the health officer and the secretary -- ought to be nominated by the board itself."

The exhaustively researched and brilliantly envisioned paper as Dr. Cochran presented it to the Association was discussed by his colleagues and given their wholehearted endorsement. It was then published in the *Transactions* of 1871.

Mobile was weary of epidemics and Dr. Cochran's lucid analysis of the causes and effects and his clear explanation of the approach to prophylaxis and cure must have seemed a Godsend to the mayor and Common Council of the city. Cochran stirred up considerable interest with his papers and that led to the adoption of a health ordinance in 1871 by the City of Mobile. He, himself, wrote the ordinance, creating a health officer and placing the sanitary supervision of the city in the hands of a Board of Health elected by the Mobile Medical Society.   He was able to follow up his Transaction -published article on "Endemic and Epidemic diseases of Mobile" with the following:

"Post Scriptum, August, 1871, -- It affords me pleasure to be able to say that the Mayor and Common Council of the city of

Mobile have approved the views which I have developed in this paper, and have remodeled the Health Department of the city in accordance with the plan upon which I have insisted."

Under the ordinance, Cochran was elected Health Officer and served for two years, 1871 and 1872.

On October 1, 1871 a sixth child, a boy, Francis Lawrence, was born amid joy. Again, deep sorrow touched the personal lives of Jerome and his family. On December 4, Jerome's fortieth birthday, their infant son, Francis Lawrence, died at two months of age, the third angel in the cemetery.

Unrealized by Dr. Cochran, the tapestry of his life had taken on a rich complexity undreamed of. His genius was to lead the medical destiny of Alabama so far into the future, that, had he but foreseen the results of his vision, he would have been amply gratified. As it was, all he could do was work hard and forge ahead with what energy he could muster.

Since the work of Dr. Cochran becomes so complicated during the years of 1870 - 1873, we have chosen to separate -- for easier reading -- his work for the profession, for public hygiene, his fight against yellow fever, and his brilliant work in the basic sciences. Therefore, Chapter VI addresses the Profession, Chapter VII addresses Public Health, Chapter VIII addresses the yellow fever epidemic of 1873, and Chapter IX addresses his study of the White Blood Corpuscle.

Chapter VI

The Profusion of Genius
The Profession

- 1870-1873 -

In spite of his poor health and domestic tragedies, in the decade of the seventies Dr. Cochran achieved his greatest accomplishments for the State and for the medical profession in Alabama:

1. Crystallizing his plan for the structure of a strong authoritative Medical Association of the State of Alabama with legal and legislative functions.

2. Passage of medical practice laws giving the Association power to control the practice of medicine in Alabama.

3. Founding of the State Department of Public Health .

4. Eradication of yellow fever.

-1870-

Cochran had long considered that the Association should take over the state's public hygiene, but he truly found the Association of 1870, totally incapable of doing so. It was loosely bound together, like most medical groups in America. As secretary of the group, he could see the weaknesses: very few duties or responsibilities, no discipline or incentives, and it was more like a men's social club than a professional society. Some drastic changes were in order.

That year, Jerome Cochran planted the seed. He became a member of the committee to rewrite the constitution and bylaws, and began working hard to replace this loose club of doctors by an organized, responsible, well disciplined, self-perpetuating body capable of performing legislative functions.

-1871-

At the March 1871 meeting at Mobile, with Dr. Frank Armstrong Ross presiding, the proposal to reform the Medical Association was again made. They discussed the constitution and bylaws. He gave an impassioned presentation of the diseases prevalent and the needs of the public. He hoped that his plan for the Health Department would give them a better insight into his reasoning for certain features of the constitution and bylaws. In about four or five months they would get their copy of the *TRANSACTIONS* with everything again spelled out for them.

The members, as individuals, could not drain swamps to prevent malaria, but as a group and with the authority of the State backing them, they could. As individuals they could not clean up filth, but, if properly guided, city, county and state authorities could. They did not have remedies for the endemic and epidemic diseases that confronted them. Even their malaria patients, under good control with quinine, would slowly weaken, and become unable to work and pay their doctor bills. Since the 1842 advent of the use of ether as anaesthesia, soon followed by chloroform, more and more operations were feasible. But, he advocated, one must hesitate to remove an ovarian cyst in a malarial patient, thus preventing cures.

Cochran wondered if the present membership actually knew what had happened to the first Medical Association of the State of Alabama. The first association had a small membership. Over half had not paid their dues: in 1855, already over a thousand dollars in debt, the Association ordered 1500 copies of the *TRANSACTIONS* to be sent to all the doctors, newspaper editors, and intelligent citizens of the State. They could not pay this bill causing printers to refuse further work. Records of the Society ceased. It was clear to Cochran that this irresponsible care of finances -- not the Civil War[1] -- had bankrupted the Association and caused its demise.

Cochran believed that his plan for a firmly entrenched organization would lessen the chance of failure. As Secretary of the Association, he would see that no funds would be wasted and few would be asked of the members or the State. Instead, he turned to advertising. For example, the *Transactions* of 1872 bears a full page ad: "Everybody Should Buy their READY MADE CLOTHING at the Mammoth Clothing House of M.P. Levy & Co., Nos. 16, 18 and 20 North Water St., Mobile, Ala."

-1872-

In Huntsville, at the March meeting, Dr. George Earnest Kumpe Chairman of the Committee on Cochran's plan of constitution, submitted his report. He had asked the other committee members to examine the material and to forward their opinions. He reported:

"Drs. Johnson, Mason, and Robert Dickens Webb expressing themselves adverse to the adoption of the new constitution, upon the ground of its being too complicated, and for the further reason that the present constitution, under which this Association had obtained to its present prosperity, was sufficient for the future. Dr. Gratz A. Moses signified his willingness to adopt the new constitution as a whole." None of the other members of the committee were at the session. Pointing up the irresponsibility of the members, Kumpe made his declaration:

"... [I cannot] believe with them, that this organization, under the present constitution, will ever remedy the evils which all complain of, and which so materially prevent the medical profession of this State from attaining that degree of prosperity and respectability to which it is justly entitled, namely, admitting of incompetent persons into the ranks of healers."

----

[1]This idea was later reiterated by Barkley Wallace Toole, M.D , Talladega, "The Annual Message of the President," *Transactions of MASA*, Selma, April 1897, pp. 20-21.

Dr. Thomas Childress Osborn of Hale County presided. The proposal seemed certain of passage. But Cochran wanted time to formulate, then present a rebuttal to those members opposed. He wanted everyone to understand the need for the new constitution and bylaws. He asked for a postponement until the 1873 convention. The Constitution was tabled.

Now in that year, Dr. Cochran was very busy: as Health Officer of Mobile, as Professor of Chemistry at the Medical College, and as Secretary of the Association with all the duties therein. He was active on various committees. In short, he had much on his plate.

He had lost three children in as many years, and Sarah Jane [at age 37] was pregnant again, due in November. He also still suffered from the lingering illness contracted in Nashville in February of 1870.

Without respite, calamities continued to follow each other. On November 14, less than a year after the death of little Francis Lawrence, the Cochrans' seventh child, a son, Lamoua B. was born and died. A fourth angel in their family grave-site. Were the children left to them, Ina Lou, aged 12, Jerome Bowling, aged nine, and Edmund Collins, aged four, to be survivors? Or would these, also, be taken from them?

-1873-

At this annual meeting, Cochran resigned as Secretary of the Association, writing: "During these five years I have done for the Association a large amount of hard work. Whether it has been done wisely and well must be left for others to judge of [sic]. One thing I can avow with a conscience void of offense, namely: that whatever I have done in my official capacity has been done solely for the honor and dignity, and advancement of the profession of medicine in this State; and not with any purpose directly or indirectly of personal advantage or of personal ambition. For the hard work and the brain work which I have done I have had no reward in money, or in money's worth. I have paid my annual dues the same as any other member. I have paid my own expenses incurred in attending the meetings of the Association; and have steadily refused to avail myself of the resolution ordering my expenses to be paid out of the Treasury of the Association." He wrote of his desire to serve the Association in the cause of professional progress in the future: "Freely I have entered this office; freely I have labored in it, freely I retire from it. I have ends in view that I can forward to better advantage in a different capacity."[2]

The Association met in Tuscaloosa in March 25-27, 1873 with Dr. George Ernest Kumpe, of Leighton, presiding. The new constitution was discussed in detail.

It is interesting to note that opposition to the adoption of the constitution was from members who did not want the formation of a strong central organization because it might impinge on their rights as individuals. Their principle objections:

1. It was too complex and cumbersome, and

2. It was aristocratic and oligarchical and, therefore, inconsistent with the genius and institutions of the American people.

Cochran had planned his rebuttal.[3] He scathingly, yet professionally replied to the first objection in a published address as follows:

"Against this plan the objection is urged that it is too complex, that it lacks perfection of simplicity which is necessary for the easy and efficient attainment of the ends in view. It is most strange to me that an objection of this sort should be urged by gentlemen who have so often feared to expose its weakness. It is stranger still that such an objection should be urged by persons claiming any decent acquaintance with the fundamental principles of comparative anatomy and physiology.

"It is strangest of all that argumentation so flimsy should be expected to influence the judgment of a body of educated physicians. Simplicity is in no case the measure of perfection. And this rule is true, without exception, and applies to all organisms of

---

[2]Annual Report of the Secretary, *Transactions of MASA*, 1874, pp. 10-11.

[3]Because this rebuff shows so much of who Dr. Cochran was and what his values were, it is presented in its entirety.

every nature whatever. It is true of the animal hierarchy. The simplest animals stand lowest in the scales; the most perfect and the most powerful stand highest in the scale. Compare, for example, the shapeless mass of jelly which constitutes the body of aureolia with the elaborate and complex apparatus of organs which is found in the body of man, fearfully and wonderfully made. It is, for example, the rude and simple habits true in social organisms. Compare for example, the rude and simple habits and laws of a tribe of African Hottentot, or bigger Indians, with the elaborate and infinitely complicated social and government arrangements of any civilized European or American nation. It is true even of machines made by human hands. Compare for example, an old-fashioned scythe with one of McCormick's reapers. I cannot now go into an extended development of this principle, but these few familiar examples must make it plain even to the commonest apprehension, and it would be an insult to the intelligence of the audience I am now addressing to suppose that further argument on this point could be needed to convince them of it, indeed, I ought to apologize to such an audience for mentioning it at all. The case is so clear that only the blind could fail to see it."

He attacked the second objection in this manner:

"The doctrines of freedom and equality furnish favorite themes of *ad capiendum* declamation to American demagogues, who as a rule care a great deal for office and the emoluments of office, and very little for the imprescriptible authority and majesty of truth; but we seek in vain for any realization of these doctrines in any of the kingdoms of nature or in any of the kingdoms of man. In the words of Pope:

'Order is heaven's first law, and this contest,

Some are, and must be, greater than the rest.'

"It certainly does not require any very lofty intelligence to understand that the rule of the wise few is better than the rule of the ignorant many. Hence it is that everywhere, whether nominally so or not, yet in fact and reality, the reins of power are in the hands of those to whom superior wisdom has given superior strength. The strong rule the States. The strong rule the churches. The strong rule everywhere, and everywhere rule by divine right. And everywhere, in the words of Mr. John Ruskin:

> 'Government and cooperation are in all things
> the laws of Life; and anarchy and competition
> the Laws of death.'"

Line by line and paragraph by paragraph, each section of the constitution was discussed, then was voted on separately. The process took two days. With strong support from the North Alabama delegates led by Dr. Kumpe, and with minor amendments, the constitution was adopted in its entirety by a two-thirds majority.

The new constitution established the organizational structure of the Medical Association of the State of Alabama that has served well for over one hundred years and appears to be permanent.

Briefly the new constitution provided for the following: an executive body with a president who exercised supervisory authority over the Association; two vice-presidents, one each for the northern and southern regions of the state. These vice-presidents were in charge of county medical societies; and there was a secretary, a treasurer, and a board of five censors whose purpose was to divest the profession of incompetent men, and" to regulate the practice of medicine so as to secure the just rights of the regular Profession, and restrict the various systems of quackery and irregular medicine within the narowest possible limits."[4] Dr. Cochran was here named as Senior Censor.[5]

One of the most distinctive features of the constitution was the role of the board of censors. All business of any nature presented to the Association, was to be referred to the board of censors without motion or debate, to be studied by the board and reported back to

---

[4]First Annual Report of the Board of Censors, *Transactions of MASA 1874*, pp. 19-20.

[5]The number of Censors was increased to ten after 1877 when it also became the State Board of Health.

the association with their recommendations and reasons, after which it was to be discussed and voted on by the Association. The board members were: Drs. Jerome Cochran of Mobile, for five years; James Guild, Sr., of Tuscaloosa, for four years; A.G. Mabry of Selma, for three years; R. F. Michel of Montgomery, for two years; and George I. Kumpe of Leighton, for one year. The legislative branch of the Association was the College of Counsellors and Delegates from the county medical societies. The College of Counsellors was limited to one-hundred in number, who had won their places through service and merit. The counsellors were elected for life by the State Association. All the officers and censors were selected from their membership.

The county medical societies were chartered by the Association and their members were the membership of the State Association. Each county medical society was allowed to send two delegates to all the State Association meetings. Anticipating the action of the State Legislature by several years, Cochran had added a supplementary "Book of the Rules," that included the following: An ordinance in Relation to the Boards of Medical Examiners; an Ordinance on Relation to the Duties and Obligations of County Medical Societies; an Ordinance Creating a State Health Officer; Ordinances in Relation to the Duties and Obligations of County Medical Societies; an Ordinance regarding the Revision of the Rolls; an Ordinance in Relation to the Publishing Committee and its Duties.

The constitution provided for a strong organization with firm centralized powers. The membership of the profession responded with renewed confidence in the Association. Membership rose rapidly so that by 1893 there were some 1,100 dues-paying members ($10 annually), and by that time there was a medical society in each of the 67 counties. The first phase of Jerome Cochran's life work had been completed.

Chapter VII

The Profusion of Genius
The Fight For Public Health

-1870-1874-

Cochran left no stones upturned in his pursuit of knowledge and understanding. His passion for the betterment of health led him to read everything he could find, looking for tidbits, however distant, however obscure. He researched -- everything. In order to understand the quest for public health undertaken by Jerome Cochran, it is necessary to view slices of the world in which he lived; meet the men -- and women -- in America and around the world who fought tough battles to improve health, and who wrote about their discoveries, their beliefs. These findings shaped Cochran's views and proved his own vision.

-Early days-

Two great epidemic diseases, cholera and yellow fever, did more than anything else to raise demands for a public health service. After yellow fever had devastated Philadelphia in 1793, doctors,

Benjamin Rush[1] among them, who believed the disease was due to local filth, persuaded the city fathers to establish a permanent board of health; the first in America. These doctors also persuaded them to clean up the city's streets, and to build the first free public water system in the country. Although Rush was wrong in the belief that filth caused yellow fever, the public health measures brought about lowered death rates from all causes, and gave Philadelphia the reputation of being the "first in the cause of sanitary reform." Other of America's great cities followed Philadelphia's lead, and the public health movement spread.

Public health and hygiene made considerable progress from the days of Sylvester Graham in the early 1800's to the time Jerome Cochran became the first Professor of Hygiene and Medical Jurisprudence at the Medical College of Alabama in 1873.

Sylvester Graham was a temperance lecturer in Pennsylvania. In 1830 he was inspired by religious enthusiasm to save all mankind. Playing the game of "one-up-manship" with the other reformers of the day, the abolitionists, prohibitionists, women suffragists etc., he included gluttony and drunkenness in his repertory of deadly sins from which he must save mankind. He looked around for more sins to add to his portfolio, and what he found amazed him. When he grasped the full situation, it fired his spirit to a white heat. Once aroused, he discovered that the problem was even more serious than he had supposed. The American people were apparently headed straight for hell, or at least to physical degeneracy. Men not only suffered from bad habits connected with food and drink, but they were committing many other sins against nature: lack of bathing, loitering at pool halls, smoking and chewing tobacco. You name the sin and it had its devotees.

Conditions in winter did not encourage bathing with well water, heated before an open fire. The invention of the cast iron stove by Benjamin Franklin in 1744 made it easier, but everyone knew that

---

[1]Benjamin Rush, a forceful figure in 18th century medicine in America, Revolutionary War hero, signer of the Declaration of Independence, strong believer in therapeutic blood letting.

bathing in winter caused colds and ague. Besides, it was not to be until the 1830's that advances in ironmaking and transportation made cast iron stoves widely available. People felt that bathing only removed dirt, and wasn't dirt a sign of honest toil and to be commended?

Graham advocated not only a vegetarianism that included whole-wheat products, notably his whole-wheat crackers. He also lauded the virtues of bathing, fresh air, sunlight, dress reform, sex hygiene, and exercise. Upon invitation, he addressed the Franklin Institute of Philadelphia. He gave lectures in New York and New England to audiences numbering as many as two thousand people. Some good came out of Grahamism. The influence of Graham's movement on personal hygiene was a factor in the improvement of public health as a whole in America.

-Old World Advances-
Elsewhere throughout the world medicine had been making slow but significant progress. In 1858 Virchow published his *Cellular Pathology*, establishing the human cells as the source of some diseases. Kékulé postulated the ring structures of some organic compounds, making it possible to explain the complex chemical formulae of organic compounds. In 1860 Lemaire pointed out the antiseptic properties of carbolic acid, paving the way for Lord Joseph Lister's aseptic surgery. The Berlin Medical Society was founded. In 1861 Pasteur discovered anaerobic bacteria. Max Schultze defined protoplasm and the cell. In 1864 Parkes' "Manual of Practical Hygiene" was published. In 1865 Gregor Mendel published his "Memoir on Plant Hybridity," the beginning of the science of genetics, and Villemin demonstrated the infectiousness of tuberculosis. In 1866 Voit established the first hygienic laboratory in Munich, Bavaria. 1867 was a significant year. Lister introduced antiseptic surgery, using Lemaire's carbolic acid as his antiseptic agent. The first International Medical Congress met in Paris. The Suez Canal opened. In 1869 Virchow urged the medical inspection of schools; Oscar Liebrich demonstrated the hypnotic effect of Chloral Hydrate. In 1871 The German Empire was

established; Darwin's *Descent of Man* was published; Weigert demonstrated bacteria stained with carmine. In 1872 the Infant Life Protection Act was passed in England. In 1873 revaccination became compulsory in Germany; there was an international Cholera Conference in Vienna; Ehrlich introduced dried and stained blood smears, and Willy Kuhne discovered trypsin.

Basic medical research was moving forward in Europe and had also begun in earnest in America. It would appear that the people of the world were becoming interested in their public health and hygiene, and in investigating the causes of disease. From 1870-1873 Dr. Jerome Cochran was preparing Alabama as rapidly as he could.

-Women in medicine-

Ever since the emergence of Homo sapiens, woman has been the hygienist, first of the family, then of the community. She was the one most responsible for nurturing and protecting the immature infant until it could fend for itself. She treated her mate when the prey he would kill for table food got the better of him. In the nineteenth century, mother treated the children's colds, cuts and bruises, made them bathe, brush their teeth, get enough sleep, saw that they were warmly clad. She also suggested when her husband needed a bath, poured out his whiskey when he drank too much, made him go outside to smoke tobacco, and not cuss in the presence of the preacher.

Much of the hygiene, and especially feminine hygiene, practiced in the nineteenth century was done by women without any medical training or scientific learning. Some women, chafing under the injustice of the system, resolved to break the lock that held them back. The Women's Rights movement and the Public Health movement ran parallel and simultaneously in America.

Clarissa Harlowe (Clara) Barton[2], (1821-1912), following

---

[2] Elizabeth Brown Pryor, *Clara Barton, Professional Angel, 1993,* University of Pennaylvania Press, Philadelphia, PA.

the practices of Florence Nightingale in the fields of nursing and hygiene, introduced military nursing by female nurses in America's Civil War. In 1881 she founded the American Red Cross, a strong force in the public health of America.

Elizabeth Blackwell, M.D. (1821-1910)[3] and her sister, *Emily Blackwell, M.D.*,[4] together in 1857 founded the Medical School of the New York Infirmary for Women and Children.

Elizabeth, after witnessing the death of a dear friend, felt that her friend could have been saved if that friend's physicians had examined her adequately. Blackwell felt that a female doctor, who would not be shocked by examining the female anatomy, might have saved her friend. She wondered how many women had been lost because of shy physicians.   After many tries and much frustration, she was accepted by a medical school and obtained her M.D. degree on January 23, 1849.   She became the first genuine practicing woman doctor in America.   At a time when there was some debate as to whether women had souls, their private anatomy was considered sacrosanct. Women were not given any instructions on their special functions. The reason given? It might make them nervous. Elizabeth Blackwell wrote and spoke many times on the female functions. She was considered in some circles to be a scarlet woman.

Marie Zakrzewska, M.D.[5], her friends and students called her "Zack," was the granddaughter of a gypsy queen, and her grandfather was a surgeon attached to the army of Frederick the Great.   At age twenty-two she became chief accoucheuse and Professor in the School of Midwifery at Berlin.   She came to America and, after more training with Drs. Elizabeth and Emily

---

[3]Arthur Selwin-Brown , Sc., M.A., Ph. D., LLD., *Modern Women Doctors: Glimpses of the Struggles of the Pioneers*, Capehart-Brown Co., Inc., N.Y., N.Y. 1928, p.208.

[4]*Ibid*, p. 209.

[5]*Ibid*, p. 110

Blackwell, moved on to Boston where she founded the New England Hospital for Women and Children.

Ann Preston, M.D.,[6] was born in 1813; her father was a Quaker minister. She graduated at the first commencement of the Women's Medical College of Pennsylvania; she remained as Professor of Physiology. She later became Dean of that college and was one of the founders of a hospital for women and children connected with the Women's Medical College of Pennsylvania.

Mary Putnam Jacobi, M.D.,[7] was born in 1842. She was the daughter of the founder of the publishing house of Putnam in New York City. Mary received her M.D. degree at the Women's Medical College of Pennsylvania. She married Dr. Abraham Jacobi. She founded the children's department of Mount Sinai Hospital in New York, and was the first woman admitted to membership in the New York Academy of Medicine and the New York State Medical Association. Her writings were admired for their literary quality as well as for their professional merit. Through her writing, she made known to the world that women are competent to study, practice, and teach medicine successfully.

Helen Webster, M.D.,[8] *née Worthington* was born in Boston in 1837 and died in 1904. She graduated from the Massachusetts Female Medical College in 1862, while Dr. Zakrzewska was still there. In an act of patriotism she gave up her plans to study in the great medical centers of Europe and went to work in a military hospital in Washington D.C., as a nurse. She met and married a young surgeon, Dr. William Webster. In 1874, she became the college physician and Professor of Physiology at Vassar College. She was the first female member of her County Medical Society.

These women doctors were pioneers. They found a way to ease

---

[6]*Ibid.*, pp. 211, 125-16.

[7]Mary Putnam Jacobi, "Shall Women Practice Medicine?" *North American Review 134*, January, 1882, p. 54.

[8]Arthur Selwin-Brown, *op.cit.*, pp. 217-19.

into the man's world of medicine against obstacles that to many people would have been insurmountable. They softened the pain and smoothed the roughness of eighteenth and nineteenth century medicine. It was not until 1893, when the Johns Hopkins Medical School admitted its first class, that women were admitted to coeducational medical schools on truly the same basis as men.

-Public health: antebellum-

Dr. Wilson Jewell persuaded the Philadelphia Board of Health to call a national sanitary convention, which was held in Philadelphia in 1857. Subsequent sanitary conventions were held annually, during the ensuing three years: in Baltimore, 1858; New York, 1859; and Boston, in 1860. Town and city officials and physicians interested in public health originally met to discuss quarantine rules and regulations. Finding that they needed to influence public opinion, and that they needed help from engineers, they also discussed getting laymen involved in the movement.

Jewell and the others became convinced that experimental studies of sewage disposal, ventilation, and disinfection were urgently needed, as well as pure food and drug laws. In 1860 at the meeting in Boston, Richard Arnold, the mayor of Savannah, Georgia, complimented the people of Boston for their hospitality, and Georgia was roundly applauded by all the assembled delegates. Union of interests was bringing union of minds. Jewell became the leading spirit in these four annual national sanitary conventions. They planned to meet the next year in Cincinnati to form a permanent national health association.[9] The War Between the States intervened. The nation had gone from the sanity of mutual interest in public sanitation to the insanity of a fratricidal civil war. The noble Dr. Wilson Jewell disappeared from the pages of history.

---

[9]We assume that Dr. Jerome Cochran, then studying medicine, would have read of these endeavors and absorbed their import.

-The War years-

At the onset of the Civil War, it became evident that ancillary assistance would be needed to support the troops. In the big cities of the North, women organized the United States Sanitary Commission, to satisfy that need. The Commission provided temporary shelters, clean bedding, wholesome food, and other services for the army's men.

Through lack of resources, the women of the South were not able to match the work of their Northern sisters. Many women's aid societies were organized paralleling the activities of the Commission. Additionally, they helped run medical supplies through the Northern blockade, and took the ailing troops into their homes.[10]

Both sides of the War Between the States lost heavily from disease. During the first year of the war eighty-five percent of the deaths in both armies were due to illnesses having no connection with the battlefield. Although much was lost to the war, including Alabama's state-supported medical school, a few principles were engraved in the minds of the medical men who were drawn into the conflict. Dr. Jerome Cochran learned that there was very little an individual doctor could do to cure the great infectious diseases then prevalent. He gained the belief that a concerted effort by everyone was indicated to prevent the diseases, with the doctors as the leaders. This belief pushed him into his life's work.

-Post War years-

In 1871, the American Medical Association had asked that state representatives create State Boards of Health according to the only existing system: the Massachusetts/California model. Dr. J. S. Weatherly, as Alabama's representative, was sent to the San Francisco meeting and subsequently brought home all papers and recommendations which he obtained.

In 1872, at the annual meeting of the Medical Association of the

---

[10]Paul E. Steiner, (1968) *Medical Military Portraits.*

State of Alabama in Huntsville, March 26-28, Dr. Cochran, having thoroughly studied what Weatherly had brought, expressed his disagreement of the model and proceeded to present his own. Weatherly stated his views in favor of the Massachusetts/California model.[11]

To the members of the Medical Association of the State of Alabama, Cochran said: "I am free to say that I have no special objections to the Massachusetts and California plan, in itself. If no other arrangement was suggested, I would very cheerfully advocate it, and do all I could to secure its adoption by the legislative authorities of the State. A State Board, so constituted, would undoubtedly render valuable service to the State, and make valuable contributions to our knowledge of the natural history of disease and of the influence of various circumstances, geological, topographical and meteoro-logical, upon the sanitary conditions of localities. If, then, I oppose this system of organizing a health department for the State, it is not because I think it intrinsically bad, but simply because I think I have a better plan to offer to your consideration."

Calling upon his experience as Health Officer of Mobile, his amassed knowledge from his research, and his farsighted vision for the State, he addressed the Association members, outlining the following for consideration:

"...I would have a general health law passed by the Legislature of the State, carefully prepared, so as not to stand in need of frequent revision or amendment.

"I would have this law to invest the Medical Association of the State with the functions, powers and responsibilities of a State Board of Health; and these functions I would have exercised through such organs as the Association which in its wisdom, might think best.

"I would have the same act of the Legislature to invest each county medical society with the functions of a county board of

----

[11]Cochran, "The Medical Profession," *Memorial Record of Alabama, Vol.II.,* Brant & Fuller, Madison , Wis., 1893., p. 129.

health, said functions to be exercised through such organs as the said county societies should, in their wisdom determine to be best."

It was decided that a committee of three would be formed to go over both propositions and report on the last day of the session. Neither Cochran nor Weatherly was on the committee. On that last day, "the discussion was conducted with much earnestness on both sides and resulted in the emphatic endorsement by the association of the new plan."[12]

Cochran's plan was in the form of a bill embodying all the details. The newly formed Board of Censors, with Cochran as its chair, was ordered to present it to Alabama's next legislative session.

Cochran did submit to the Legislature of the State of Alabama a bill "containing the form of an act to invest the Medical Association of the State with the functions of a State Board of Health, in accordance with the plan submitted by me to the Association at the Huntsville meeting and which the Association saw fit to approve and endorse."[13] The act was referred to the Legislature's Committee on Municipal Organization in 1873, and again in 1874.

Also in 1872, Cochran was a member of the committee that met in New York City Health Commissioner Stephen Smith's office and organized the American Public Health Association.

At the annual meeting of the Alabama Association, Tuscaloosa, March 25-27, 1873, Cochran's plan for a Board of Health was endorsed by the Association by unanimous vote .

For the General Assembly, Cochran put the proposed legislation into words. It was finally enacted into a law of the State on February 19, 1875. This law makes the State Medical Association, the State Board of Health and the County Medical Societies in

---

[12]*Ibid.*

[13]*Transactions of MASA,* 1873, p. 10.

affiliation with it, the "County Boards of Health."[14]

Meanwhile, in 1873 in Mobile, the opposition party came into control of the city. They abolished Mobile's Board of Health, and with it the office of Health Officer. Jerome Cochran was fired. These officials instead created an Advisory Board of Health and a City Physician. This organization was composed of purely political appointees and the tragedy is that they failed to prevent a yellow fever epidemic in the city in 1873. The practicing physicians regarded this political advisory board as nothing more than a nuisance and a waste of time and refused to cooperate with it. The Advisory Board quit functioning.

Jerome Cochran was out of a job. He had had to give up most of the patient care aspect of his practice of medicine due to his own ill health, and the loss of income must have been a blow. He was not permitted to treat the city in the face of the worst yellow fever epidemic that ever hit the area. This epidemic raged for months. The quarantine practices Cochran had installed were not pursued effectively and unnecessary deaths occurred.[15]

But in this year, 1873, Jerome had definitely decided to pursue public health as a specialty. He closed his Mobile office on the corner of Dauphin and Hamilton and listed his residence and his office at 114 St. Francis, the fourth house south of Jackson.[16]

---

[14]These provisions had been incorporated in the Rules and Bylaws of the Medical Association of the State of Alabama as already adopted by the Association.

[15]For extensive detail, see next Chapter.

[16]City Directory of Mobile, 1874.

Chapter VIII

Basic Science

That Jerome Cochran was a genius, there is little doubt. There are many definitions of genius, but we see in Cochran's case, a man of superior intelligence and with superb self-confidence and tremendous drive. Many features of intelligence are inherited, the self-confidence is, to some extent, an ethnic trait. It may be believed that a tremendous driving force is the true mark of genius. A brief perusal of Cochran's family tree reveals fairly marked intelligence; his sons who survived to adulthood were successful business men; two of his grandsons, Schamyl and Walker Cochran, were graduates of the United States Naval Academy and achieved rather high rank as naval officers. Each retired after serving in two world wars with the rank of Commander. Jerome Cochran was Scotch-Irish. There is no other ethnic group in the world so stubborn.

Where did Cochran get that tremendous drive? Ill health in infancy and early childhood may have been a factor. Whether severe ill health is more frequent among geniuses is difficult to say, but there is a long list of unquestionable persons of genius who were so burdened by disease that the wonder is that they ever accomplished anything. This can be said for the German poet Heinrich Heine, as well as of Elizabeth Barrett Browning. Voltaire was sickly to the point that his parents despaired of his life. Most of his work was done lying in bed. Immanuel Kant was so frail that it was feared that he might be blown away by a strong wind. De Quincey, Thomas Carlyle, Charles Darwin, John Keats, Robert Louis Stevenson, Moliere, Chopin, Chekhov -- to name but a few -- suffered chronic, debilitating illnesses, yet their genius and accomplishments cannot be denied.

Certain psychologists, notably those of the school of Alfred Adler, stress the influence of bodily defects on the personality. These defects, such as Cochran's fairly small stature, his sallow complexion, (and possibly more imagined bodily failures) would qualify. It seems that these defects give rise to an inferiority complex. The feeling of inferiority causes the individual to compensate by extraordinary efforts, even to the point of achieving genius. To prove their point, the Adlerites point to blind John Milton, deaf Beethoven, clubfooted Byron, shrunken-legged Sir Walter Scott, stuttering Charles Lamb; to dwarflike Alexander Pope, whose grotesque body was said to "resemble a question mark." Of a different stripe, Kaiser Wilhelm II of Germany was born with a withered left arm that drove him to attempt to gain recognition as a military leader, and to attempt world conquest.

Jerome Cochran was chronically ill all his life. Many of the doctors of that period suffered guilt feelings because of their inability to heal sick people. That feeling drove J. Marion Sims to research. It drove John Wyeth to a second M.D. degree and the founding of the New York Polyclinic Medical College -- the first post-graduate medical school in America. This professional guilt feeling also drove both Walter Reed and Jerome Cochran to achieve double M.D. degrees.

-1873-

Dr. Cochran had just completed engineering the acceptance of the constitution and by laws which he had written for the Medical

Association of the State of Alabama. He was suffering from an unknown malady that had first affected him like rheumatism, then invaded the alimentary canal, and finally assumed a more neuralgic character that had hung on for three years and showed no sign of letting up.

He had been forced out of public health by Mobile's new government, a fact which frustrated him mightily, especially in the face of the yellow fever epidemic. He wound up, true to his analytical logic and his convictions, in the midst of a debate about what he considered the inadvisability of the Medical College faculty taking over the City Hospital from the religious order of the Daughters of Charity who held it under lease from the city. He quit his position as chemistry professor.[1] He was, therefore, out of two jobs. Over the previous four years he had sustained the deaths of three children. He was emotionally and physically tired.

His reaction to this situation? Simple. He plunged into literature. He wrote a learned scientific paper on "The White Blood-Corpuscle in Health and Disease."[2] The unusual features of this endeavor were:

1. The paper had little to do with the chemistry that he had been teaching.

2. It had nothing to do with medical legislation or politics.

The paper was a comprehensive review of the basic science of biology as it stood in 1873, and as such, it was pointing the way toward the philosophy and research tools that were to bring on the renaissance of scientific medicine in the next century.

Cochran's paper should be on the reading list for anyone who would like to probe the thought processes of this illustrious man. One must remember that in 1873 there were no motorized vehicles; Thomas Alva Edison did not invent the incandescent light bulb until 1879; the typewriter had not yet come into use; Ehrlich would

---

[1]"Doctor Jerome Cochran of Alabama," *Op.dit.*, p. 7.

[2]Jerome Cochran, M.D., "The White Blood-Corpuscle in Health and in Disease," *Transactions of MASA*, 1874, pp. 231-255.

introduce dried blood smears with improved staining the following year -- 1874; Landsteiner would not discover the blood groups until after the turn of the century. Cochran was dealing with unstained, rather amorphous microscopic globs of jelly-like substance, the structure and function of which had only recently been partially clarified.

He was aware that most of his readers did not possess microscopes, nor were they able to keep up with the basic science literature. Even Cochran had had difficulty finding sufficient current scientific literature.

He began his work by asking the question, "What is a white blood corpuscle?" He answered the question in his characteristic dogmatic fashion by stating:

"There is no more important question than this in the whole of the broad realm of philosophical biology.

"...As the result of recent investigations the white corpuscles have been invested with properties and powers of such unexpected and comprehensive character as to necessitate the revision, and even the entire reconstruction, of many of the most important of physiological and pathological doctrines.

"We know now that the white corpuscle is not simply a geometrical solid, granular and spheroidal, except when it is dead or dormant; that it is not a comparatively unimportant constituent of the animal body, without any definite physiological history, and without any special work to do in the economy of animal life. On the contrary, in current biological speculation, it has risen not simply to a position of comparative importance, but to a position in which it overshadows all other anatomical and physiological elements. The stone so long rejected of the builders has become, indeed, the chief of the corner -- the foundation stone upon which must be constructed the whole edifice of the physiology of the future.

"Let us see, then, if we can get some adequate conception of what this marvelous physiological factor is.

"In composition it is albuminous and colloidal. This much we have already settled. It is a mass of living protoplasm -- a lump of animated jelly, colorless, translucent, homogeneous without shape, and without ascertainable structure. It is the typical animal cell in its highest and freest development. It eats and drinks and grows. It breathes and lives and moves. It is obedient to the primal mandate, and multiplies its generations under the sun. In very truth it is a living creature. It belongs to Haeckel's kingdom of the Protistae. It is allied to the amoebae. Yes, verily, it is an amoeba; but an amoeba of marked characteristics, one of which is that it has its habitat in the fluids of living bodies, another, that it lives not for itself but for the service of the bodies in which it is found.

"In order that this summary description of the white corpuscle of the blood may be adequately understood, I must give some account of the modern doctrine of cells; and some account of the natural history of the amoeba."

Cochran defined protoplasm as:

"...the living matter of living creatures; the matter through whose agency all their tissues and organs are constructed; the matter through whose marvelous endowments all vital functions such as growth, development, movement, metamorphosis, and reproduction, are accomplished. This thaumaturgic matter of life is always and everywhere of the same nature. The most refined methods of chemical, physical, and physiological analysis have not enabled us to distinguish the protoplasm of animals from the protoplasm of plants.[3]

"The demonstration of protoplasm as the one sole form of living matter in all the kingdoms of organic nature and the origin of all the tissues and organs of plants and of animals in multiform metamorphoses of protoplasm, is the most important achievement of contemporary physiology. It is to physiology what the law of gravitation is to astronomy."

---

[3]Dr. Cochran recognized that not all albuminous colloids are living material. He referred to Dr. Lionel Beale, who distinguished two kinds of matter. first as germinal matter or bioplasm, corresponding to living protoplasm; second, which he called formed material, which has passed into the structural elements of tissues and ceased to be truly living.

Cochran reviewed the work of Felix Dujardin, who in 1835 referred to the substance which he saw in lower life forms as sarcode. He then referred to the work of Max Schultze who noted the similarity of sarcode to the contents of cells of higher animals. Then he named Unger, Brucke, Haeckel, Kuhne, Huxley, and Beale, pioneers in the field who seemed to prove "-- that living matter is always and everywhere of the same identical nature, -- the same in its chemical constitution, the same in its physical properties, the same in its vital endowments."

There was no way Cochran could have anticipated Thomas Hunt Morgan's work on chromosomes and the subsequent discovery of DNA and the genome of animals. Cochran reviewed in some detail, the history of the cell theory from Aristotle, Galen and Fallopius through the early microscopists, with their imperfect instruments; from Swammerdam 1658; Robert Hooke 1667; Malpighi 1670; Leeuwenhoek, 1687, who described accurately the blood corpuscles in man and in animals, to Schleiden and Schwann, who formulated the cell theory in 1838-1839. He interpreted Schleiden and Schwann as believing in the spontaneous generation of cells. After lavishly praising the pioneer cytologists Cochran says this of them: "Nevertheless, there is hardly a single point of their description of the genesis and structure of cells which has not been either altogether overthrown or else largely modified by the results of later investigations."

He felt that more primitive cells might not have nuclei or cell walls. He believed that, "...their investing wall is caused by the consolidation of their most external portion, while the nucleus is due to a new growth of younger protoplasm within the original mass."

Cochran didn't follow Virchow in his *omnis cellula é cellula.* He preferred the theories of Dr. Beale. He preferred to call the living matter bioplasm, and he designated the cell as a bioplast. He held with the school of Virchow, that living matter, and living matter only, can generate living matter; and that therefore, every cell must originate in the proliferation of some pre-existing cell. He held further, that:

"... all cells, or bioplasts are in the beginning simply extremely minute, solid, homogeneous, and individualized masses of living matter or bioplasm; and that all bioplasts grow, not by superposition of additional bioplasm upon their external surfaces, but by the genesis and integration of bioplasm in their central parts; so that in every bioplast the central parts are always the youngest and most vigorous; while the peripheral parts, being older and feebler, grow continually less and less active in the discharge of vital functions, and at last cease in any proper sense of the word, to live at all."

Of the amoeba he has this to say:

"In their simpler forms they exhibit no structural differentiation whatever, not even a contained nucleus nor an investing membrane, but are homogeneous throughout. They can hardly be called organisms, because they are entirely destitute of organs. In brief, they are extremely minute masses of protoplasm -- little microscopic lumps of living jelly.

"Still they manifest all the essential phenomena of life. They move; they eat; they grow; they reproduce their kind. They are sprawling things, without any definite or abiding shape, and go crawling about, in no particular direction, and with no obvious purpose. They thrust out any portion of their jelly like bodies into an improvised arm or foot; and this may be immediately retracted, and another thrust out in some other direction, or its extremity may become fixed and drag the whole body after it. If they come in contact with a particle of food, mouth and stomach are improvised for its appropriation, the soft body of the creature opens to receive it, and flows slowly around it so as to inclose it completely; and when all the nutritive material has been extracted from it, opens again, and the indigestible debris is rejected through an improvised vent which immediately disappears. If one of them is separated into any number of fragments, each fragment becomes a complete amoeba, -- lives and grows, and pursues an entirely independent career. Like Milton's angels, they are vital in every part, and cannot but by annihilating die. Per contra, if two or more of them come together they immediately fuse into one, and neither joint nor seam remains to mark the place of union. A large number thus fused together into a considerable mass constitutes what is called a plasmodium. ...The soft homogeneous protoplasm inside the investing membrane undergoes a process of segmentation exactly analogous with the segmentation of the mammalian ovum during the initial stages of foetal development. But the subsequent history of the segments is different. In the mammalian ovum all the segments concur towards the formation of a single complex organism; while every separate segment of the encysted amoeba develops into an individual living creature."[4]

"...There is good reason to believe that the amoeba may arise in still another way, -- that it may arise spontaneously in fluids holding organic matter in solution. ...What I have said applies chiefly to the lower amoebae, such as the Amoeba porrecta of Max Schultze; the Protamoeba primitiva of Haeckel; and the Protomyxa aurantiaca of the same author. ...I hope that I have said enough to indicate the true character, and the biological relations of these creatures, -- enough at least to show that there is ample warrant for the statement which I made a little while ago to the effect that the white blood-corpuscle is an amoeba. ...Under the microscope some forms of the amoeba and some forms of the white blood-corpuscle resemble each other so nearly as to be absolutely indistinguishable."

In the effort to explain the origin of the white corpuscle, Cochran combined them with the so called lymph-corpuscles and pus corpuscles and used the name leukocytes, suggested by Robin. He liked the word bioplast, introduced by Dr. Beale, "... it is of still wider application, comprehending all living cells whatsoever."

Cochran thought the observations by Wharton Jones and Dr. Addison in 1835 and in 1841, that blood leukocytes put out pseudopods like amoebae; and the observations that blood leukocytes from the blood-current passed through the walls of blood-vessels, by Dr. Addison, were tremendous, but:

"They failed to grasp the conception that the leukocytes were

---

[4]Unknowingly, he had described the life cycle of the malaria parasite.

endowed with independent amoeboid vitality and the faculty of spontaneous locomotion. They were consequently unable to give a rational explanation of the phenomena of which they were the first witnesses. They stood upon the threshold of the discovery which has revolutionized both physiology and pathology; but with the doors of the temple of life wide open before them, they saw nothing but shadows. Their observations bore no fruit, and very soon fell into oblivion."

Cochran believed that the discovery of anaesthesia and curare made the study of living preparations possible, and by using them, certain valuable observations were made by Professor von Recklinghausen in 1863:

"In this memoir von Recklinghausen established on a firm basis the following propositions:

1. That leukocytes exhibit rapid amoeboid changes of form.

2. That leukocytes possess the power of moving from place to place through the meshes of the soft tissues.

3. That leukocytes are capable of flowing around minute solid particles of any kind so as to imprison them completely or partially in the soft protoplasm of their amoeboid bodies.

"...I add here the account of what he saw in his own words:

'The corpuscles differ very strikingly in their form from those from which the ordinary descriptions are taken. No globular forms present themselves, -- only jagged ones, and the prongs vary both in length and number. But what strikes one even after very brief examination is, that each corpuscle is constantly changing its shape. While one prong withdraws itself into the body of the corpuscle, another juts out. Each prong is at first a delicate, homogeneous, somewhat slimy thread; but it soon thickens at the base, lengthening at the same time. Then gradually the substance of the corpuscle tends more and more towards it, becoming smaller as the process gets larger, the whole thus assuming an oblong or protracted form. During this transformation the tip of the process is rounded off and subsides into the contour of the corpuscle; or new thread-like processes shoot out and again undergo the same changes.'"

Having stated that the white blood-corpuscle behaves like free living amoebae, Cochran attempted to prove that:

"...they are also of the same identical nature with the germinal vesicle, with the segmentation spheres of the developing ovum, and with the so-called cells of the blastodemic layers of the embryo, out of which are developed all the tissues and organs of all the higher orders of animal creatures, and it will be seen that I had ample warrant for the assertion that the stone so long rejected of the builders, has become the chief of the corner, -- that it was upon the foundation of the white blood-corpuscle that the physiology of the future was to be constructed."

In the discussion of the metamorphoses of leukocytes, Cochran expanded still further. He dropped the term leukocytes that he had used for white blood corpuscles and now he referred to them as bioplasts:

"We are now ready for the discussion of the metamorphoses of bioplasts, -- that is to say, for the discussion of the genesis, the growth and development of living tissues, and of living creatures, for all these questions will be found to be involved in the metamorphoses of white blood-corpuscles, or of their biological equivalents."[5]

Cochran next went into the reproduction of unicellular animals, then multicellular, primitive animals, then coelenterata, various insects and mammals, then mankind. He exhibited his vast knowledge of his subjects and drew some very interesting conclusions which seem logical. He made the observation that the germinal tissue of higher animals differentiates early in the developing foetus.

Cochran's essay on the White Blood Corpuscle was a classic of

---

[5]Viewing Dr. Cochran's essay after the passage of over one hundred and twenty years, one cannot help but be amazed at his conclusions. It is hoped the above quotations from it will suffice to show his reasoning, his tendencies to philosophical speculation and his lucid writing.

its time.[6] It was widely read by Alabama doctors and added to his reputation as a learned professor and physician.[7] This reputation for scholarship may have gained for him the following he needed for the legislation and professional rulings he was attempting to push through the State's General Assembly and the Medical Association of the State of Alabama.

Characteristically, Cochran felt he was missing something; that there was more depth to the knowledge and understanding than he could, at the time, conceive and convey. Therefore, he ended the essay on an apologetic note in which he stated:

"Here, for the present, this paper must close. I am fully aware how incomplete and defective it is, and would gladly make it better if circumstances were more auspicious. It has been written hurriedly, in the midst of many pressing engagements, and, worst of all, with but scanty access to books and authorities.

"Nevertheless, I am satisfied that the statements of facts will be found to accord very generally with the latest observations. For the scientific or speculative use which I have made of the facts, I am, of course, responsible. If my speculations are sometimes a little startling, I am not the less satisfied that in the main they will turn out to be the true interpretations of many recondite problems in physiology.

---

[6]One must admire the way he handled the basic sciences that had developed up to that time and were still developing. Current research has shown that an ovum taken from an unborn mammalian fetus may be combined with a sperm from an unborn male fetus and the resulting union can be carried to term in the uterus of a surrogate mother, and the resulting individual may be born from parents that never existed.

[7]Recently (1994) this writer (Dr. Morris) had the occasion to compare the most recent textbook of hematology with the one he used as a medical student in 1942. He was astounded by the immense mass of knowledge that had accrued in just fifty years. Dr. Cochran was using facts current one hundred and fifty years ago. Never mind that his conclusions were sometimes inaccurate. Christopher Columbus thought he had discovered India. We do not think the less of Paul Ehrlich, who examined 707 compounds before he discovered Salvarsan, the first effective cure for syphilis and the first chemotherapeutic agent, even though it is not used today as a treponemacide. By the time Domagk received his Nobel Prize for Medicine, his Prontosil, the second chemotherapeutic antibacterial agent, was no longer in use.

"It may be that sometime the opportunity will be afforded me of returning to the subject; and of filling up several gaps which occur in the physiological sketch which I have attempted; and, what is still more needed, to discuss in a way more nearly commensurate with their importance, the pathological relations of the white blood-bioplast, which so far have only been incidentally touched upon.

— April, 1874"

Chapter IX

In Righteous Anger
Yellow Fever Epidemic of 1873

When the Board of Health was abolished and the Advisory
Board of Health set up by the opposition party, Cochran was
forbidden to do more than any private physician to aid the City of
Mobile during the savage yellow fever epidemic of the year of 1873.
The Advisory Board, mostly political appointees with no medical
experience and with only one physician "advisor," became like
many other Southern Boards of Health: concerned with the
commerce cut off by quarantine.

In the summer of 1873, almost simultaneously, the fever was
brought to New Orleans and Pensacola on two ships from Havana.
It subsequently spread through many Southern cities. The
mismanagement by the Advisory Board in Mobile left no one in that
city to direct the overall effort to fight or to control the disease. The
Board acted, but ineffectively, and too late.

Yellow fever, so named because one of its effects was a yellow
hue to the skin and sclera of its victims, was a terrifying scourge,
especially in the South and along the Atlantic seaboard. Thought to

be contageous and due to filth in cities, sanitation efforts were stressed. As early as the 1840s, physicians began to realize the disease was being imported. Local origin versus transmission theories were to rage until after the turn of the 20th century. It was noted, however, that during the naval blockade of the Civil War, there were no outbreaks of yellow fever -- except in North Carolina and Key West, Florida due to blockade-runners' success.

Two ships left Havana in June, 1873: the Golden Dream to arrive at Pensacola on June 10, but because of illness and death on board during the trip, was quarantined 500 yards from the dock until July 3; and the Valparaiso to arrive at New Orleans on June 26, twice disinfected en route, healthy, un-quarantined. The spread of yellow fever from these two cities is as follows: from Pensacola to Montgomery by railroad on the 10th of August; and from New Orleans by the steamboat Bee to Memphis on August 10, by boat to Shreveport on August 12, and by railroad to Mobile on August 17. From Shreveport, the disease traveled to Calvert by railroad on September 3.

As evidenced in the 1871 reading of his paper to the Medical Association of the State of Alabama, Dr. Cochran was convinced of the transportability of the disease. While he did not completely agree with Dr. Nott's belief that mosquitoes were the carrier,[1] he strongly advocated quarantine. This advocacy resulted in his being put in charge of Mobile's Health Department and thereby its quarantine efforts. Since that time, all the physicians of Mobile accepted his plan, and his methods of treatment.

Frustrated, knowing he could have done a much better job of containing the disease, Cochran was determined to learn all he could about the epidemic. He compiled the information from all involved cities on their outbreak of yellow fever. Late in 1873, using this data, his wide research [even into European points of view which were beginning to advocate -- as was Cochran -- the transportability

---

[1]J.C.Nott, "Sketch of the Epidemic of Yellow Fever of 1847, in Mobile," *Charleston Medical and Surgical Journal*, 1848.,Vol. 3, pg. 4.

rather than the contageous theory,] and his personal experience, he wrote the paper on "The Yellow Fever Epidemic of 1873." He bylined himself as Jerome Cochran, M.D., Professor of Public Hygiene and Medical Jurisprudence in the Medical College of Alabama, which, in later decades, gave credence to his work. He read the paper at the 1874 Medical Association meeting. It was published in the Transactions of 1874.[2]

The report on "The Yellow Fever Epidemic of 1873" is important as the first paper Cochran published as an epidemiologist. He, along with New Orleans doctors Stanford Chaille and Joseph Jones, are recognized as the most prolific writers on the subject of yellow fever.

The paper immediately established his authority in the field of public health. It is written in the typical Cochran manner, quite detailed and therefore quite long. The following exerpts from the 62 pages highlight the horror of the disease and are important in understanding the genius of the man and the significant role he played in Alabama's fight against the disease.

The paper is divided into "Part First. The History of the Epidemic" and "Part Second. The lessons of the Epidemic." In his typical way, he collected all data, outlined it, then with brutal honesty, discussed the epidemic as it occurred in the entire widespread area and criticized the earlier observers of the epidemic (especially the Advisory Board) as follows:

"...It is true,[sic] that many accounts of the epidemic have been published, especially of its behavior in those cities which have suffered from it most severely. But the more these accounts are studied [by myself], the more they are found to be superficial, uncritical, and unsatisfactory; and sometimes they are still worse -- that is to say, they are equivocal, sophistical and false.

"If the field of the inquiry afforded by the recent epidemic had been more industriously and more wisely cultivated, it is hardly to

---

[2]Jerome Cochran.M.D., "The Yellow Fever Epidemic of 1873," *Transactions of M.A.S.A.*, 1874., pp. 112-173.

be doubted that valuable contributions would have been made to our knowledge of the natural history of yellow fever; and to the protective resources of public hygiene. But even as it is, the careful study of such facts as I have been able to collect will be found to yield us some items of important information."

Cochran gave a tabular statement of the numbers of cases and the number of deaths in the various major cities afflicted by the disease. It is interesting that Memphis, Tennessee had 10,000 cases with 2,000 deaths while Mobile reported only 210 cases and 35 deaths. Although he could not know it until he undertook his exhaustive collection of data, even though Cochran had been relieved of his duties as the Mobile Health Officer, some of the measures he had originated were still in operation. In spite of the misaction of the Advisory Board of Health, it was the adherance to these measures by the physicians of Mobile that continued to prove Cochran's worth. For he estimated that there were, in the entire epidemic, in excess of 20,000 cases "while the aggregate of deaths would exceed three thousand five hundred," truly a plague of horrifying proportions. Reading Cochran's account admits one to the justified, stampeding fears of the people of the day; and makes us realize, all the more acutely, his amazing accomplishment in the face of a lack of precise knowledge of the cause of the disease.

"THE EPIDEMIC IN NEW ORLEANS"
"...The first case of yellow fever in New Orleans in 1873, which was also the first in the Mississippi Valley, occurred in the person of J. M. Arrua, mate of the Spanish bark Valparaiso. The Valparaiso left Havana on the 15th of June, in ballast, with twenty-one souls on board, all in good health. ...She was thoroughly disinfected, twice with chlorine, and twice with carbolic acid. The disinfection was done both between decks and in the forecastle, and at night hatches were left open for ventilation. She reached the city on the 26th or 27th of June, and was docked at pier 48, at the head of Second Street, in the Fourth District, two miles above Canal street."

He reported that Arrua was taken sick on July 4, and stayed on board for two days before being "taken down to the Third District, a distance of three miles, to 448 Moreau Street, where he died on the 8th of July." The Valparaiso and the house in which he died, were both subsequently disinfected. No other case of the disease followed. Cochran observed that "Arrua may have contracted the disease, as the captain of the vessel insists, in New Orleans."

The steamboat Belle Lee lay about 100 feet above theValparaiso. "The mate of this boat, Edward Hynes by name, was taken sick with yellow fever on the 12th of July, and died on board on the 20th. Subsequently, a carpenter and a painter, who had been employed on the Belle Lee, also sickened and died. In the meantime the boat was moved to the lower port of the sixth district and moored between Louisiana and Napoleon Avenues, at which point a new focus of infection was established, about which clustered thirty-seven cases and twenty-five deaths."

The steamboat W.S. Pike was docked at the same time. She had three cases of yellow fever. From August through October several other vessels docked in the area "also suffered severely, a considerable number of cases occurring on board of them, with several deaths. Several of these vessels were removed, like the Belle Lee, three miles below, to the Third District, and seem to have conveyed the infection to the wharves of that locality."

Cochran made a depressing observation: "About half the cases occurring in the Third District originated on shipboard; and it is worthy of special remark that disinfection here utterly failed to check the progress of the disease. Dr. J.T. Newman, Sanitary Inspector of the District, tells us that the forecastles and holds of infected ships were treated in the same manner as infected houses; but fresh cases occurred on the same ships even after the process of disinfection."

Cochran wrote that general disinfection in the city was practiced constantly "on a more extensive scale than has ever been attempted anywhere else in the world. What was the result? Simply this: that the disease maintained the conflict on its chosen battlefield until the coming of the frost, unterrified and defiant to the last."

Cochran also observed that Charity Hospital of New Orleans

admitted and treated 105 of the worst cases of which 68 died. He reported that no disinfection was carried out and that the disease showed "no disposition whatever to spread; and only two cases originated within the hospital."

"THE EPIDEMIC IN MEMPHIS"

"Yellow fever was brought to Memphis in 1873 by the steam towboat Bee, which ran between New Orleans and St. Louis. She had been with her barges in New Orleans at the infected wharf of the Fourth District, in the same neighborhood with the Valparaiso and the Belle Lee. Three or four of her crew, along with the captain, were taken sick with the fever during her trip up the river. She reached Memphis on the 10th of August, and remained there several hours. Two sick deck passengers were put ashore at the foot of Market street in the neighborhood afterward so famous in the annals of the epidemic known as Happy Hollow. One of these, whose name is not known, staggered into a shanty near the wharf, occupied by an Irishman named Riley, and died there the next day. The name of the other man was W.W. Davis, who lived in Lauderdale county, Alabama. He passed the night in the Adams Street station-house, where he died the next morning. There were two deaths, therefore, on the 12th. The captain, C.B. Goll, remained on the boat and died the next night at Oscola, Arkansas, ninety miles above Memphis. His body was brought back to Memphis and shipped by express to St. Louis. The infection did not spread from either Mr. Davis or Captain Goll, but proceeded first to make the conquest of Happy Hollow. ...The first victim claimed from the population of the city was a young man, name not given, who had rendered some humane assistance to the poor stranger who died at Riley's. Riley himself was then stricken down and soon died.

"During some weeks its depredations were confined to Happy Hollow" (A low, unhealthy, slummy area near the river on the north side of the city.) "I have no information of the number of persons inhabiting this locality; nor of the number of deaths occurring among them; nor of the rate of mortality."

The epidemic apparently was confined to the area of Happy Hollow for about three weeks, then, from the first to the 14th of September the epidemic spread to the entire northern third of the city, and from there to the rest of the city.

Cochran observed: "It is worthy of remark, however, that the jail, which was in the heart of the district which suffered most severely, escaped invasion until the 8th or 10th of October, when one of the prisoners, Fred Brooks by name, was attacked. He was removed to the Walthall Infirmary, where he died. Another case occurred shortly afterwards, which was treated in the jail and recovered. There were quite a number of cases of sickness in the jail which were regarded as dengue, all of whom recovered. The average number of prisoners was about one hundred and twenty-five. It was surrounded by a wall fifteen feet high. It is to the high wall and non-intercourse that Dr. Erskine, who had charge of it, attributes its comparative exemption."

There was a puzzling phenomenon of the Memphis epidemic. The first frost was on November 5th. New cases of the disease, with the usual percentage of deaths, continued to occur until the middle of December. Cochran wrote, "Some of these, I am unable to state how many, were among returned refugees. This unusual persistence of the pestilence after there had been several times severe frost and ice, is one of the remarkable features of its history."

Of the terror struck into the hearts of residents, Cochran's report gives evidence. "The population of Memphis at the advent of the epidemic may be stated at about 45,000. In the general exodus that ensued it is estimated that 20,000 persons sought safety in flight, leaving 25,000 at the mercy of the pestilence. The number of cases is roughly estimated at from 7,000 to 10,000. ...I have seen a list of the deaths containing 2,000 names."

"THE EPIDEMIC IN SHREVEPORT"

For the epidemic at Shreveport, Cochran was obliged to depend on reports of Drs. A.B. Snell, D. P. Fenner, and J.F. Davis, made to the Howard Association, and the report of Dr. Henry Smith to the Louisiana Equitable Life Insurance Company of New Orleans. Of these he says, "The scanty detail of facts, as I have given them, leaves the origin of the epidemic enveloped in some doubt. Much stress has been laid on the filthy and unsanitary condition of the city on account of defective drainage and neglect of scavenging. But this unsanitary condition of the city has existed for many years which have not been marked with epidemics. Besides, while defective drainage and filth may render yellow fever more malignant, it is well known that they will not of themselves produce it."[3]

Many of the city's panic-stricken inhabitants fled. Cochran noted that many had unknowingly already been stricken. "It is said that more than half the cases attacked in this way died...." These persons also spread the disease into other epidemics "-- as for example in Calvert and in Marshall." Ever the statistician, Cochran observed that "about four thousand five hundred persons, black and white, remained in Shreveport. The number of cases is estimated at three thousand. The number of deaths was seven hundred and fifty-nine. The blacks were attacked almost as generally as the whites, but the mortality amongst them was very much less -- six hundred and thirty-nine whites dying , and one hundred and twenty blacks. ...The ratio of deaths to cases was about twenty-five percentum. ...The average period of incubation seemed to be about seven days; but in some it was as short as three days and in some as long as three weeks."

"THE EPIDEMIC IN PENSACOLA"

The yellow fever epidemic in Pensacola was traced to the ship Golden Dream. This vessel had lost three of her crew at Havana, and eight more while at sea. She reached the harbor of Pensacola on the 10th of June. Cochran wrote, "She was therefore placed in quarantine, cleaned, fumigated, and whitewashed, and detained for twenty-four days before she was allowed to approach the city. She

---

[3]Twenty-seven years later Walter Reed and his Yellow Fever Commission would have to learn this fundamental lesson again in Cuba.

was anchored about five hundred yards from the central wharf. This brings us to the 3rd of July. A month elapsed without any event of importance, when a sailor who had been eight days on board the Golden Dream was taken sick with the fever on the 2d [sic] day of August. He died with black vomit on the 5th. The Golden Dream sailed on the 16th of August, and was lost at sea on the 30th, in consequence, it is said, of 'getting short of hands,' her crew having been stricken down by the pestilence."

On August 6, three cases occurred in Pensacola, all in the same house, "the residence of Mr. W. Mckenzie, Deputy Harbor Master, on Romana street, two squares distant from the water's edge. On the next day, the 7th, four other cases occurred on Romana Street, near Mr. Orthing's house. The first death in the city was that of Mrs. Nasite, who arrived in Pensacola from New Orleans on the 22d of July, was taken sick two weeks after, namely, on the 7th of August, and died on the 13th. Between the 7th and the 14th several stevedores who had been employed on the infected vessel contracted the fever, and communicated it to their families, thus establishing almost at the same time several different centers of infection.

Interpreting the data he had gathered, Cochran followed a logical train of thought, then made an astute observation. "It will have been remarked that the first eight cases in the city had no direct communication with the Golden Dream. How, then, did they become infected? Mr. Orthing had visited the vessel repeatedly, but, while the inmates of his house were stricken down, he himself escaped. He might have brought the poison with him in his clothing, even as Dr. McDonald, the author of the article on Yellow Fever in Reynolds Practice, tells us that he often trembled to think that his monkey jacket might become a vehicle of infection. But the more probable opinion seems to be, that it was in the wings of the invisible swift winds that the seeds of the pestilence found agents of transportation.[4] We are told that the wind, from the 28th of July until after the fever became epidemic, blew steadily every day, between the hours of five and ten P.M., from the south-west, sweeping first over the infected ship, and then over that portion of the city in which these cases made their appearance, the distance to be traversed being about half a mile. We are also told that the disease spread rapidly for more than a mile towards the north-east, the direction traveled by the wind, along a narrow belt about one square in width; and that it was confined almost exclusively to this belt for some ten days. Afterwards it spread all over the city."

To what did he attribute the subsequent spread of the disease? He noted that "The atmosphere was damp and humid. ...There were but three entirely fair days in June, ten in July, and twelve in August. The rain was abundant, and fell in torrents."[5]

Once again he remarked on the panic of the inhabitants, "The population was reduced by stampede to about three thousand, of whom about one thousand were liable to the disease. The number of cases is estimated at six hundred. The number of deaths was sixty-one, -- ten percentum. ...I am indebted to Dr. Hargis, of Pensacola, for most of the facts given in this sketch."

"THE EPIDEMIC IN MONTGOMERY"

Cochran's account of the spread of yellow fever from Pensacola to Montgomery spared no details. The unsuspecting the citizens who thought they were ready for the poor weather, all conspired to spread the epidemic. Vividly, he recorded that "...It is believed that the disease was brought from Pensacola by a white woman named Mollie Jackson, and by Mr. D.H. Cram, President of the Pensacola and Louisville Railroad. Mollie Jackson had been living in Pensacola opposite the hospital. It has been stated in the account

------

[4]How close Cochran came to describing the mode of spread of the disease! The seeds were the yellow fever virus; the agent of transportation was the wings of Aedes aegypti mosquito swept by the prevailing winds.

[5]An atmosphere perfect for breeding mosquitoes.

of the epidemic in Pensacola, that yellow fever had made its appearance there in three cases on the 6th of August, and in four cases on the 7th, and that it had traveled in the direction of the wind with extraordinary rapidity. Mollie Jackson left Pensacola on the 9th, and had therefore been sufficiently exposed to the infection. She arrived in Montgomery on the 10th sickened on the 17th, and died on the 26th. During the first four days of her illness, she was seen by a physician who did not suspect that he had a case of yellow fever. The fever subsided and the physician saw her no more; but notwithstanding her apparent recovery, she relapsed in a few days and died. The extreme yellowness of the dead body, together with information derived from the nurses, afterwards satisfied the physician in question that it was really a case of specific yellow fever. One of the nurses went to West Point, Georgia, was very ill with fever, and is stated to have thrown up blood from the stomach.

"From the house, situated near the intersection of Clay and Dickerson streets, in the First Ward, in which Mollie Jackson died, as a focus of infection, the fever spread through the surrounding neighborhood. Almost every house in the three adjoining blocks was invaded, and death after death by black vomit proclaimed the character of the malady.

"Mr. Cram's residence was at the corner of McDonough and Madison streets, in the Fifth Ward. He left Pensacola on the 14th day of August and reached Montgomery on the 15th. His office in Pensacola was in the infected region. He got sick somewhere between the 17th and the 20th with a fever which lasted several days. Its character does not seem to have been accurately determined; but on account of his Pensacola exposure, and of subsequent events in his neighborhood it is presumed to have been yellow fever. Here at any rate was in some way established a new focus of infection. The husband of Mr. Cram's nurse died soon after in the same yard of yellow fever -date of death not given. On the 4th of September the house next to Mr. Cram's on Madison street, which was occupied by Germans, was invaded, and up to the 25th five deaths had occurred in it. Next to Mr. Cram's on McDonough street, is a row of brick buildings, not one of which escaped."

Cochran stated that there were about 500 cases in Montgomery of which 102 died. Montgomery had measures of disinfection against cholera in operation before the epidemic struck, "such as lime in gutters and foul places and the use of carbolic acid in the vaults of privies, and the city was considered to be in a good sanitary condition. While the fever was in progress large quantities of coal tar were burnt in the streets, but the fumes evolved exhibited no power to check the march of the pestilence."

"THE EPIDEMIC IN MOBILE"

Mobile was Home. Cochran was very familiar with the lay of the land, and utilized his knowledge with precision in attempting to follow the course of, and thus perhaps make some sense of, the epidemic in his city.

Mobile was clear of the disease until a Mobile and New Orleans railroad employee made a round trip to New Orleans on August 6-7. He became ill on August 21 and died of "black vomit" on August 26. His death occurred at a residence on the east side of Hamilton Street, between Palmetto and Charleston. It was to be five weeks before another case showed up in this area.

The second case came into the city from a man who worked near Shreveport. He came to Mobile via New Orleans, already ill. He apparently went on across the bay on September 10, but returned to Mobile on September 11, now very ill. He was found near the wharf by a policeman, who was directed to take him to the City Hospital. He died on the 13th "of unmistakable and malignant yellow fever." Cochran wrote that it was from this case that the epidemic ensued.

Cochran insisted that "In order that its dissemination may be easily understood it is necessary to premise a few topographical details.

"The City Hospital, the focus of infection, is just one mile from the river in the north-west quarter of the city. The streets here that are parallel with the river run very nearly from north-west to south-east. Of this range of streets we shall have occasion to mention Wilkerson, Jefferson, and Broad, the last being the most remote from the river of the three. Other streets cross these at right angles, running from the river to Broad street and beyond, and consequently pursuing a direction nearly from north-east to south-west. Of these we shall have occasion to mention St. Antony, Congress, and Adams. The City Hospital lies between Broad and Jefferson, on the north-east side of St Antony. To the north-east of the City Hospital and separated from it by a high brick wall is the jail, which also lies between Broad and Jefferson, fronting on Congress. In the same range, south-west of the City Hospital, on the opposite side of St. Antony street, is Providence Infirmary. On the same side of St. Antony street as the City Hospital, separated from it by Jefferson street, and so lying one square nearer to the river, is the Marine Hospital. Each of these institutions occupies an entire square. Across Broad street, just beyond the City Hospital and the jail, are several squares that are very nearly vacant. Sweeping past the south-west corner of Providence Infirmary, in a direction a little north of west, is the Spring Hill Road. A few hundred feet further towards the south, and very nearly parallel with the Spring Hill Road, is the Spring Hill Shell Road. To reach the Spring Hill Road from the City Hospital by the shortest route it is necessary to cross one square in a diagonal direction. To reach the Shell Road two squares must be crossed diagonally. Passing down Broad street towards the south-east, we come, at the distance of eight squares, to Canal street. Here Broad street changes its direction, and runs almost directly to the south, bearing however slightly to the west. The next street after crossing Canal is Palmetto -- which is thus nine squares from the City Hospital. Next west of Broad in this part of its course, and parallel with it, is Marine street.

"The infection confined itself chiefly to a narrow belt extending from north to south, almost along Broad street, with the City Hospital near its northern extremity, and Palmetto street near its southern boundary. Along this belt there were established three special yellow fever centers -- the first at the City Hospital, the second beyond Broad street, on the Spring Hill Road and the Shell Road, the third also beyond Broad, and about the intersection of

Palmetto and Marine. ...Nine other cases occurred in the Hospital, making ten in all, with five deaths. One of these was Sister Xavier."

On September 15, a Sister at Providence Infirmary became ill and died on the 18th. She was one of four cases, three of whom died. There were several cases in the neighborhood of the Infirmary. Cochran noted that carbolic acid was used extensively in this neighborhood, to no effect.

A very interesting oasis from disease was discovered and commented on by Cochran. "Passing along the infected belt towards the north-west, we find that the jail escaped infection altogether. Not a single decided case occurred within its walls during the season. There was one doubtful case in the person of the Jailor, Mr. J.E.Collins, who had a mild attack of some sort of fever commencing November 2d.[sic] It is stated that this institution has always enjoyed a similar immunity during all previous epidemics. It is surrounded by a high brick wall, and necessarily has but little communication with the rest of the city, There were a few cases still further north than the jail, but they require no special mention."

There was only one case among the blacks, a woman who died on November 17.

Cochran could find absolutely no benefit from the use of carbolic acid or any other disinfectant. The meteorological table for the year presented nothing unusual. There was a concomitant, and more extensive, epidemic of dengue, but it was impossible to ascertain the number of cases. There were no deaths due to the dengue.

He decried the handling of the epidemic. "In consequence of the epidemic there was complete prostration of business, and from eight thousand to ten thousand of our people went away to escape the infection. The excitement was out of all proportion to the danger. All of the most populous parts of the city escaped with comparative impunity. There was inside of the infected neighborhoods indeed, considerable danger; but outside of the infected neighborhoods the danger was very slight. I sincerely believe that our commerce ought not to have suffered interruption; and that strangers could have visited with perfect safety, and at any time during the season, any of the business parts of the city. Because yellow fever prevailed about the City Hospital, and in a narrow belt beyond Broad Street, a mile or more from the river, it does not follow that pestilence was lying in ambush among the dry goods and grocery houses of Water and Commerce streets, and the hotels and restaurants of Royal. A few strangers did venture into the city during the reign of the epidemic, and I have not learned that any of them suffered on account of their temerity.

"A quasi quarantine was established against the West Indies, New Orleans, and Pensacola. But it was not put into operation until the disease which it was intended to exclude had already entered the city. It was moreover of such imperfect character that it was easily evaded, and in point of fact was evaded repeatedly. It is therefore unnecessary for any purpose I have in view to give any detailed account of it. If however, I were writing a history of municipal folly it would be worthy of special mention."

Cochran succinctly summarized his report. He noted that he received information and statistics from several leading physicians of Mobile. He stated, "I am aware that it differs very widely from the report of our Advisory Board of Health; but not for that reason is it any the less worthy of confidence. Doubtless the Board of Health did the best they could under the circumstances; but circumstance were singularly unfavorable to them, inasmuch as most of our physicians persistently refused to report to them, or to recognize them in any other light than as public nuisances."

Cochran felt that the political "Board of Advisors" and the "City Physician" (replacements for the legitimate Board of Health and himself as the health officer) had been responsible for some of the deaths in the epidemic and he was determined to expose them to as many people as would read his writing. Here is his verbatim account:

"THE REPORT OF THE ADVISORY BOARD OF HEALTH"

"But it is necessary that I should be a little more explicit concerning the report of the Advisory Board of Health, or rather, the report of the Medical Officer of that Board.

"This report bears date the 1st day of November 1873, and was published under the auspices of the Board in the Daily Register, newspaper, of the 27th of the same month. The material portions of it had been communicated to the American Public Health Association, at its session in New York, on the 12th of November, and is to be published in the Transactions of that body. It is, moreover, the only official account of the late epidemic which has been given to the world, and will naturally be made use of by medical historians and statisticians. In the interests of historical and scientific accuracy, therefore, it becomes important that its mistakes should be corrected and its deficiencies supplied.

"I quote verbatim the summary of cases and deaths:
cases treated in the city, as officially reported, is as follows: Sixteen cases occurred in the hospitals, of which number seven died and nine recovered. Outside of the hospitals there were twenty-two cases, of which number twelve died and ten recovered. Total number of cases in the city, forty; total number of deaths, nineteen; and of recoveries, twenty-one.'

"These statements may be in entire harmony with the reports made officially to the Board of Health. But they are certainly very wide of the mark as to the real facts of the epidemic, and so are false and misleading.

"Not sixteen cases, but twenty-one cases, occurred in the hospitals; and the deaths in the hospitals numbered eight at least, instead of seven. Instead of twenty-two cases with twelve deaths, at least one hundred and seventy-nine cases were treated in the city outside the hospitals, with twenty deaths certainly, and perhaps one or two more. For I happen to know that some yellow fever deaths were assigned to other causes of dissolution; and I know also what sort of influences were sometimes used to determine the character of the certificate of death.

"Sixteen cases inside of the hospital, plus twenty-two cases outside of those institutions, would make, according to the ordinary principles of addition, an aggregate of thirty-eight cases. But the arithmetician of the Advisory Board makes out of these addends a sum equal to forty; and forty therefore let it be. Of these forty cases they tell us that twenty-one recovered, and that nineteen died; a dreadful percentage of mortality indeed. I have shown, however, that instead of an aggregate of forty cases in Mobile during the season there was really five times that number, namely, two hundred cases; and that instead of nineteen deaths we had thirty, making the percentage of mortality fifteen, instead of forty-seven and a half.

"Now, it is true that the report of the Advisory Board of Health bears the date of November the 1st, although it was not published until November 27th; and that a certain number of the cases and deaths included in my statistics occurred after the first of these dates; but the epidemic was then so nearly over that corrections made with reference to this fact would afford but little help to the Board, except in the single item of the number of deaths.

"The conclusion of the report is of the nature of an apology, for carbolic acid disinfection; and an assertion, without proof of its prophylactic value.

"Every step of the argument, if that may be called argument which is really no argument at all, is disingenuous and sophistical. No attempt is made to arrange the facts connected with the disinfecting of the various localities which were treated with carbolic acid so as to show their bearing on the questions at issue; but we are told in general terms that Mobile and New Orleans used carbolic acid with persistence and assiduity, and escaped any general epidemic; and that Memphis and Shreveport and Pensacola did not invoke the prophylactic agency of carbolic acid and suffered frightfully; and from these premises, by some logical legerdemain which passes my comprehension, the conclusion is drawn, that, therefore, carbolic acid disinfection arrests the progress of yellow fever. Now, in the first place, the premises are false; and in the second place, even if they were true they furnish no logical warrant for the conclusion which is drawn from them.

"With how much accuracy this Report has been prepared, may be further judged of when I call attention to one little fact of omission. The streets and grounds about the City Hospital were most elaborately disinfected. The air of the whole region was kept reeking for weeks with the foul fumes of carbolic acid, the frogs were killed in the gutters, and the grass was scorched and blasted as if the hot breath of the sirocco had fallen upon it. And yet this Report affords not the slightest intimation that any disinfection at all was practiced there.

"But what were the real results of the disinfection? What did the carbolic acid accomplish? The answer is short and easy, if not very elegant and refined. It made a great stink, and it did nothing else. It did not check the disease in the City Hospital. It did not prevent its migration across St. Anthony Street to the Providence Infirmary. It did not keep it away from Mr. Thompson's in the acute angle between Broad Street and the Spring Hill Road. It did not check its march on the Spring Hill Road along which it traveled steadily from house to house until it passed beyond Pine street, and was met by the frost. It did not interfere with its passage from the Spring Hill Road to the Shell Road, nor with its dissemination along that thoroughfare. It did not fence it out of the McCann neighborhood, nor check its ravages after it got there. In one word, seriously and deliberately spoken, it utterly failed to accomplish any good whatever; and this is the verdict of every medical man in Mobile of whose opinion I have any knowledge. Whether it was equally impotent for evil is not so easily settled."[6]

In his "Part Second -- The Lessons of the Epidemic, Cochran put together worldwide facts known about germs, comparing and contrasting this knowledge with what was then known about yellow fever. "While there is good reason to believe that the infectious germs of small-pox, cow-pox, and several other eruptive diseases have been actually demonstrated under the microscope, it can not be claimed with any confidence that anybody has ever really seen the

---

[6]We now know that yellow fever is carried by the Aedes aegypti mosquito, in Alabama. This mosquito doesn't ordinarily fly more than 200 yards away from its breeding area; but it is easy to see how it could be blown a half mile or so in a flat area such as surrounds Mobile. The mosquito lives as an adult for only 20 - 30 days. the female can lay up to 3,000 eggs. These eggs lie dormant in cold weather and will hatch in two to three days in warm weather. When the insect bites an infected person, the yellow fever virus rapidly matures in the mosquito. It lives there the rest or the mosquito's life, and is transmitted to each person that the mosquito bites from then on.

germs of yellow fever. Nevertheless we do not hesitate upon analogical grounds to affirm that such germs do exist. There is no other theory capable of explaining the phenomena of the disease." He reiterated the proof of migration (transportability) of the disease. And he stressed that with the continued improvement in travel and "intercommunication" from the seaboard inland, that the danger to inland dwellers became that much more dreadful.

What could be done to prevent such disaster, he wondered. "There are two measures of public prophylaxis which have recently attracted much attention, namely, Quarantine and Disinfection." He proceeded to outline these in his presentation. He included the difficulties of control due to "feverish commercial activity," that precluded the use of absolute quarantine, those of local administrations, [due to lack of funds or ineptitude] and the "imperfections of our scientific knowledge." He had, in 1872, been part of the beginning of the American Public Health Association, and, therefore, held an enthusiasm for a national outlook toward what could be done to further public health. Later events would alter the focus of the following view, but at this early time in his public health career, Cochran felt that quarantine against foreign countries would be better handled by the "general government" [of the United States.]   "It is through the various channels of commercial intercourse that foreign epidemics are brought to our ports; and it would seem to be evidently expedient that the power which regulates commerce should also have the regulation of quarantine." He went on in this paper to tell of a bill presented to Congress by Mr. Bromberg of Mobile "to prevent the introduction of infectious and contagious diseases into the United States," that had been well adapted to the report of Assistant Surgeon Harvey E. Brown, of the United States Army who had been commissioned by the Congress to "make investigations with a view of 'providing for a more efficient system of quarantine on the Southern and Gulf coasts.'"

Regarding disinfection, Cochran enumerated the types of disinfection, how it worked, and then gave examples of yellow fever epidemics in New Orleans in which disinfectants, burned into the air to purify same, failed abysmally. He concluded that frost was the only true killer of yellow fever.

It would seem that the mishandling of the epidemic of yellow fever in Mobile in 1873 propelled Cochran deeply into the specialty of Public Health and, therefore, is one of the prime reasons for Alabama obtaining its great Public Health Department.

Chapter X

The Turning Point

-1874-
-- A challenge is hurled --
In the Prologue of this book questions were posed:
Who was this man who was attempting to revise and improve medical education; improve the quality of medical practice and its practitioners by making them show their competence on examinations given by practitioners who had proved their own competence; create a health department that would protect the citizens of the state by bringing all the legitimate practitioners into its fold?

Who was this man who was attempting to wrest authority away from politicians and give it to the professionals to whom it belonged? Who was this man who was attempting something that had never before been attempted, and in the process challenging his fellow physicians to lend their expertise and strength to the task?

The answer is, as you have read thus far, complex. Again, a review of the most recent facts sees that in this year of our Lord, 1874, Dr. Jerome Cochran was beset by difficulties. Not permitted to oversee and direct the health care delivery to the people of Mobile for which he was appointed in 1871 then removed by the new government in 1873, he, nevertheless, continued to gather data.

In ill health, he continued to push himself for the good of his fellow man. Standing up for his beliefs, he had resigned from his professorship at the Alabama Medical College. The College, however, unwilling to lose such an excellent teacher, created a chair for him in Public Hygiene and Medical Jurisprudence -- his undeniable area of interest and expertise -- which he accepted and began in the first term of 1874. Grieving for his four lost children, he supported his family. He gave himself to God, knowing in his heart that God would provide the means for him to continue his dedication to serve and improve the lot of mankind.

At the April, 1874 annual meeting of the Medical Association of the State of Alabama in Selma, Cochran exhorted his fellow physicians to heed the call to reason. He reminded the group that "At the annual session of the Association in Huntsville, in 1872, the plan of a general system of Boards of Health for this State, which was submitted by Dr. Jerome Cochran for the consideration of the Association, was discussed and endorsed. It was also again endorsed by the unanimous vote of the Association at the annual session in Tuscaloosa in 1873."[1]

He informed those assembled that "A bill has been prepared, embracing the details of this plan, and was presented to the General Assembly of the State during its last session. It was received with a considerable amount of favor; but for reasons not necessary to be explained, it was never voted on. We believe that this bill, if its provisions should be adopted, is calculated to be of great service to the State, and to the prosperity and influence of this Association. It is therefore presented here in full."

Cochran then presented the above as Document "A," An Act to Establish Boards of Health in the State of Alabama, and Document "B," An Act to Regulate the Practice of Medicine in the State of Alabama. In his speech, Cochran hurled this challenge to his fellow physicians: "To fold our hands passively and take things as they

------

[1] Jerome Cochran, M.D., "First Annual Report of the Board of Censors of the Medical Association of the State of Alabama," *Transactions of MASA*, 1874, p. 19.

come -- this is not our mission; but to shape events for ourselves and to compel circumstances to pursue such course as we may believe to be wisest and best. ...But if we act under the influence of petty passions and selfish ambitions, then verily shall we find that we have sown dragon's teeth, which will spring up into armed men, and destroy us." A long discussion ensued. As a result, the Board of Censors was ordered to present Document A of these Acts to the next State General Assembly.

His Act To Regulate the Practice of Medicine in the State of Alabama, however, they felt needed more work. It, too, was discussed at length by the Medical Association, but, as was later reported, "was brought forward with some improvements at the session in Montgomery in 1875; and still again, with some additional improvements, at the Mobile session of 1876."[2]

--Vindication--

In the spring of 1874, a dread disease became epidemic because of negligence on the part of the politically appointed City Physician, who was not public health oriented. By November, small pox -- that had begun in four or five different foci -- had spread over the entire city.

The Board of Trade, a real power in the city, became alarmed because shipping was coming to a halt. Other ports would not allow their ships to unload and ships from other ports would not land in smallpox infested Mobile. She, being a significant seaport, was recovering financially from the War Between the States faster than were the other cities in Alabama. However, the financial situation was desperate. Officers of the Board of Trade paid the mayor a visit, whereupon that official promptly revived the original Board of Health, consisting of Drs. Geo. A. Ketchum, Wm. H. Anderson, E.P. Gaines, John T. Gilmore, and C.C. Sherrard. Dr. Ketchum was elected President, and Dr. Sherrard as Secretary of the Board. Cochran was re-selected as the executive officer of the Board, with

---

[2]"Doctor Jerome Cochran of Alabama," *Op.cit.*, p. 20.

the title of Health Officer. The board was given full power to act during the emergency.[3]

The Health Officer was notified of his selection at 2 o'clock on the 12th of November, and was instructed to prepare the outlines of a plan of action to be submitted to the Board at half past seven o'clock that evening. Cochran promptly submitted his plan, which the Board immediately accepted.

He demanded two clerks to do the paper work, seven vaccinating physicians, a disinfecting corps, and a detail of policemen as a back-up in the compulsory vaccination program and for general inspection. The entire city was surveyed to find the number and location of the cases. Every man, woman and child was compelled to be vaccinated. Houses that contained smallpox cases were isolated, houses from which smallpox patients had left were fumigated and disinfected, and a new pesthouse was built to care for all the cases that could not be adequately cared for at home.

The vaccinators met a wide variety of resistance. There seemed to be a mortal fear of it among the blacks. They had been told that vaccination was a form of voodoo practiced by the white folks and caused serious difficulties with their reproductive function.

Cochran was quite concerned that the blacks, especially, should be vaccinated. He had found that they were twice a susceptible as whites to the disease, and the mortality rate among them was much higher than among whites.

Some of the whites believed vaccination abridged their constitutional rights. Many, both black and white, were simply afraid of the needle. They tried by every means conceivable to avoid vaccination. But Cochran insisted, and persisted.

Smallpox was a terrible disease. It ranged in severity from the mild disease of the incompletely immunized, who had only a few itchy pimples (which were as contagious to the non-immune person

---

[3]Jerome Cochran, M.D. of Mobile, "On Smallpox Epidemic in Mobile," *Transactions of MASA*, 1875, pp. 232-313.

as full-blown disease) to the fulminating "Black Pox" which was universally and very quickly fatal. Visiting a pest house where every possible agony of every stage of death was presented would be too demoralizing for the general public. Only a few laymen other than survivors ever witnessed such a scene. Cochran had seen these forms of death, and he was becoming more convinced that epidemics of this nature were a public responsibility. But how was the public to assume this task? He had just had a tragic demonstration -- during the smallpox epidemic -- of the failure of the democratic process in handling it. There had to be people who would dedicate themselves to the public's hygiene and health. The public's health must be taken out of the hands of the electorate and placed in the hands of the health professionals.

Under Cochran's firm hand and brilliant management, the smallpox epidemic slowly ground to a halt. When the last crust of the last pustule of the last victim had been shed, the workers took stock. What they saw was a miracle such as had never before been recorded in world history. Certainly the epidemic could have been stopped early in its course by prompt attention to the first few cases. But this one had been allowed to take a firm grip on the city and was in full sway. Cochran did not take over until winter, the time of year most favorable to the disease's spread. He and his assistants had stopped it in its tracks. 990 cases in 614 households with 262 deaths had been recorded.[4] Yet, due to Cochran's work, thousands of people had been spared horrible deaths and the economy of the port had been restored.[5]

---

[4] Jerome Cochran , Montgomery, "The Medical Profession," *Memorial Record of Alabama*, Vol. II, 1893, Bryant & Fuller, Madison Wis., p. 111.

[5] Louis Pasteur and Robert Koch would come later. Cochran and his crew had performed their great achievement without any knowledge of the etiological agent of Smallpox. The germ theory, though thoroughly understood and explained by Cochran, was not a respected theory among most Alabama doctors at the time. Cochran, however followed the example of Edward Jenner of England, who, in 1796 developed vaccination using cowpox germs.

In the midst of organizing his fight against smallpox, he also had to honor the Association's order to give his approved Document A to the November session of the General Assembly.

"The distinctive features of the Alabama system are as follows:[6]
 (1.) That in it the state medical association, as organized under its constitution of 1873, is made the state board of health, with a general supervision of the county boards of health.
 (2.) That the functions of county and municipal boards of health are invested in the county medical societies holding charters from the state association, thus virtually engaging all the doctors of the state in the sanitary service of the people and in the administration of the health laws of the state.
 (3.) That the extent and character of the sanitary work, to be done in any county, city, or town, is made a matter of negotiation and agreement between the county and municipal authorities, on the one hand, and the board of health on the other hand.
(4.) That in all these agreements the full control of all appropriations for sanitary purposes is reserved to the county or municipal authorities; while the selection of all the agents to be employed in sanitary work, such as county and city health officers, quarantine physicians, sanitary police, etc., is reserved to the boards of health. This arrangement, in effect, makes the county and municipal authorities component factors of the boards of health, while it places the appointment of the health officials, and the administration of the health laws, entirely beyond the reach of political influences."

However, instead of simply giving the Act to a legislator to present, Dr. Cochran was invited to speak before the General Assembly, a distinct honor due, no doubt, to his reputation as a learned physician and brilliant speaker as well as the author of the bill to be discussed.

-1875-

43 years old, Cochran wound down the fight against small pox.

---

[6]Jerome Cochran, Montgomery, "The Medical Profession," *op. cit.* p.129.

While continuing his professorship in a subject in which he deeply believed, and continuing his dedicated efforts to see passage of the laws affecting public health and the medical association, Jerome Cochran kept busy and happy. He refused to give in to his ill health. Sarah Jane, at age 41 was pregnant with their eighth child.

He was very proud when, on February 19, the Alabama Assembly passed into law his Act to Establish Boards of Health. His hard work had paid off. This was the first State to have a legislated Board of Health that was made up solely of physicians.

In reporting this in his Second Annual Report of the Board of Censors of the Medical Association of the State of Alabama in Montgomery on Thursday, April 15, 1875, Cochran reminded the members that they had charged the Board of Censors, at the session held in Selma the preceding year, to present for consideration to the General Assembly the bill to establish Boards of Health in the State of Alabama.

He related to the assembled members the form of the presentation to the General Assembly such that:

"Nos etiam Sperarumus meliora."

"To the Honorable the Senate and House of Representatives of the State of Alabama, in General Assembly convened.

"We, the Board of Censors of the Medical Association of the State of Alabama, at the last annual session of the Association, which was held in the city of Selma on the 13th, 14th, and 15th days of April of the present year (1874), were charged with the duty of presenting for the consideration of your honorable bodies the subjoined draft of "A bill to establish Boards of Health in the State of Alabama." In the performance of this duty we would most respectfully state:

1. That the need of legislative enactments for the promotion of the public health has been recognized in almost all civilized communities, health-boards and health-laws being a part of the regular machinery of government in most European countries, and in several of the States of the American Union.

2. That here in the State of Alabama thousands of deaths and tens of thousands of cases of sickness occur every year from diseases

which might be prevented, entailing on the people an amount of physical suffering and of pecuniary loss, which it would not be easy to exaggerate.

3.   That the Medical Association of the State, after mature deliberation, has unanimously endorsed the plan for the organization of a health-system, which is now presented to the General Assembly.

4. That this plan will secure the co-operation of the entire Medical Profession of the State.

5.   That the expense to the State which it involves is extremely small.

6. That the expense to the several counties and cities of the State which it involves, is left entirely to the proper legal authorities of such counties and cities as choose to avail themselves of its advantages."

Cochran explained to the Association that, as the State Board of Health, their duties for the present would be chiefly advisory. Later, he recognized, that as the State became more populous, and wealthier, the duties of the Board would become more executive in character. He advised prudence and wisdom in their actions.

Cochran understood his audience. He let them know that even the august members of the medical profession had, as yet, a very inadequate appreciation of the ends, aims, and especially of the actual resources of sanitary science. With a possible ironic smile, tilt of his head and lift of one shoulder, he added, "This being true, what can we expect of the members of the General Assembly and the general public?"

One can imagine Cochran noticing a slight rustle among the audience. Perhaps George Ketchum whispered something to Dr. Anderson who smiled broadly, or perhaps his unexpected humor made the whole audience laugh.

Cochran continued, "Wise sanitary legislation will be difficult to obtain, and appropriations for sanitary purposes will be made with hesitation and reluctance. All these things must be remembered and we must not expect too much in the way of public appreciation and encouragement."

There probably were, again, knowing smiles. He might have acknowledged them, and gone on with his serious talk. "In order to facilitate the action of the Association in reference to this matter[7] we have prepared the following resolutions, and respectfully recommend their adoption:

Resolved, that the Medical Association of the State of Alabama hereby accept for themselves and for the County Medical Societies under their jurisdiction the provisions of an act entitled An act to establish Boards of Health in the State of Alabama, and approved by the Governor on the 19th day of February, A.D. 1875; and will endeavor to discharge the duties assigned to them in said act in good faith and with earnest purpose, to be of service to the people of Alabama.

Resolved further, That a copy of these resolutions, properly certified by the President and the Secretary of the Association, be transmitted to the Governor of the State."

Cochran, then set up the "plans of procedure, and determine the organs, the special machinery, through which our health functions can be discharged with the best prospect of facility and efficiency of action."

With the adoption of the above-referred-to ordinance and resolutions, and its writing into a bill for presentation to the State legislators, Cochran knew that they all understood the situation and that the future of public health in Alabama was assured.

It may be added here that the eighth --and last -- child, a son Louis, was born in March of 1875. It is not known if he was premature, but on May 5, Louis became the Cochran's fifth angel. He joined his two sisters and two brothers in the family plot.[8]

---

[7]The acceptance by the Association of the bill in its present legally certified form.

[8]In his dissertation on "Vital and Mortuary Statistics," —1887 — Dr. Cochran laments bitterly the fact that, "in the entire nation, wherever statistics were taken, they have shown that half the children born did not live to be five years old." The Cochrans had eight children born, the oldest of the last four died at age three.

The bill on public health was a fact. With this law, the five Censors of the State Medical Association, along with five other members elected from the House of Counsellors, became the State Board of Health. The county medical societies, in affiliation with the State Medical Association, became the County Boards of Health. These County Boards of Health were under the general supervision and control of the State Board. The right to elect or appoint the officers and servants employed in the administration of the sanitary regulations was, in all cases, reserved to the Board of Health. All questions relating to salaries, appropriations and expenditures were reserved to the appropriate authorities in the legislature. The one big link between the legislature and various boards was the purse strings. The Legislature controlled them, and so the State Health Department always seemed strapped for funds.

During that summer, thoroughly worn out, Jerome finally had to take time for himself if he hoped to continue the Herculean tasks to which he had set himself. He decided to take a well-earned vacation and make an overdue visit to his brother, William Lewis Cochran and other relatives in Indian territory in Oklahoma/West Texas. His father, Augustus Owen, and mother, Frances (Bailey) Cochran had, by this time, also moved to Stonewall, Chickasaw Nation, Oklahoma.

Born January 11, 1834, William was 2 years Jerome's junior. In Oklahoma, William blended well with the Indians. His wife Jincy (Bohannon) was half Chickasaw. William was liked by the Indians and his other neighbors. He even joined the Confederate Army for the duration of the war, in spite of having lost his left leg in a war effort in Nicaragua. His obituary in 1913 states: "Few men ever lived in Oklahoma who held the confidence and esteem of all who knew him to the extent enjoyed by Mr. Cochran. With a big heart and generous nature he extended a helping hand to many a man whose luck was against him."[9]

---

[9]*Genealogy*, by Mary Gregg

When Jerome visited William in 1875, it is not documented whether he took the whole family. Knowing Jerome as we have come to do, it seems highly likely that they all went.[10] Instead of thinking of himself and how tired he was, it might have been Jerome's intention to give Sarah Jane a much needed vacation after the trying loss of their last child.

At this time William had accumulated considerable wealth. He operated a general merchandise store, and owned a ranch of several thousand acres on which roamed over fifteen hundred head of cattle. He had ample leisure to hunt and "rough it" with his older brother, Jerome.

The visit was just what Jerome needed. The two brothers hunted deer and antelope, camped out in the open air, slept on the ground, cooked over a campfire, and killed a few rattlesnakes. They spent hours on end telling tall tales about their adventures in the war and their successes in their respective undertakings since they had last seen each other. Jerome gradually lost his sallow complexion, gained some weight, and began to feel better than he had in many years. In three months, with his wife and children, he returned to Mobile much improved and enthusiastic to continue his work. He promised himself and his family in Oklahoma that they would come back again soon.

We do not know whether they made it back before, but they probably did go back for the burial of Jerome's father, Augustus Owen, who died on April 19, 1877 at the age of 72. He was interred in the Frisco cemetery. Jerome's mother, Frances, did not die until January 20, 1893, just 11 days before her 85th birthday[11].

Work. Back to work. Once again he was the Alabama Medical Association's representative to the annual meeting of the American Medical Association just as he had been in 1874. As Mobile's

---

[10]It is a known fact that Jerome Bowling and Edmund Collins both wound up in Texas -- a result of their relatives? or their travels?

[11]*Genealogy*, by Mary Gregg.

Health Officer, Cochran resumed a busy schedule. The Medical College was back in session. He began working on his scientific paper: "Yellow fever in Relation to its Cause." He continued to compile data for his annual report as Senior Censor. He worked on making the Act To Regulate the Practice of Medicine in the State of Alabama even better. In other words, he was again working at his usual driven pace.

Chapter XI

Prime Example

-1876-

At age 44, Dr Jerome Cochran was in his prime. That his prime was to continue for so many years should not have surprised anyone. His peers, both county and state, genuinely came to rely on him.

Following the rules of his own constitution of the Medical Association of the State of Alabama, Cochran, at the state level, had served as Counsellor and Censor since 1873. To aid the reader of this biography in appreciating and understanding how extremely busy these duties kept him, and how deeply committed he was to his cause, the roles of each of the officers of the Association is described as follows in his authored work found in the Memorial Record of Alabama, Volume II, 1893:[1] [The misspellings and lower case designations are Cochran's own.]

"(1) The officers of the association are: one president, two

---

[1]Jerome Cochran, Montgomery, "The Medical Profession," *Memorial Record of Alabama*, Vol. II, Brant & Fuller, Madison Wis., 1893, pp. 107-140.

vice-presidents, one secretary, one treasurer, and ten censors. None of these positions are sinecures; every one of them has a considerable amount of work and responsibility to it; and every one of them involves a considerable expenditure of both time and money. Every officer is expected to pay all the expenses of his office out of his own individual pocket, with the exception of two, the secretary and the treasurer, who have small salaries.[2]

"...(4) One of the most distinctive features of the organization is the Board of Censors. This Board is composed of ten counsellors; the term of service for each one is five years, and two are elected at each annual session to fill vacancies occasioned by expiration of terms. ...This board is the general executive committee of the association. All business of whatever character, which is presented to the association, is referred to them without debate and without motion, to be by them reported back to the Association with their recommendations and the reason therefore, after which said business is discussed and voted upon by the association." [3]

The first Board of Censors chosen were: "Drs. Jerome Cochran of Mobile, for five years; James Guild, Sr., of Tuscaloosa, for four years; A.G. Mabry of Selma, for three years; R.F. Michel of Montgomery, for two years; and George E. Kumpe of Leighton, for one year.[4]"

A great undertaking, indeed - yet Cochran seemed amazed, and/or justly proud of the work as evidenced in the next statement: "It is a remarkable fact that from its organization up to this time - some twenty years - no recommendation of the board of censors has ever been overruled by the association."[5]

---

[2]*Ibid.* pp. 123-4.

[3]*Ibid.* p. 124.

[4]Howard L. Holley, M.D., *A History of Medicine in Alabama.* The University of Alabama Press,1982, p. 218.

[5]Jerome Cochran, Montgomery, "The Medical Profession," *op. cit.*, p.124.

He continued to delineate the role of the Censors as follows: "To this board, also, is referred the annual message of the president, the annual reports of the vice-presidents, the annual reports of the secretary, and of the treasurer and the publishing committees, and all reports of special committees. During the intervals between the sessions they attend to all the business of the association, which is, in such matters, bound by their action."[6]

Cochran served as Senior Censor from 1874 to 1878 and was reelected each time thereafter for the remainder of his life.

Regarding the College of Counsellors, he explained:

"(5) Another very distinctive feature of the association is the College of Counselors, which is limited to 100 members on the active roll. The position of counsellor is intended to be permanent, but it may be vacated by death, by resignation, by removal from the state, by losing membership in a county society, by impeachment, and by failure to pay dues or to attend meetings of the Association. The great burthen[*sic*] of the work and expense of the association rests on the shoulders of the counsellors. All the officers of the Association are selected from their ranks. They are the old guard, the Spartan band, the Roman Legion of the Association. After twenty years of consecutive service they are transferred to the life roll, retaining all the privileges of the counsellorship, but relieved of all its compulsory obligations."[7]

Cochran, one of the 100 counsellors from the beginning, was elected Grand Senior Counsellor in 1884 and remained so for life.

The county societies also had a board of censors:

"(6) The Association is composed of the affiliated county societies of the state, each of which holds a charter from the association prescribing their duties and their privileges. The county societies are organized on the same plan as the state association, so far as circumstances admit of it. Every county society is the board

---

⁶Jerome Cochran, Montgomery, "The Medical Profession," *op. cit.* p. 124.

⁷*Ibid*, p. 124.

of health of its county; is entitled to send two delegates to all the sessions of the association; and its members are *ipso facto* members of the association. Every county society, also, has a board of censors composed of five members, each one elected for five years, one very year, which is the general business committee of the society, the committee of public health of the county, and the county board of medical examiners."[8]

The counties who applied for a charter from the State Association were: 1875 - Autauga, Butler, Dallas (which succeeded the Selma Medical Society in 1874), Hale, Perry, and Talladega; 1876 - Lowndes, Mobile, Morgan, Sumter and Walker; 1877 - Elmore, Jefferson, Lamar, Lawrence, Limestone, Madison, Marengo, Monroe, Shelby and Tuscaloosa; 1878 - Barbour, Blount, Etowah, Montgomery, Pickens, Pike, Randolph, St. Clair and Wilcox;[9] and in 1879 the rest of the counties.

With brilliant determination, Dr. Jerome Cochran continued the weaving of the medical profession's tapestry. With imagination soaring, energy streaming, he continued to pull himself and his peers onward, upward, through the weft.

As well as expending time, energy, and his own money dedicating himself to the performance of his many duties -- Senior Censor, Counsellor, Health Officer for Mobile, active in the American Medical Association, active in the Mobile Medical Society, teaching in the Medical College of Alabama -- his further dream, the regulation of the practice of medicine in Alabama, was still that -- a dream. He had worked longer, harder, and with more against him than he had in creating the Board of Health. Because in *this* endeavor he had had to enlighten the doctors themselves; convince them that it was to their benefit to get behind him. He had already spent years at the task, spent a small fortune in time, papers

---

[8]*Ibid.*, p. 125

[9]Holley, *op. cit.* p. 219.

and speeches purporting his vision to his peers, widening their knowledge and understanding of what he knew to be the best way to establish the medical profession's authority.

In 1873, after approving his constitution, the Association had approved the concept of a bill that would legislate the practice of medicine. Through his continuing zealous work, Cochran did improve on that bill -- tabled year after year at his own insistence until he had it perfected. Finally he deemed it the best he could do and, at the annual meeting of the Association, held in Mobile in the spring of that year of Our Lord, 1876, he presented the final form of his bill to his peers. He expounded, using the best of his speech-making ability. Could his personal example of dedication move them? Would they finally approve his vision?

It did. They did. The Association unanimously accepted the proposed law, and instructed the Board of Censors to present it to the Legislature that November. Also, in 1876 the government of Mobile adopted Cochran's Medical Practices Act.

In November, the Board of Censors presented the bill to the General Assembly. It met with general acceptance in the Senate. One clause the Senate struck, however, raised the complete ire of the faculty of the Medical College of Alabama. The clause struck was one providing that the faculty should be one of the boards of medical examiners. The faculty, therefore, encouraged organization of active opposition in the House of Representatives.

-1877-

Soon, "after some modifications and an active canvass, the bill passed both houses of the general assembly" on the last day of the session. The Governor signed it on February 12, 1877, and it became law. The Medical Practices Act of 1877 was the first law passed in America in which "the organized medical profession of the state is invested with the power to fix the terms of admission into its own ranks, and to prescribe the character and amount of the qualification which shall entitle any one to practice medicine in the state."[10]

Cochran summarized "the leading features of the law ... as follows: [11]

"(1.) That the board of censors of the medical association of the state of Alabama, and the boards of censors of the county medical societies holding charters from the state association, are constituted authorized boards of medical examiners.

(2.) That the standard of qualifications and the rules for the government of the authorized boards of medical examiners are such as may be from time to time prescribed by the medical association of the state.

(3.) That all persons legally engaged in the practice of medicine in the state at the time of the passage of the law, are continued in the enjoyment of that right under certain regulations.

(4.) That no one shall be allowed, under fines and penalties, to begin the practice of medicine in Alabama until he has passed a satisfactory examination before some one of the authorized boards of medical examiners, and had registered the certificate thereof in the office of the probate judge of the county in which he proposes to practice."

"The rules for the government of the examining boards at present in force maybe briefly summarized as follows:

(1.) All examinations must be in writing, and must comprise ten different branches, namely: chemistry, anatomy, physiology, natural history and diagnosis of diseases, physical diagnosis, principles and practice of surgery, mechanism of labor, obstetric operations, hygiene, medical jurisprudence. Materia medica, therapeutics and the practice of medicine are intentionally omitted from this schedule.

(2.) The examinations are conducted by a paid supervisor, who can not be a member of the board, in such way as to make consultation

---

[10]Cochran, "The Medical Profession," *op. cit.*, pp. 126-7.

[11]*Ibid.*, p. 127.

of books or persons impossible. The questions are prepared and the answers valued by the members of the examining board. Each answer is separately valued. The values range from one hundred, which indicates a perfect answer, down to zero, according to the judgement of the examiner; and for a successful result the final average of the values of the answers must reach seventy-five. The time consumed in an examination is usually from four to six days.

(3.) Every written examin[a]tion made by the county boards is sent up to the state board, is reviewed by them, and their opinion of it is transmitted in annual reports to the state association. Neither the state board nor the state association can reverse the decision of a county board; but if the association is not satisfied with the way a county board does its work, a reprimand or censure will secure better work in future.

(4.) Examinations are accorded only to regular graduates of reputable medical colleges; and all examination papers are bound and kept on file so that they can be produced, if needed for testimony, in the courts or for other purposes.

(5.) If any applicant believes that he has not been fairly treated by any county board, he can at any time appeal to the state board, which gives him a new examination. If any applicant is rejected by any county board, he cannot have another examination by the same or by any other county board until after the lapse of twelve months.

"Eclectics and homeopaths must pass the same examinations as regulars. Our law, indeed, does not recognize sectarian differences amongst doctors; that is to say, the state knows nothing about regulars, Eclectics, or homeopaths, but puts them all on the same legal footing and requires the same standard of qualifications for all. All legal doctors, of whatever name or school, have the full legal right to membership in our medical societies, and all are eligible to be members of the examining boards. All legal doctors, also, are freely admitted to consultations, and to all other professional privileges.

"The strong point in this system, that which secures and guarantees its efficiency, is the supervision of the state medical association. Any one, not familiar with our work, would very naturally suppose that its weak point would be found in the large number of our county boards. But our county boards give us strength other ways, and in practice we find it easy to hold them up to quite a sufficiently high standard. At the worst, they can not fall below the standard of the medical colleges. As a matter of fact, the rejections average about twenty per centum of the examinations."

One of the amazing things about the way Cochran set up the examination process was that, due to difficulty of travel, the administration of examinations by the county medical societies was much more expedient, yet he strongly believed that "the thoroughness of examination is not the only thing we have to consider. Indeed, strange as it may seem, it is not even the principle thing we have to consider. Our great aim is the organization and discipline of the medical profession throughout the state; and the most potent of all the factors we are able to invoke in the accomplishment of this object grows out of the fact that the county medical societies, through their board of censors, have been made the agents of the state for the administration of the law to regulate the practice of medicine."

Ten years later, in 1886, the president of the Medical Association of Georgia appointed Dr. William A. Love of Atlanta to "look thoroughly into the workings of the Alabama Association." Dr. Love attended the annual session of April 13-16 in Anniston, Alabama and reported back to his president as follows:[12]

"...that the Medical Association of Alabama is a representative body, that its working is at once unique and complex, its very complexity giving it strength. It has united the profession of the State as one man; its influence for good is felt throughout its jurisdiction. From irregular [practitioners] it has met [strenuous] opposition. These for a time played upon the prejudices, the credulity, and gullibility of the people, and brought what at times seemed to be formidable opposition to it, but its intelligent officers

---

[12]Holley, P. 222.

... have so far guided it safely to a condition of prosperity and power that would seem to vouchsafe a successful future ... They are united in peace, they are working in harmony, and their social and political standing and influence is such that it is a sufficient guarantee that in the future, as in the past, they will be amply sustained by the enactments of the General Assembly in all their efforts for the common good of a confiding community."

Early in 1877, when the Senate struck lines from Cochran's bill regarding the faculty of the Medical College as one of the boards of medical examiners, raising the opposition of the faculty to the bill, "Dr. Cochran, preferring the interest of the profession to the interest of the college, and not willing that any fancied allegiance to the faculty should embarrass his efforts with the general assembly, immediately resigned his professorship, which put an end to his connection with the college."[13]   Though it probably tried his constitution to the utmost, the fact that these men were his colleagues and friends did not stop him from doing what he felt in the best interest of the state medical association. "He has been known to persevere in his convictions in regard to an important public professional interest, and struggle for their ascendancy, notwithstanding it involved the alienation of friends and the sacrifice of private interests with which he could ill afford to part."[14] His justification of his position favoring the act anticipated the findings of the Abraham Flexner Commission by forty years.[15]

As Senior Censor, Dr. Cochran was able to report to the annual Association meeting the passage of the Medical Practices Act. Firmly, he had to explain the changes that had been made by the

---

[13]Personal Memoirs, Montgomery County, "Jerome Cochran, M.D.," *Memorial Record of Alabama.* Vol. II, 1893, Brant & Fuller, Madison, Wis., p. 651.

[14]*Ibid.* p. 654.

[15]See Glossary, Flexner.

Legislature, but he, and subsequently the members of the Association, decided they could live with the changes. By his example, he led them.

Aside from all the duties attendant upon him as Senior Censor of the Association, he was active in the American Medical Association and he was Health Officer for Mobile.[16] By his own rules for the City of Mobile, his plate was full. As Health Officer alone, he had -- besides the reports due weekly to the Board of Health of all the business of his office -- "To supervise the administration of all the health laws of the city; to examine into all cases of malignant, pestilential, infectious and epidemic diseases which may occur in the city, and the causes thereof; to examine into all such nuisances as may tend to endanger the health of the city, and take such steps as may be necessary for their removal; to exercise a general supervision over the sanitary regulations of all the municipal institutions, including hospitals, markets, asylums, prisons, and public schools; to superintend all matters pertaining to quarantine and the Quarantine Physician, and direct all measures of detention, disinfection and purification of vessels, cargoes and passengers coming from ports against which quarantine many have been proclaimed.[17] ... That the Health Officer shall be the executive officer of the Board of Health, and, under the direction and control of the Board of Health, shall exercise a general supervision over the sanitary interests of the city; that he shall make a circuit of observation at least once in every week, to every part of the city;[18] ... that he shall keep on hand at all times, so far as possible, a supply of reliable vaccine virus, which he shall furnish to the physicians of the city, free of charge; that he shall also vaccinate all indigent

---

[16]A health ordinance written in 1875, after passage by the General Assembly, establishing Boards of Health in Alabama.

[17]Jerome Cochran, M.D., "An Ordinance to be Entitled An Ordinance to Secure the Public Health," *Transactions of MASA*, 1876, p. 346.

[18]*Ibid.* p. 349.

persons who may apply...."[19] "shall keep a book, to be entitled 'The Register of Deaths,'"[20] for such patients as come under the public health jurisdiction; and "shall examine all persons who make application for admission into the City Hospital,"... "who are "fit subjects for public charity."[21]

In addition to his duties as Health Officer -- he was elected in November as County Physician for a term of three years.[22] He held this position for the rest of his life at a salary of $125.00/month.[23]

Under different circumstances, Jerome Cochran might have become a great biologist instead of the Senior Censor of the Medical Association of the State of Alabama and the Health Officer and County Physician for Mobile. He had all the instincts of a biologist. But the same could be said of him as a medical researcher, or a poet, or a lawyer, a surgeon, a philosopher, a novelist, a historian. Although MASA had become the Board of Health, Cochran was determined that the sphere would remain broad. Public Health would be all-embracing, not a narrow specialty. Therefore, in 1877 he rehashed a paper he had worked on before and submitted it for publication in the Transactions for 1878.

He seemed fascinated by the revelations the microscope was bringing to light, and the relatively new explanations of Huxley, Darwin, and a newcomer, Edward Van Beneden. Actually, in all his facets -- and Dr. Cochran was a polyparametric man -- his interest was in life itself.

Hermaphroditism (individuals presenting the organs of both

---

[19]*Ibid.* p. 349.

[20]*Ibid.* p. 350.

[21]*Ibid.* p. 351.

[22]"Jerome Cochran of Alabama," *op.cit.* pp. 15-16.

[23]*Transactions of MASA*, 1880 pp. 136-7.

sexes, in a more or less perfect state of development) seemed to be a subject of universal interest. In his report titled: "HERMA-PHRODITISM,"[24] he didn't claim originality for the article except for a few suggestions that were not found elsewhere. The subject was not new, but it was of considerable interest, and it had not been covered very adequately in the manuals of physiology current at the time.

"Perhaps," Cochran wrote, "there is no influence operative in the world of organic nature, of wider potency, or of more multifarious affiliations than that mysterious attribute of living creatures, which in our language, is designated by the word SEX." He went on to state that it is "paradoxical ... that the two sexes, male and female, may be united in the same individual.

"As a matter of fact, however, we soon learn that individuals presenting the organs of both sexes, in a more or less perfect state of development, are occasionally to be found even in the human family. These creatures of monstrous birth, and of double sex, are called Hermaphrodites, and the condition itself is called Hermaphrodism, or Hermaphroditism."

He went to Greek mythology "as told in mellifluent verse by Ovid in his Metamorphoses -- a book which has been one of the delights of fifty generations of scholars" to explain the use of the word used to describe such individuals. Simply restated: Hermes (also known as Mercury) had an illicit affair with Aphrodite (also known as Venus.) The male child -- named for both of his parents -- was Hermaphroditis. He was of such irresistible charm and strength that his first affair, with a water nymph Salmaela, was consummated with such ardor and passionate energy that the two melted into one body, retaining the genitalia of each of the original individuals. The influence of Classical Greek among all scholars gave us the appellation to all creatures of double sex.

For many of the facts Cochran uses, he gives credit to the

---

[24]Jerome Cochran, "Hermaphroditism," *Transactions of MASA* 1887, pp. 209-239.

Brochure, published in French by Edward Van Beneden in 1874, to Huxley's latest classification of the animal kingdom, to Haeckel, of Germany, and -- to give things the latest twist -- his translation of a French article in January 1878 which quoted Waldeyer as proving the reality of the hypothesis of Eirstock und Ei, Leipsig, 1870, "that the embryo of superior Vertebrates presents, at an epoch little advanced of its development, a hermaphroditic condition and that it carries the rudiments of the two sexes."

Cochran, quoting all the above, went through the explanation of the embryonic germ layers, the reproductive zooid, fecundation, the union of the sperm and egg comparing them to the union of hydrogen and oxygen. After explaining all the premises, Dr. Cochran gave the following "classification of hermaphrodites in the entire metazoal animal sub-kingdom: [25]

1. Animals which exhibit both the male and the female organs of generation, fully developed in the same individual, and which are self-fertilizing. Of these animals, the variety is very great, including some with vaginas and intromittent organs; as, for example, the well known Tenia solium.

2. Animals which exhibit both the male and the female organs of generation, fully developed in the same individual, and which are not self-fertilizing -- animals in which two individuals reciprocally impregnate one another, by a double sexual congress; as, for example, our common snails.

3. Animals which individually exhibit only one set of generative organs, the male organs being developed exclusively in some individuals, and the female organs being exclusively developed in other individuals.

"...When it is the sexual elements of the ectoderm, that participate in the evolution, the resulting sex is male; and when it is the sexual elements of the endoderm that participate in the evolution, the resulting sex is female. It may seem to be rather a lax use of terms to call these creatures hermaphrodites, when in them, as a rule, one

---

[25] *Ibid.* p. 226.

of the sexes remains impotent and undeveloped; but both sexes are potentially present in the germ.

"...There sometimes occur exceptions to the rule -- cases in which, amongst these highest animals, both sexes are developed at the same time, in the same individual. These are the cases which constitute my fourth class of hermaphrodites; and so far as human creatures are concerned, it is to these cases alone that the name is ordinarily applied. These creatures, in whom the sexual development reverts to a far distant ancestral type -- a type which is general and normal amongst all the lower animals -- these are the hermaphrodites of our human physiologies, of our systems of medical jurisprudence, of theological casuistry, and of poetry and popular tradition."

This article is classical Cochran. He takes a perplexing problem, applies all the recent scientific developments he can find, adds his own reasoning and boldly formulates his conclusions.

As is always the case in scientific endeavors, one is playing with a deck in which the face cards may be added at a future date. One can hope to add a small one with his efforts. In Cochran's present effort, the entire science of genetics was added later, as was the science of endocrinology, and psychology. Embryology was in its infancy, the chromosome awaited the researches of Thomas Hunt Morgan, genes were unheard of, gene splicing undreamed of. DNA and RNA were unnamed and unsuspected. Cochran played a good game with a deck in which all the face cards were missing, and the deck was full of jokers -- all wild!

In December of 1877, at the time of his 46th birthday, his beloved wife Sarah Jane was 43, to be 44 on December 11. Ina Lou would be 18 on January 25, Jerome Bowling had just turned 14 on November 9, and Edmund Collins was 8. His family was growing up. These authors do not know the extent of the family's social life. With Dr. Cochran being one of the foremost medical men of the city, it is assumed they attended any and all functions of importance, as well as attending the activities of their Catholic church. Neither is it known whether Ina Lou was courted. She never married. This year, also, Dr. Cochran lost his father. It is assumed the family traveled to Oklahoma for the funeral.

Chapter XII

Jousting With The Saffron Knight

-1878-

At the State Medical Association's annual session in Eufaula in April, Dr. Benjamin A. Riggs, the orator of the medical association, had this to say:[1]

"As Bichat and Hunter were the geniuses of the origin of the new era which we have attempted to briefly portray to you tonight, and Sims and Sayres are its choicest fruit and greatest modern exemplars, so there sits within the sound of my voice one whom we may appropriately style the genius of medical organization. Our medical association, with its complex machinery already in operation, and an adumbration of more, owes its present excellence and preeminence largely to the zeal, fidelity and energy of one mind. Patient, far-reaching, tenacious, learned, indefatigable, oftentimes misunderstood, and sometimes misrepresented, Dr. Jerome Cochran

---

[1]Benjamin A. Riggs, M.D., "Annual Oration," *Transactions of MASA*, April 1878, p.172.

builded wiser than he knew in erecting the plan of the State Association. He deserves to rank as the apostle of medical action in the new era. As the British Medical Association has come to the United States for a code of ethics, so have older States in the American Union, and others are still to come, sought inspiration in studying our plan [of] organization."

The Saffron Knight -- or as yellow fever was also known by the natives of Mobile: Yellow Jack -- came once again to joust with Dr. Jerome Cochran. In 1877 Cochran had described the three main contemporary schools of thought concerning the source of infectious disease:[2]

1. The school that thought that factors causing diseases were offsprings of climatic agencies such as heat, humidity, and organic decomposition.

2. The school that admitted that malaria was not caused by the same type of poison as yellow fever but argued that malaria was the result of climatic conditions.

3. The school that endorsed the germ theory of communicable diseases.

To Cochran, the third school was the only one that was tenable. He spoke very clearly of yellow fever: "Yellow fever is a special infectious disease, propagated by a. ... poison composed of organic material particles which live and grow...and which can be transplanted...from place to place. Yellow fever poison is not indigenous to the soil of Alabama.... Whether sporadic or epidemic in form, it is always due to importations from abroad of the specific disease germs which are necessary to its production.... It has no relation whatsoever with malaria which is endemic." In projecting his views, Cochran pulled no punches.

Before 1900, the only known defense against yellow fever was quarantine. When the yellow fever epidemic of 1878 hit Mobile,

---

[2]Jerome Cochran, "Endemic and Epidemic Diseases of Mobile,"*Transactions of MASA,* 1871, pp. 238-241.

Cochran was selected to be the physician at the lower quarantine station at Fort Morgan, and was invested by the Board of Health with very large discretionary powers.[3] As quarantine officer of the Port of Mobile, he found that the existing quarantine laws, while effective, were unnecessarily stringent. With his superior knowledge of yellow fever, he was able to tighten up the laws in certain places and be more lenient in others. Through acute observation and experience, Cochran had found that most unopened cartons of cargo were not contagious, even if coming from ships with many cases of yellow fever aboard. Therefore, he allowed certain cargoes to be unloaded coming from yellow fever ports (principally Havana), so that tropical goods could be imported the year round. This was good economics; and the Board of Trade and the people in general appreciated it. Also, the quarantine became more reliable and was easier to enforce. In 1878 the employment of Cochran's rules for quarantine of Mobile and Alabama saved countless thousands of lives from importation of the disease from Havana, New Orleans and Memphis where disease was spreading rampantly.

Also at this time the federal government, realizing its responsibility to its citizens, appointed a National Yellow Fever Commission. The members of this Commission were recommended by the American Public Health Association(APHA) and included Dr. Samuel M. Bemiss of New Orleans as Chair, and Cochran probably took on the duties of secretary.

On September 30, Cochran resigned his post in Mobile to accept a place upon this Commission, which was tendered him by Dr. John M. Woodworth,[4] the Surgeon-General and chief physician, of the Marine Hospital Service.[5] He at once proceeded to New Orleans, where the commission first assembled for organization, and in the

---

[3]"Doctor Jerome Cochran of Alabama," *Op. cit.*, p. 16.

[4]See Glossary, Woodworth, John M.

[5] "Doctor Jerome Cochran of Alabama," *op.cit.*, p. 16.

discharge of his duties...after two weeks spent in hunting up the histories of the earlier New Orleans cases, he visited the New Orleans quarantine station. Then he visited (in Mississippi) Port Eads, Osyka, McComb, Jackson, Water Valley, Granada, Grand Junction. He then went to Memphis, Tennessee, following the spread of the disease, and making at every one of these places he visited, such as his time allowed, researches into the introduction and dissemination of yellow fever amongst the people. The object was to trace the causes of the progress of the pestilence in time and space, in such a way as to furnish reliable indications for protective legislation.[6] In the Great Epidemic of 1878 over 200,000 people contracted yellow fever. The usual mortality rate was 20% to 30%. Although no accurate figures are available, there must have been as many as 40,000 deaths due to the disease.

Vadah Cochran related: "Jerome came to Holly Springs and Marshall County, from Memphis, during the yellow fever epidemic." What he found there must surely have devastated him. Between late August and early November, when Cochran arrived, both his twin brother and sister, Eugene and Ann Florence, had died of yellow fever at the age of thirty.

"He visited the Clark T. Cochran place where he saw many refugees from Holly Springs camped in front of the house. His uncle Clark Cochran, whose plantation was somewhat north of Holly Springs, was providing food for them. He slaughtered a cow every day and continued feeding them for nothing -- as did plantation owners all over the county. The cost ruined some of the owners.[7]

The inability to stay longer and render valuable assistance must have frustrated Cochran enormously. But he had been ordered by Dr. Bemiss to attend the session of the American Public Health Association at Richmond, Virginia on November 19 to present the

---

[6]*Ibid.*

[7]Vadah Cochran, Personal Conversation with Dr. John T. Morris

Commission's report.   He had to leave his relatives in Holly Springs.[8]

While in the Memphis area, Cochran may have met a young medical student from Bellevue Medical College, who was attempting to get into Memphis to help with the patient load. His companions called him W.C., and he was bitterly disappointed that the "shotgun quarantine" wouldn't allow him to go beyond Moscow, Fayette County, Tennessee. After the first exodus from Memphis, no "unadapted" person was allowed to go in and no one was allowed to leave Memphis. The young man was William Crawford Gorgas.[9] Dr. Gorgas was to become the one man who eradicated yellow fever in both Cuba and the Panama Canal zone in the first decade of the 20th century.

The following (indicative of what all cities went through) is an account of the 1878 epidemic at Holly Springs:

Interesting facts present themselves. Moscow, Tennessee and Holly Springs, Mississippi, former residences of Jerome Cochran, were badly hit by the epidemic.

The story of Memphis, and surrounding area (including Moscow) during the Great Epidemic of 1878 has been told and retold. It is the story of a disaster striking a great city, and is stark horror. The same epidemic struck little Holly Springs with a population of 3500 and was no less a horror story. In Holly Springs there were 1440 cases of yellow fever with 304 deaths.[10]

Initially, the epidemic had come to Grenada and Memphis, bypassing Holly Springs. On August 12, 1878, Holly Springs had

---

[8]*Ibid.*

[9]John T. Morris, B.S., M.D. "Josiah Clark Nott and the Heroic Age of Alabama Medicine," *Alabama Medicine, Journal of MASA, Vol. 62, No.7*, January , 1993.

[10]J. M. Keating, *A History of Yellow Fever, Memphis, 1879*, Printed for the Howard Association, pp. 244-46.

set up a Board of Health consisting of Dr. F. W. Dancy and two other members. Colonel H. W. Walter and other prominent citizens believed that Holly Springs' "air was pure," and that her elevation would protect her. They urged that the gates to the city be opened to refugees from Grenada and Memphis. Drs. Dancy and Compton strenuously held out for a quarantine, but they were overruled, and the refugees poured in.[11]

W. J. L. Holland lived in the little brick house that had been the land office. He moved out and gave it up to some people from Grenada, and some of them were the first to die of yellow fever. Mayor Goodrich, "The First Citizen" of the town was the first townsman to die.[12]

There was the usual panic and exodus from the city when one case of the fever occurred. People scatterd in all directions, by train, by carriage, and on foot. From a population of 3500 before the fever began, 1500 remained: 300 whites and 1200 blacks. 2,000 people had left the city.[13]

From those who remained, there were fine examples of courage. Colonel H. W. Walter, who had been a member of the Board of Health, and had argued for mercy on the pilgrims from Memphis and Grenada, sent his wife and the younger children to Chattanooga with Mr. Henry Myers, husband of his daughter, Minnie. With his three oldest sons, all recent graduates of the University of Mississippi, Colonel Walter elected to remain amidst the fever. Jimmy took charge of the post office, and they opened their beautiful home to the suffering, trying to aid in whatever way they could. The old gentleman and his three sons died within a week.[14]

---

[11]Dunbar Rowland, LL.D.,L. *History of Mississippi, Heart of the South,* S.J. Clarke Pub. Co. 1925, pp. 214-271.

[12]*Ibid.,* p. 215.

[13]William Baskerville Hamilton, *Holly Springs, Mississippi, to the Year 1878,* pp. 49-51.

[14]*Ibid.*

Trains soon refused to stop in the stricken city of Holly Springs. They pulled up three miles south of town. A funereal quiet settled over the city. "It was left deserted to the dying and the dead."[15]

A relief committee, headed by W. J. L. Holland -- he who had given up his home to the victims from Grenada -- obtained help from the Howard Association of New Orleans.[16] This New Orleans organization, which did yeoman service in the entire area of the great epidemic, sent, on September 5th, doctors, nurses, a telegraph operator, druggists, and assistants.

They established a hospital in the Courthouse. Some of the immune doctors who came in were: Drs. Walter Bailey and A. R. Gourrier, of New Orleans; R.M. Swearinger of Texas; and J. W. Ross of the United States Navy. Drs. Manning and Lewis, of Texas were not immune; both of them died during the first weeks. Dr. B. F. McKie stayed with the town. Dr. W. M. Compton, who had argued so vehemently for quarantine, stayed with the town and died.[17]

"In the streets there was no sound save, perhaps, the frantic clatter of horse's hoofs as someone rode in from the country to implore the attendance of a doctor, or the rapid roll of the hearse's wheels as a corpse, followed by no mourners, was borne to the grave."[18]

Volunteers had to take charge of all necessary posts, such as the telegraph office, the post office, and the commissary. Mr. George Myers was in Atlanta when he read in the *Atlanta Constitution* of the tragedy that had befallen his people. He came home, but was forced to get off the train some distance below Holly Springs. He walked, carrying his luggage, back to the town past the cemetery,

---

[15]*Ibid.*

[16]Rowland Dunbar, LL.d., L. *op.cit.* p.216.

[17]Keating, *op. cit.* pp. 244-46.

[18]Dunbar, *op.cit.*, p. 216.

where Mr. Gus Smith was being buried. Upon his arrival, Holland put him in charge of the express and telegraph offices. Kelly, an "immune" from New Orleans, relieved him there, and Myers went to work at the commissary.

The people of the nation responded to the dire need of the South, and supplies -- everything from clothing to champagne -- rolled into Holly Springs. Negroes and whites alike were furnished with the necessities for the well and the ill. The "foreign" doctors, those who had come into Holly Springs to help, were aghast at the waste of champagne on uneducated, as well as ex-slave palates. They commandeered this luxury to keep themselves going.[19]

Real heroes in this pest-house-of-a-town were more the rule than the exception, but several specific instances have been handed down in tradition. "Probably the most awful of these was the sacrifice of the Catholic School in the town.

"The Priest was Father Oberti, and the six nuns were Sister Stanislaus, Sister Stella, Sister Margaret, Sister Victoria, Sister Lorentia, and Sister Corinthia. In the hospital, where the black and white lay side by side, the nurses were the Sisters from the local Catholic School.... Like angels of mercy they hovered over the loathsome sick day and night, caring not who the patient might be.... One by one the sisters fell until all six of them, along with the faithful priest, lay dead."[20]

Kinlich Falconer was Secretary of State in Mississippi. At the outbreak of the fever in his town, he immediately raced to its aid, asking the governor to appoint to his post his friend Myers in case he did not return from the city of the dead. The Saffron Knight did, indeed, take him, as well as his own brother, Howard, and Holland, his press colleague. There is in the cemetery at Holly Springs a monument to Falconer, Holland, and four other members of the Mississippi Press Association who died during the epidemic. They

---

[19]Hamilton, *op.cit.*, pp. 48-51.

[20]*Ibid.*

are: J.P. Allen, of the *Meridian Gazette*; the editor of the *Vicksburg Herald*; W. K. Adams, of the *Enterprise Courier;* and O. V. Shearer of the *New Orleans Times.*[21]

Oxford, Mississippi, only 35 miles south, was strictly quarantined. No trains stopped or started in the town and no one was allowed to enter by any other means. Oxford had not one case of yellow fever.

Winter came, and with it a lifting of the terror, but Holly Springs was exhausted and crippled. Dr. Dancy "conservatively" estimated the cost of the epidemic to Holly Springs at $439,000. Mr. George Myers said that every merchant in the town was ruined. Many emigrants did not return, many immigrants did not leave after the epidemic ended.[22] The character of the town changed forever.

There was further reaction:

"This epoch in 1878 changed the lifestyle, as the war had changed the old lifestyle. It was followed by even greater relaxation of high standards. Night life in Holly Springs was lurid and lasted much of the night. Ladies seldom ventured on the square at night unless there was something on at 'the hall.' Saloons were more openly operated; the front doors were dutifully locked on Sundays but the rear doors were open. One saloon, occupying the entire M. and F. building operated its poker games upstairs and bar below day and night.

Excursion trains of ten or twelve packed coaches often ran there from Memphis on Sundays; when the saloons were over-crowded, porters with waiters of whiskey would be sent out to peddle them on the square.

"It was the extreme revulsion of taut nerves from the horrors of the epidemic. Such phenomena may follow all such disasters." [23]

---

[21]*Ibid.*, p. 21.

[22]*Ibid.*

[23]*Ibid.*

Cochran, in Richmond, along with the several members of the Commission made to the American Public Health Association preliminary reports of their investigations, which were then referred to special committees for their consideration. The other members of Cochran's committee described the work done by him as almost super-human.[24]

The Commission's chairman, Dr. Bemiss, indicated that he, Cochran, Howard, and Col. Hardee would continue the inquiry "as long as funds were available,"[25] also stating that it would be several months before the first volume of its findings would be published. Howard resigned, but Cochran may have taken a break and gone home from Richmond, stopping in Chattanooga, Tennessee in an official investigative capacity on the way to Mobile.

When his family visit was over, Cochran traveled to Louisiana, then to Meridian and Okalona [what war memories those stops must have evoked!] He then proceeded to Holly Springs. Finally, he traveled into Alabama, visiting Tuscumbia[26] and Florence before finishing in Decatur.

The press across the country helped raise an uproar for national quarantine. President Hayes addressed this matter in his December 2 annual message to Congress. On December 16, the Senate and House of Representatives' committees on epidemic diseases -- committees named as a result of resolutions by the APHA requesting a further detailed study of yellow fever -- created a Board of Experts.

The Board of Experts was chaired by Dr. John Woodworth chairman of the Commission on Yellow Fever, and Supervising Surgeon General of the Marine Hospital Service. The Board was comprised of Drs. Bemiss [of New Orleans, who was also the editor

---

[24]"Doctor Jerome Cochran of Alabama," *op.cit.* pp. 16-18.

[25]New orleans *Picayune*, November 23,1878.

[26]Helen Keller, Alabama's "First Lady of Courage," was born in Tuscumbia the very next year.

of the *New Orleans Medical and Surgical Journal*] and Cochran [of Mobile,] Col. T.S. Hardee, [N.O. civil engineer,] Dr. Sanford C. Chaillé [of New Orleans, who, like Dr. Cochran, soon became a prolific writer on yellow fever,] Drs. T.S. Craft, and Samuel Green [unknown hometowns,] Dr. Robert W. Mitchell [of Memphis who had headed the Howard Association's yellow fever relief mission of Memphis during the epidemic of 1878,] Dr. R. M. Swearingen [of Texas,] and Dr. Jacob Mosher [unknown hometown.] The homeopath that was on the Board of Experts at the insistence of the Homeopathic Association was Dr. Louis Falligant.[27]

"At Florence he [Cochran] received notification of his appointment on the Board of Experts established to aid the Congressional committees of the Senate and House of Representatives in the investigation of the epidemic of 1878. The proceedings of those committees, and of the Board of Experts, is a portion of the public history of the Forty-fifth Congress. By far the greater portion of the field work for the collection of data used by the congressional committees and the Board of Experts had already been done by Drs. Bemiss and Cochran, and by Colonel T.S. Hardee, civil engineer, whilst [sic] members of the Yellow Fever Commission, so that the principal work of the Board of Experts was to give their information to the committees, and to formulate the conclusions warranted by the researches already made. Dr. Cochran was made Chairman of the Sub-Committee of experts on the Origin, Cause and Distinctive Features of Yellow Fever and Cholera."[28]

The first meeting of the Board of Experts was held on December 26 at the Peabody Hotel in Memphis. Although rail travel had become much faster, imagine Cochran having to again leave his family, this time probably on Christmas Day after early Mass, in order to arrive in Memphis on time for the meeting!

During this year of 1878, in addition to all that his demanding

---

[27]J.M. Keating, *A History of the Yellow Fever : The Yellow Fever Epidemic of 1878 in Memphis, Tennessee* (Memphis, 1879), p. 27.

[28]"Doctor Jerome Cochran of Alabama," *op. cit.* pp.16-18.

work schedule entailed, he wrote another scientific paper: "What is Puerperal Fever?" This was published in the 1879 Transactions.

-1879-

From December 30 to January 6, the Board of Experts met in New Orleans to determine: 1) if the disease of yellow fever was endemic or imported [they decided it was definitely imported] and 2) to decide upon a system of quarantine that was both effective, yet economy-saving, for quarantine and business did not go hand-in-hand. They spent the next few weeks readying and polishing the report. On January 30, the Board presented its report to Congress in Washington.

Of Cochran, it was written, "His committee [subcommittee on the Origin, Cause and Distinctive Features of Yellow Fever and Cholera] was the first to report, and the report was adopted by the full board substantially as written. The thirty-four propositions -- all of those in relation to yellow fever, of the conclusions of the Board of Experts -- are especially Dr. Cochran's work, and constitute such summing up of what is known of the natural and secular history of yellow fever as is nowhere else to be found."[29] The Board recommended a national system of quarantine, isolation of the sick, dispersion of the healthy, and establishment of refugee camps.[30]

The Board of Experts was dissolved on the 3rd day of February, 1879.[31]

None of us lives in a vacuum. The members of the Commission on Yellow Fever, and the members of the Board of Experts, many of them the same people, had had time to take each others' measure. Cochran could not help but be very aware of the nationwide outcry

---

[29]*Ibid.* p20.

[30]"Conclusions of the Board of Experts," New York Times, January 31, 1879. pp. 21, 23, 26.

[31]"Doctor Jerome Cochran of Alabama," *op. cit.* p. 20.

for a national board of health that would make quarantine efforts uniform and, hopefully, prevent future epidemics. He would have also been aware of the two factions seeking to create such a board: the Marine Hospital Service headed by Dr. John M. Woodworth, and the American Public Health Association, whose president was Dr. James L. Cabell of Charlottesville, Virginia. Cochran was a charter member of the APHA.

Dr. Cabell and the APHA had been busy formulating their idea of the form and composition of a national health board which precluded consultation with state and local health boards.

While the Board of Experts was in Washington giving their report, they probably discovered that various proposals for a national health board were submitted, yet died in committee on Capitol Hill.

On February 24, the McGowan bill was finally enacted by Congress creating a National Board of Health. It was a weakened version that gave the Board virtually no power except to investigate and report to Congressional Committees. And, it was given only four *experimental* years in which to show what it could do. The members were to be appointed by President Hayes within a month. However, the Marine Hospital Service was effectively cut off as the agency of choice to become the national health board. Dr. Woodworth, who had hoped to be THE POWER in national health, was bitterly disappointed. He died a short time later. His replacement to the position of Supervising Surgeon General of the Marine Hospital Service was John B. Hamilton, a rather brusque man.

Also in February, Cochran was asked to appear before the Alabama Legislature in Montgomery, regarding the annual appropriation of $3,000 for health purposes to be expended under the direction of the State Board of Health. He spoke to the floor during the regular session. "Those conversant with the usages of a legislative assembly will appreciate how signal a tribute of respect was conveyed in such a proceeding. After the address, the House became almost as unanimous for the bill as before they had seemed to be against it.

"In no other State has [sic] such powers been intrusted to the medical profession, and the fact that it is so in Alabama is due almost entirely to the sagacity and professional devotion the subject of this memoir."[32]

On April 1, the executive committee of the National Board of Health (NBH) was appointed by the President. Among those who were appointed were Drs. Bemiss and Mitchell. Dr. Bemiss was made chair until elections could be held the next day, at which time Dr. James Cabell was elected President. Committees were set up. The Board members knew their function was chiefly cooperative (with state and local boards) and advisory. They set up a scientific study of investigation and collections of public health issues and information by hiring qualified persons, both medical and sanitarian.[33] All they needed now was the approval of Congress with appropriations for same.

"On the 11th of April, at the MASA annual meeting, Dr. Cochran was unanimously elected the Medical Association Health Officer of the State of Alabama for the term of five years."[34]

Not one to sit back and accept others' rules for him, on May 21-22, probably as a result of attending the AMA convention in Atlanta two weeks earlier, Cochran called into special session in Montgomery, the Committee of Public Health. The committee members were Drs. J. B. Gaston, J.S. Weatherly, S. D. Seelye, C. H. Franklin, C. D. Parke, and M. H. Jordan. The purpose of this special meeting was to 1) formulate rules for preventing the spread and yellow fever, and 2) assure the compliance of county medical

---

[32]*Ibid.* p. 20.

[33]Minutes of the Executive Committee, National Board of Health, I, 1, April 2, 1879, pp. 4-5, RG 90, National Archives.

[34]"Doctor Jerome Cochran of Alabama," *op. cit.* p.18.

societies regarding sanitation and vital statistics.

In July, 1,000 copies of the rules regarding yellow fever were sent to physicians throughout the State and Circular No. 1 "Rules for Preventing the Introduction and Spread of Yellow Fever."[35] This document is divided into two parts: "The Quarantine of First Cases of Yellow Fever" and "The Quarantine of Railroad Cars and Passengers."

In the first topic, seven rules were set forth: 1. Isolation without delay of any suspected case of yellow fever, with a line and guard to assure compliance.

2. Disinfection without delay of any clothing, etc. capable of becoming a means of spread of infection. This included bathing the patient.

3. Only those persons necessary to take care of the patient(s) would be allowed across the line, and must routinely bathe, champoo [sic], put on fresh clothes and disinfect those clothes worn when caring for the patient.

4. Anyone else coming into contact with the patient prior to isolation was to be required to bathe, shampoo, don fresh clothes, disinfect those clothes worn, then be isolated for a minimum of five days [maximum incubation time of yellow fever] from the last time of exposure to the infection.

5. After removal of the patient (or his body) from the place of isolation, that place was to be completely disinfected and closed until after the frosts of November.

6. The corpse was to be buried as soon as possible with no one in attendance except the burial detail, then the burial detail was to be disinfected as prescribed above.

7. Since there was no proof at the time that body excretions were not the source of the spread of infection, and recognizing that this knowledge was incomplete, Cochran prescribed the exact treatment and disposal of same.

---

[35]Cochran, "The Report of the Board of Censors," *Transactions of MASA*, April, 1880, pp.117-119.

As to the quarantine of the railroad cars and passengers, it was decided that the simplest and most inexpensive was mandated. Therefore,

1. No stopping in infected towns, keeping everything closed up on the way through. Mail from the infected town was to be heated at 240° before being shipped.

2. Passengers from infected towns had to be inspected, disinfected and isolated for five days.

3. Merchandise, likewise, was to be disinfected.

As a result of his work for the Yellow Fever Commission and the Board of Experts, he compiled his scientific paper "Sanitary Administration, and the Theory and Practice of Quarantine," and published it as a pamphlet for Alabama's State Board of Health. It was also included in the *Transactions* of 1880.

In order to appreciate the convoluted events of August, 1879, we must here learn that on April 30, in accordance with his appointment to the NBH, Dr. Mitchell called a meeting of physicians of the Mississippi Valley. They set up the Sanitary Council of the Mississippi Valley. Their primary concern was the relationship between commerce and public health. They pledged themselves two objectives: promoting state sanitation, and preventing the spread of epidemic diseases -- these in wholehearted cooperation with the NBH.[36]

The Sanitary Council met in Atlanta on May 5, timing their meeting with the conventions of the NBH and the American Medical Association. Cochran probably attended the AMA convention.

In the meantime, Senator Harris, one of those whose bills died in committee, set about to strengthen the existing law that had created the NBH. What he did manage to do was get an appropriation on June 2 to approve the appointment of skilled professionals and

---

[36]Resolution of the Sanitary Council of the Mississippi Valley to Congress, May 5, 1879, House Select Committee on Epidemic Disease, 46 Congress, First Session., HR 46-H26., National Archives.

sanitary experts to conduct a series of systematic sanitary investigations to find out the actual hygienic conditions of ports that were potential sources or avenues of infection. These men would receive$10/day plus expenses for their work.[37]

The NBH agreed that the inspections would continue throughout the entire yellow fever season. Of the eight inspectors named, Cochran was given the Gulf Coast from Key West Florida to Pensacola, Florida. Included in the duties of these inspectors was to furnish copies of the NBH Quarantine Rules and Regulations. Should the States fail to execute the Board's R&R, it was then the responsibility of the President of the U.S. to force compliance. In the contingency plans, an investigator could be temporarily assigned to assist at the place of an epidemic, should one arise. In which case, he was to insist on the isolation of the sick and immediate burial of the dead. All reports were to be made public in the *Bulletin*.[38] Cochran assumed these duties along with those of his office as Alabama's State Health Officer, and Health Officer of the City of Mobile. -- for whom also he was the Quarantine Officer.

In July, Yellow Fever struck Memphis. Dr. Mitchell telegraphed the NBH and was ordered to trace the origin. On July 11, the NBH wired Mitchell asking if the city was dangerously infected. They sent additional inspectors to Memphis, and telegraphed Illinois, Tennessee, Mississippi, and Kentucky Legislatures to quickly adopt the NBH Rules and Regulations so they could be assisted monetarily by the Board when requested to do so. (The law stipulated this requirement of adoption before assistance could be rendered.)[39] He was also ordered to cooperate fully with the health authorities throughout the valley. He, therefore, could advise, but had to assist the Quarantine Officer, Dr. John Johnston. Since there was a severe

---

[37]NBH *Bulletin*, I (1879), Supplement 2, NBH Annual Report, 1879, p. 4-5.

[38]*Ibid.*

[39]New York *Times*, June 20-25, 1879; NBH Annual Report, 1879, pp. 17-18; Executive Committee minutes, I, 27, July 10, 1879, pp. 3-5.

shortage of funds, especially after the devastation of 1878's epidemic, Dr. Johnson recommended depopulation. Mitchell requested monetary assistance from the NBH as soon as Tennessee adopted the R&R. Mitchell was also under the NBH authority to destroy all sources of infection and attempt to isolate all fever cases.[40]

On July 18, Mitchell notified the NBH that Memphis was dangerously infected. The main means of defense has been mass evacuation; it was effective, but expensive. Money was needed desperately and had been requested through the proper channels.[41]

On August 8, Cochran was sent to Memphis. What he found must have horrified him. Cochran had been running the quarantine operations of Mobile since 1871. He knew what worked. He was used to people following the rules. His papers, and his reputation proved him a man of science who knew all there was to know about yellow fever and the treatment of its victims and environ.   On August 9, he met with the local health authorities and urged them to adopt a 5 point program to halt the fever. However, he acted in anger. He gave the impression that members of the NBH were not harmonious, but openly criticized each other, when he accused Dr. Mitchell of failing to carry out the Board's policy of isolation and disinfection. Cochran failed, perhaps, to consider that Memphis was still suffering a severe lack of funds after the 1878 epidemic.

Mitchell, probably exhausted, in a rage, fired off his resignation to the NBH. The Board wrote back asking him to reconsider, as resignation might be seen as an admission of guilt.[42] Mitchell

---

[40]New York *Times*, July 11, 1879; Executive Committee Minutes, I, 29, July 12, 1879, Letters I, 154-55; NBH to R. W. Mitchell, Washington D.C. July 12, 1879 Letters I, 289-90.

[41]R.W. Mitchell to NBH, Memphis, Tennessee, July 18, 1879, NBH Correspondence Undesignated Communication 816; Mitchell to NBH, Memphis Tennessee, August 2, *ibid* 1334, NBH to J.D. Plunkett [in Nashville], Washington D.C. August 6, 1879, Letters I, 289-90.

[42]NBH to Mitchell, Washington, D.C., August 21, 1879, Letters I, 376-7.

agreed to stay, and Cochran was swiftly removed from Memphis. Cochran said he had been confronted with the threat of an epidemic in Memphis and that passion had overcome him.[43]   Cochran, however, wrote in his report to the Alabama Board of Health in 1880, that the NBH had a glorious opportunity for action during the Memphis epidemic, but lost it. Instead of taking active measures such as isolation and disinfection, the Board was stricken with paralysis. The confinement of fever to Memphis was attributed not so much to the NBH as to the policy of mass exodus and non-intercourse quarantine placed on the Bluff City as soon as the fever appeared. He admitted he was all the more devastated because he was an employee of the Board and familiar with Memphis activities.

On August 12, Dr. Johnston wired Washington with a complaint: that it had been 30 days since the outbreak, and still no effort "worthy of the name" had been given by the NBH to check its spread. Johnson wrote, "When the time comes, I hope the National Board will be ready, but before that time comes, the battlefield will be much nearer the office of the National Board."[44]

The end of the story of the Memphis epidemic of 1879 is that Dr. John Shaw Billings, VP of the NBH (and future president of the APHA,) and Surgeon of the U.S. Army, met in McKenzie, Tennessee with Dr. Mitchell and Dr. J.D. Plunkett, President of the Tennessee State Board of Health in Nashville, to try to settle ruffled feathers and clarify misunderstandings. But it was to be the beginning of September before a systematic disinfection process

---

[43]Jerome Cochran to NBH, Memphis, Tennessee, August 13, 1879, NBH Correspondence, Inspectors Report 1644; Cochran to NBH, New Orleans, Louisiana, September 6, 1879, *ibid.* 2162.

[44]John Johnston to NBH, Memphis, Tennessee, August 13, 1879, NBH Correspondence, State Report 1581; J.D. Plunkett to NBH, Nashville, Tennessee, August 11, 1879, *ibid,* 1489.

was initiated when the NBH assigned Dr. J.M. Ross as inspector.[45]

When the yellow fever season was over, Dr. Cochran got to go home for more than a day or two at a time. He was 48, graying, somewhat plump. He had his picture made -- the only picture available of him -- for the Memorial Record of Alabama. For such a great figure, there is remarkably little personal and family information. It only proves that, while he dedicated himself to the improvement of medicine, he was, in truth, a very retiring person. Was he all business at home as he was in his career? Or did he relax and become a doting husband and loving father?

Of his wife, Sarah Jane, we have no information. Was she slender? Or was she, also, plump? That she lived in Jerome's shadow is evident. But who were her friends? Being a devout Catholic, she most likely entered into parish activities. And living with, and loving a dedicated man like Jerome had to have rubbed off on her. She probably gave of herself where needed -- taking her turn at caring for the ill, the elderly, the needy under the wing of the Church, at times leaving the care of her boys to Ina Lou. It was written of her that she loved flowers. It is probable that she spent a great deal of time making her own gardens. It is also probable that she donated many of these to the Altar Society to beautify the altar on Sundays and Holy Days.

Was she, like many mothers today, wrapped up in her children's activities? Since Jerome was absent so much of the time, this is probably the case. That both her boys became very fine men -- as records do indicate -- she had to have been a great influence, for mothers' gentility rubs off on male children regardless of circumstances. She evidently taught her daughter very well, for Ina Lou became the rock of the family.

Was Sarah Jane well these last months of her life? Or was she ill? She died on January 3, 1880 at the age of 46, the month Ina

---

⁴⁵New York *Times*, August 29, 1879; J.W. Ross to NBH, Memphis, Tennessee, August 29, 1879, NBH Correspondence, Inspectors Report 1898.

Lou turned 20. It can be inferred -- due to an exhaustive work on "The Zymotic Diseases in the Relations to Public Hygiene" written in 1879, that Jerome spent that time fairly close to home. Other than his necessary travels as State Health Officer, at least she had her beloved husband near her.

It was then that Ina Lou had to take over the running of the family home, for Jerome Bowling was 17 and Edmund Collins was only 11. Jerome had suffered the excruciating loss of his helpmate.

Chapter XIII

Eminent Physician
- Of Loss and Plodding On -

-1880-

In spite of his deep grief at the loss of Sarah Jane, Jerome kept busy, motivated by his sense of duty and his strong conviction that he was needed by his profession and the people of Alabama and America.

At the April meeting of the Medical Association of the State of Alabama, Cochran presented his compiled information of yellow fever.

There had been a flurry of reaction from southern physicians to several proposed bills to strengthen the authority of the National Board of Health. With full understanding of the working of the NBH, and being convinced that any federal control over quarantine would interfere with states' rights, Cochran took action. During the meeting of the Medical Association of the State of Alabama, the Committee of Public Health, with Cochran as leader and as State

Health Officer, made a request of the Association: [1] that they be permitted to prepare "a memorial in relation to the proposed legislations to increase the efficiency of the National Board of Health, for presentation to the United States Congress;..." Permission was granted.

Cochran received word that Dr. Billings, VP but virtual leader of the National Board of Health, had made a derogatory comment:[2] "...The opposition which has developed in Georgia and Tennessee against it [the contents of the Harris and Young bills] by two or three comparatively weak and ignorant men who have no standing as sanitarians, shows that the medical profession of the South and the people have not yet learned what a quarantine is or what the National Board of Health is trying to do, and until this ignorance can be enlightened and the Board has some substantial basis of popular opinion to rest upon, it will always be in a very precarious position."

The statement probably strengthened Cochran's already firm resolve. The Committee, after due deliberation, on May 10, 1880, sent a memorial to the United States Congress, and published it in the Transactions of 1880, to press in August, for the members to read. It was a piece of brilliantly worded, persuasive work. [Because the authors of this biography strongly feel that the placement of the entire piece now will be of significant benefit to the reader of this biography in following the subsequent occurrences, it is placed here in full, rather than attached as an appendix.][3]

---

[1]"Report of the Board of Censors," *Transactions of MASA*, 1880, pp. 123-4.

[2]NBH to Jerome Cochran, Washington, D.C.April 29, 1880, Letters II, 729-30.

[3]Report of the Board of Censors," *op. cit.* 1880, pp. 225-6.

"THE MEMORIAL OF THE BOARD OF HEALTH OF THE STATE OF ALABAMA

To the Honorable the Senate and the House of Representatives of the Congress of the United States of America:

"The Board of Health of the State of Alabama, having duly considered the scope and tendency of the several bills now pending in the Congress of the United States "To increase the efficiency of the National Board of Health, have reached, in reference to the same, the following general conclusions, namely:

(1.) That it is the duty as well as the privilege of every community, as well as of every individual, to take care of itself to the full extent of its ability to do so, and, amongst other things to protect itself against the invasion of epidemic diseases.

(2.) That the practical questions involved in the establishment and management of quarantines, are of such grave importance, and affect so intimately and so profoundly the material interests of the State, and of the local communities within the State, as to make it neither wise nor prudent for us to intrust the administration of quarantine to the hands of any other health authorities than those who are of our own appointment and directly responsible to our own people.

(3.) That while the several bills now pending in the national congress "To increase the efficiency of the National Board of Health," do not interfere with the right of the State and local authorities to proclaim and enforce such quarantine regulations, in addition to those of the National Board, as to them may seem advisable, they are still open to objection from the fact that they give to the National Board the power to establish and administer quarantines within the limits of the State against all commerce and travel of which one of the terminal points lies outside of the State, and this without the consent of the local authorities, and even without consultation with them.

(4.) That it seems to us to be a proposition clearly self-evident to all persons of competent judgment in questions of this kind, that the State can not afford to allow this large grant of power, so nearly affecting the welfare of our people, to be placed in the hands of the

National Board of Health, or of any other agent of the federal government, without making earnest efforts to prevent it.

(5.) That without entering into the discussion of the principles and circumstances under which it may become advisable for the general government to extend to State and municipal authorities pecuniary and other assistance toward the establishment and maintenance of quarantines, it still seems perfectly clear to us that the proclamation and administration of quarantines should, in all cases, be reserved to the State and municipal authorities.

(6.) That it also seems to us to be true, beyond all reasonable question, that no uniform system of quarantine regulations, suitable to all times and places, can possibly be devised; but *per contra*, that the quarantine regulations that are applicable to one place will often prove entirely unsuited to the wants of another place; and that in different seasons even the same place will require widely different regulations.

(7.) That it is the circumstantial details of quarantines that present the practically difficult and important problems of quarantine administration; and that these cannot be wisely ordered nor wisely managed except by experts, who are intimately acquainted with local and surrounding conditions.

(8.) That these propositions being admitted, it follows that the rule established last year by the National Board of Health, to the effect that assistance should be extended only to such State and municipal boards as had first adopted the national rules and regulations, is very gravely objectionable, both in principle and practice, and ought not to be continued.

(9.) That the only wise and expedient rule in this regard is this, namely: That such State and municipal boards as desire the assistance of the National Board, should be required to submit their own local regulations to the National Board for examination, and that if these are found by the National Board to be of reasonable thoroughness and sufficiency, the needed assistance should then be granted.

(10.) That the National Board ought, properly, to have the general direction and control of quarantines against foreign countries; but that even these international quarantines could be most wisely and efficiently administered through the agency of the State and municipal boards having local jurisdiction over our seaport cities.

(11.) That we are in no sense antagonistic to the National Board; but, contrariwise, appreciate very fully that it has for the exercise of its legitimate functions a wide and important field of usefulness, within which the State and municipal boards have no jurisdiction, and this without emasculating and weakening the State and municipal boards, and without absorbing directly or indirectly, their most important functions.

(12.) That holding these opinions, we should very much regret to see the power and usefulness of the National Board, in its own proper field of action, diminished or destroyed by the withholding of the appropriations for which it has made application, and which are indubitably necessary for the successful continuance of the scientific investigations, sanitary surveys, and other works of sanitary administration and research which it has auspiciously begun.

"All of which is respectfully submitted, in the name and behalf of the Board of Health of the State of Alabama.

"Done in the City of Montgomery, on the 10th day of May, *Anno Domini*, 1880." The ten signatures, Drs. Jerome Cochran, J.B. Gaston, S.D. Seelye, J.S. Weatherly, M.H. Jordan, George A. Ketchum, C.D. Parke, P. Bryce, J.J. Dement and George E. Kumpe, were affixed followed by "*Committee of Public Health*"

On May 24, the City of Montgomery added their perspective to the growing clamor against the bills to strengthen the NBH. The City Council firmly stated that the proposals were in flagrant violation of the Constitution of the United States.[4]

"At the date of this writing [probably July, 1880] we are in possession of information which authorizes us to believe that the Harris Bill, the only one of the three bills pending that could have commanded a hearing in Congress, has been withdrawn and will not

---

[4]Resolution of the City Council of Montgomery, Alabama to Congress, May 24, 1880, House Select Committee on Epidemic Diseases, 46th Congress, 2nd session, HR 16A-H26, National Archives.

come up for consideration again during the present session of Congress. We also have the assurance that the objectionable features of the proposed legislation have been definitely abandoned, and will not be included in any future bill."

The success of the request to "kill the bill" or as Cochran put it, "memorial" request again put Cochran in the forefront of fighting for the rights of states to handle their own problems as deemed fit by the local men, both of medicine and government.

He also published, in the 1880 edition of *Transactions*, his work on "THE THEORY AND PRACTICE OF QUARANTINE," written in 1879 and published in 1880, that fully explains his views and the suitability of these fundamental principles.

There is a summary of contents at the beginning of this treatise that typifies Cochran's perfectionistic handling of the topic. It is as follows: Introduction, international quarantine, the infection of ships, the disinfection of ships, the disinfection of cargoes, the disinfection of passengers and crews, the quarantine of ships, quarantines of non-intercourse, modified quarantines, inter-state quarantine, railroad quarantines, intra-state quarantines, municipal quarantines, disinfection, segregation, personal prophylaxis. The following sums up his introduction:[5]

"The word Quarantine is synonymous with prophylaxis; the "summing up in one systematic body of doctrine all possible schemes of protection against the introduction and dissemination of infectious maladies."

Yellow fever is a specific disease, not indigenous to Alabama. Because it had been frequently studied by many people of various walks of life over many many years, because of its widespread ravages, and because the practices developed in its study can be applied to the whole of infectious diseases, Cochran stated that he would present the"Theory and Practice of Quarantine as it stands in relation to the protection of our Alabama communities against this

---

[5]"Report of the Board of Censors," *op. cit.* 1880, p.329.

pestilence, under five principle heads, namely:

(1.) International Quarantine; or quarantine against the introduction of disease from foreign countries, and against invasion by sea.

 (2.) Inter-State Quarantine; or quarantine against the introduction of disease from neighboring States, and against invasion by land.

 (3.) Intra-State Quarantine; or quarantine for the protection of one part the State against another part of the State, after the disease has crossed her borders and effected a lodgement upon her territory.

 (4.) Municipal Quarantine; or quarantine for the protection of the uninfected population of any city, town, or neighborhood after the advent of disease therein in one case or in a few cases; or the municipal and domestic management of epidemics.

 (5.) Personal Prophylaxis; or the protection of exposed individuals against the consequences of infection."

All that Cochran had learned, through his own studies and through his extensive work with yellow fever, through his understanding of germs and the spread of disease; of his knowledge that filth spreads disease, and the possible chemical destruction of such disease; of his extensive studies of other countries and their successful fight against plagues, all went into the brilliant, forward-looking, almost clairvoyant proposition for the prevention of epidemics through strict adherence to laws of quarantine therein outlined. For his knowledge and his methods predated scientific findings by 20 to 40 years.

He wrote of the mandatory reporting of disease within twenty four hours:

"...This proposition is advanced as scientifically, although I am quite aware that popular apprehension would very much embarrass its application to the actual practice of quarantine. And yet it is in this direction that the greatest of all possible advances is to be made in the quarantines of the futures. I do not hesitate to affirm that by the wise application of this principle, at least three-fourths of the annoyances and inconveniences caused to the commerce and travel of our Southern cities might be avoided, and this without greatly increasing the chances for the introduction of the yellow fever infection."

Cochran ended the paper by telling the very recent tale of the Excelsior, a ship from Rio de Janiero, whose crew did not become ill until they transferred the cargo of coffee from the ship's hold into the warehouse, i.e. disturbing the cargo. He felt that, "when the ship was loaded in the far away South American city; that it lay there in ambush among the sacks of coffee boxed up in the hold during the voyage; that, by possibility, it found favorable environment there and multiplied abundantly; and that the sailors were attacked by it only when they went down into the hold and disturbed the cargo.

"Cases of this sort are not of frequent occurrence; and they constitute one of the most embarrassing problems that arise in the practical administration of quarantine. For such emergencies there is but one remedy outside of a commercial embargo, and that one remedy is thorough and efficient disinfection-- disinfection not in name only, but in fact -- such disinfection as will certainly destroy the whole congregation of yellow fever germs. Such disinfection is not to be accomplished by sulfur fumigations. I believe that it could be accomplished by refrigeration.[6] If the whole hull and hold and cargo of the Excelsior had been refrigerated down to zero, and kept at that temperature for several days,. . . I believe that the infection would have been utterly destroyed . . . in the case of the refrigerating warehouse, a focus of contamination might be created between the warehouse and the wharf; and from this suggestion it follows that such warehouse should be built over the water so as to avoid, as far as possible, all the complications of the environment."[7]

Thoroughness and honesty were immediately noted in Cochran's spoken and written words, bringing about a clarity that is most pleasant. Cochran was a great health officer because he had the instincts of a great physician. He loved truth. He despised rumor. He was thorough down to the most minute detail. This was a trait ingrained in his character.

---

[6]Chemical refrigeration was discovered and was in limited use after the Civil War.

[7]Hindsight in this instance, foresight in many others.

Once when he was investigating a case in Decatur, Alabama, several local physicians had differed in their diagnosis. Some of the physicians believed the case to be yellow fever, others were equally sure it was not. The man had been dead and buried for several days. Cochran, as State Health Officer, had the body exhumed and did an autopsy on the rotting corpse. Only then was he certain that the patient had died of yellow fever. He announced his findings, and made suggestions on how to manage the threatened epidemic. Nobody panicked.

After this, and with the interstate agreement to be honest with each other, people learned to trust the announcements of their health departments. Threatened epidemics were more easily managed, to the benefit of all.

Jerome's wife, his love, was gone. The light of his life shone now from heaven. His life would never be the same. He had his work, and it took him all over the State. It kept him very busy. But his family, now diminished to three of his children, looked to him for succor. Was he there for them? Did he give of himself to his family as he must to his work? Was he able to spend any decent time with them? Or did he withdraw into his work? That he was shocked by the death of Sarah Jane was obvious. Both the "Theory and Practice of Quarantine" and the "Sketches of Yellow Fever on the Gulf Coast of Florida," published in 1880 and 1881 respectively, were written before Sarah Jane's death. While he made his reports as Health Officer of Mobile and of the State -- and they were meticulously done -- and carried out his duties, in writing where necessary, the office of Senior Censor -- also meticulously done -- it wasn't until 1883 that Jerome again began to write on topics of his own.

Jerome Bowling was old enough to go to college. He soon left for the University of Alabama at Tuscaloosa for his BA degree. Perhaps seeing how much his father had to be absent from home, he did not wish to follow him into medicine. It could also be -- as is often the case when someone grows up in the shadow of a great person -- that, initially, self-actualization must come when out from under that shadow. Jerome Bowling inherited his father's urge to independence. That family ties in Oklahoma and Texas were strong

is evidenced by the fact that, when he graduated in 1882 at the age
of 20, he promptly left for Texas to join the insurance firm of O.L.
Cochran, his second cousin (first cousin of Dr. Cochran; son of Dr.
Cochran's father Augustus Owen's oldest brother Owen J)[8]

And so there were three. It was very much the common duty of
the times for Ina Lou to become the lady of the house, relinquishing
any personal dreams, putting herself to managing her father's house
and raising her young brother. It is presumed that Dr. Cochran was
able to hire efficient household personnel. They probably lived
comfortably with a black maid as companion for his daughter and
son. Dr. Cochran had always been friendly and sympathetic toward
black people from the days when he worked beside them on his
father's farm. Throughout his writings it is noted that he paid
particular attention to blacks and their care, not only in his private
practice, but in his fights against epidemics.

So 1880 passed.

---

[8]*Genealogy*, by Mary Gregg.

Chapter XIV

Eminent Physician
Of Working and Valediction

-1881-

In this year, Cochran saw passed into law his bill to collect vital
and mortuary statistics. The session of the State Board of Health
decided that the collection of these vital and mortuary statistics of
the several counties should commence from the first day of July,
1881. The State Health Officer was authorized to have provision
made for supplying the necessary books, blanks, and instructions.
As State Health Officer, Cochran left nothing to chance!

"Accordingly, in the month of May[,] I [Dr. Cochran] forwarded
to the Health Officers of the several counties the following books,
blanks, etc.: [1]

(1) One Register of Births, appropriately bound, ruled, and lettered,
for the use of the County Health Officer.

(2) One Register of Deaths, appropriately bound, ruled, and
lettered, for the use of the County Health Officer.

---

[1] "The Report of the State Board of Health," *Transactions of MASA*, 1882, p. 168.

(3) A supply of loose sheets for the Register of Births for the use of the assistant health officers.

(4) A supply of loose sheets of the Register of Deaths for the use of the assistant health officers.

(5) A supply of blank certificates for the return of births.

(6) A supply of blank certificates for the return of deaths.

(7) Blank forms for the monthly reports of the State Board of Health.

(8) Copies of Circular No. 5 of the State Board of Health explaining the duties of the county boards of health and the methods to be employed in the collection of vital statistics.

(9) Copies of a letter of instructions to the county health officers from the State Health Officer."

In the course of his duties he "wrote and mailed over one thousand letters in ... correspondence with the county health officials, and with the physicians of the counties in the interest of the right administration of the health laws." He "paid personal visits, for the purpose of conferring directly with the County Health Officer and the county boards of health, to the following counties, namely: Barbour, Blount, Bullock, Butler, Calhoun, Chilton, Conecuh, Dallas, Jefferson, Lawrence, Limestone, Lowndes, Madison, Mobile, Montgomery, Morgan, Perry, Shelby, Tuskaloosa [sic]. ...in alphabetical order, not in the order of the visitations. ...on account of want of time I was not able to visit all the organized counties...." He "...had the honor to deliver public lectures on the subject of public hygiene in Evergreen, Greenville, Eufaula, Selma, and Birmingham. At Birmingham, also, I had a conference with the municipal authorities in relation to the drainage, sewerage, and general sanitation of the town."[2]

One of the unfortunate things Cochran found in his visits was that "...many of the Societies were badly organized, that their meetings were few and far between, and that their officers seemed to realize very imperfectly the obligations imposed upon them by

---

[2] *Ibid.*

their official positions. Very especially, I found, that in a majority of instances the Boards of Censors, acting as Committees of Public Health, seemed to think they had done their whole duty when they had designated some one to fill the position of County Health Officer." He found that some "seemed to think they had little else to do than to sit in their offices and receive and transmit reports." He was, however, very pleased to find that some of them, "from the very beginning proved themselves to be active, enterprising, sagacious, and efficient. These," he wrote, "are deserving of all praise." "In the majority of cases the result of my visits was to infuse new energy into the health officials, and to secure notable improvement in the subsequent monthly reports." [3]

December 4, 1881 was fairly cool. There had been several frosts, and the threat of yellow fever was over for the season. Cochran could relax and enjoy his 50th birthday. He spent part of the day working on his "Valedictory Address to the Mobile County Medical Society," which he was to deliver on December 17, 1881. He had been the president of the organization during the year now approaching its end. Turning 50 gave him pause for reflection on his accomplishments. He wanted to do so many things for the Mobile Society. It had taught him a great deal, and he had wanted to bring it up to the high standards he had for it.

The Saturday night meetings were enjoyable. Unfortunately, he had been unable to attend most of the meetings, because his duties as State Health Officer had called him out of Mobile during most of the year. He knew that, unfortunately, the meetings had not even been well attended by the young doctors. Cochran felt they must be somehow, strongly urged to increase their attendance. He also recognized that he must express to the vice president his congratulations for a job well done in the efficient supervision of the administration of the Society during his, Cochran's, too frequent absences. The vice president had done well, but Cochran knew he,

---

[3]*Ibid.*

himself, should have done better.

Yet dues had been paid, and the treasury was filled. Most of the projects had been accomplished. The annual reports of the Secretary, the Treasurer, the Board of Censors, the Board of Medical Examiners, and the Committee of Public Health, were in great shape, and the exhibits to be shown at the first meeting in January would cause none of them to be ashamed.

He thought briefly of the cause of this society's success. Probably the same thing that made the Medical Association of the State of Alabama successful. Yes, this Mobile County Medical Society was different. But what made it different?

In his address he finally verbalized his thoughts:[4] "The success of Societies like this depends in large measure upon rules and customs that would seem to many to be of very small consequence. One of the rules of this Society which has contributed in my opinion very greatly to our success is that which prescribes weekly meetings, and fixes those weekly meetings on Saturday evening. Would not any other evening in the week serve our purposes as well? I think not. It seems to me to be the most natural and proper thing in the world for our doctors to get together on Saturday evening, and to wind up the week's work by a general interchange of views and discussions of cases; and this going on from year to year becomes a habit, so that we doctors go to the medical society on Saturday night, just as people generally go to church on Sundays."

Cochran had a strong feeling of almost religious intensity toward the medical profession. He took very seriously the sentiments expressed by Hippocrates in his great "Oath", the basis of medical ethics.

As he spoke, he warmed to another subject. He felt he must mention that the members should be more conscientious about writing up their cases and reporting them to the journals. He knew that the busiest doctors always seemed to find time to do those

---

[4]Jerome Cochran's Valedictory Address to the Medical Society of Mobile County, December 17, 1881. *(see* appendix 5)

things, and they were the ones everyone wanted to hear from. Cochran was of the definite opinion that the least busy doctors never had time to write, and hearing them would be a waste of time anyway, because they didn't do enough to find the unique cases. He stated strongly that: "It is the young practitioner, or the old practitioner who has but little to do -who is fortunate if he gets three of four calls a day- who is always too busy to come to the meetings, always too much pressed for time to prepare himself to lead in a debate. Now I hope nobody will take offense if I say that such excuses are not simply paradoxical, but are in fact, misleading and untrue. It is not want of time, but want of will that keeps our younger men so generally away from the Society meetings. ...But it would be better for the Society if the meetings are always well attended; and I am sure that our meetings are always sufficiently interesting and instructive to make it worth while for all these younger members always to be on hand. They should remember that always, in the end, it is doctors that make the reputation of doctors- that the doctor cannot achieve any very large or very brilliant success amongst the people without the endorsement of his professional brethren. I hope I may be allowed to quote, without a suspicion of irreverence, a very striking declaration of Holy Writ: 'Seek first the kingdom of God, and His righteousness, and all these things shall be added unto you' ...All these things -that is to say worldly honors and temporal successes. And so I say to every young man who desires to achieve success in the practice of medicine. Seek first to win the confidence and respect of the medical profession itself, and then popular confidence and popular patronage will come to you of themselves."

How like Cochran to compare the medical profession to the kingdom of God. This was not a Freudian slip. The medical profession of Alabama, as he had structured it, was Cochran's version of God's kingdom on earth. He was a religious man. Not meant to be blasphemous, never-the-less his words and attitude, in many ways, bespoke the idea that he thought of God as holding in heaven the same position that he, Doctor Jerome Cochran, held in the Alabama medical profession: Senior Life Counsellor, Chairman of the Board of Censors, Chairman of the Board of Medical Examiners, State Health Officer.

Cochran controlled every aspect of organized medicine in Alabama. He, Chairman, with the other Censors, could approve or deny any doctor the right to practice medicine in the state. He could approve or disapprove all projects of the State Medical Association. He could control all the discussion to come before the House of Delegates. In short, during the 1880's Jerome Cochran *was* "Alabama Medicine." Yet, while he upbraided and encouraged, he did not do so in a demeaning or lordly way. For in no period of its history had the profession progressed so smoothly or so rapidly. The Medical Association of the State of Alabama went from its reorganization with twenty four members in 1868, to over 1,000 members and 100% of the counties belonging in 1888. It went from zero influence on the public health and hygiene of the State, to almost complete control of such serious functions as quarantine, licensing of doctors, licensing of midwives, draining of malaria-sodden swamps, disposal of sewage, purifying of water, etc., with great improvement in the health of the people.[5]

Cochran continued his Valedictory address: "Oh yes, I must say a few words about ethics: Now I do not hesitate to assert that the ethics constitute the very soul and life blood of the profession and that the abrogation of the ethics means neither more nor less than the dissolution of all professional organization.

"In the great west the ethics have become almost dead letters and the profession of medicine has degenerated, almost completely, into a trade. At the recent session in Savannah of the American Public Health Association, I had occasion to discuss this state of affairs with several distinguished western physicians; and I inquired of them if they were satisfied with the result. Very emphatically and with one accord they said, No! That the resulting state of affairs was most dishonoring and calamitous but that they were obliged to recognize established facts."

---

[5]Cochran, "The Medical Profession," *op.cit.*, p. 122.

Now, how could Cochran, without offending, remind the doctors of some of their deficiencies in such a way that they would see and correct them? And how could he make them understand that the care of the poor need not be done by becoming contract physicians in the employ of the government?

"In our own State, as you all know, the State Medical Association and the County Medical Societies have been endeavoring for the last twelve years to implicate the authority of the ethics in relation to professional charges, and in condemnation of all forms and fashions of contract practice. I am glad to be able to say, and I say it with tolerable definite knowledge of what is going on in various sections of the State, that our efforts in this direction have been attended with a large measure of success. But the whole battle is not yet won. For example, in Birmingham, the practice of employees is now done by contract. I had occasion not long ago to discuss this whole question with the Jefferson County Medical Society, and with the result that, the Society resolved to make war against the evil practice, without truce or favor, until it shall be utterly suppressed. They have a hard struggle before them. But if they act with sufficient firmness, resolution, and prudence they will win the fight in the course of time."

At this point there probably was some squirming among the Mobile doctors. He needed to put them at ease, then scold them for weakness they had shown.

"In reference to this abomination of contract practice, the Mobile Medical Society had a record of which we have good reason to be proud. In all of its grosser forms contract practice in Mobile is a thing of the past. Nevertheless, I very much fear that the unholy and unprofessional leaven out of which the contract system sprang into mischievous activity in the beginning -that is to say the hankering after illegitimate loaves and fishes- is not even yet utterly dead and buried amongst us. It needs watching still. In the words of a famous outburst of patriotic eloquence, 'Eternal vigilance is the price of Liberty;' and Josh Billings in his homely way clinches the nail when he adds, 'and of everything else that we've got and expect to keep.'

"Last Spring, feeling how important it was to push the war against medical contract to its utmost possible limits, I had the honor to present to this Society a set of resolutions condemning the appointment by the Board of Police Commissioners of a City Physician to treat the sick poor in their homes. To my surprise -in the light of subsequent events, I cannot add- to my gratification, the resolutions were adopted by a large majority. I say in the light of 'subsequent events' because you all know how, when the hour of trial came, the Society was not brave enough to stand squarely up to the high position it had assumed. It split hairs in the way of compromises with a dexterity at least, that was admirable; and I think made a mistake in doing so. "Recently in Atlanta, I have had occasion to see a practical illustration of the evils and abuses that may grow out of this system of contract practice for the poor in their own homes. In that city there are six ward physicians paid by the city to look after the poor. They are paid from two hundred to four hundred dollars each, and out of the paltry salaries they are expected, not only to give their medical services to the poor of their respective districts, but to furnish them also with all the medicines they may stand in need of.

"Of course, no capable man could undertake to do such services for such pay. But in Atlanta doctors are found who not only are willing to accept these appointments, but who enter into competition with one another, and bring to bear all the political and personal influences they are able to command, to secure them. The testimony of the physicians of Atlanta generally is that the system is a cheat and a show, and altogether mischievous and demoralizing." [6]

---

[6]This writer has often wondered how the founding fathers of Alabama Medicine would view our present involvement with health insurance, including Medicare and Medicaid. Is it not a form of contract medicine? But what practicing physician could possibly get along without it? And what patients could survive without some effective form of medical insurance?

-1882-

At the annual meeting of the Medical Association of the State of Alabama in Mobile on April 11th-14th, Cochran gave the report of the State Board of Health.[7] He was not happy with the way things were.

He reported what he had found in his travels during the year in his official capacity. "I am still very sorry to have to say, that in a majority of the counties in which County Boards of Health have been organized the law has not been administered with a satisfactory degree of thoroughness and efficiency -- in a word, that it is only in a few counties that the statistics of births and deaths have been collected with a sufficient completeness to make them of any real value. ...that the work so far done grows out of the fact that the health authorities charged with the administration of the law have been weakly and culpably negligent of their duty. ...By the parties concerned I mean:

(1), The several County Medical Societies in their capacity of County Boards of Health;

(2), The several Boards of Censors which have been created Committees of Public Health by the County Societies and charged with the immediate supervision of their public health functions; and

(3), The several County Health Officers."

Cochran chastised these physicians soundly. He exhorted them to prove to be successful in the administration of this law of public health and the collection of vital statistics and the delivery of monthly reports to the respective County Medical Societies.

He then discussed the salaries that "A considerable number of the counties in which the County Boards of Health have undertaken the administration of the law for the collection of vital statistics,...." He, himself, as State Health Officer, was paid $125.00 a month. For the County Health Officers, he found that "The smallest appropriation is one hundred dollars a year; and the highest, one thousand dollars." He spoke with fervor, "I know thoroughly well

---

[7]The Report of the State Board of Health, *Transactions of MASA*, p. 168.

the amount and character of the work that devolves on the County Health Officers, and have therefore decided opinions as to the amount of compensation they ought to receive. ...The majority of the counties ought to pay about three hundred dollars. Five hundred dollars is not too much to be paid by the larger and wealthier counties. But these several sums ought to be paid only on the assumption that the Health Officer does his work with thoroughness and efficiency. If he does his work in any other way, he is in strict justice entitled to very small pay." Cochran sternly reiterated that the Health Officer should get out to the neighborhood at least once in every month. "Duty is duty, and it shall not be shrunk from because it is unpleasant."

In this year he began his researches on the use of Quinine in treating disease. It was also the year that Congress gave back to the Marine Hospitals Service the tasks previously assigned to the National Board of Health.[8] Cochran was out of his job of inspecting ports from Key West to Pensacola.

In this year, also, the family attended the graduation of Jerome Bowling from the University of Alabama at Tuscaloosa. Shortly thereafter, they bid him Godspeed in his venture to Texas. For Edmund Collins, age 11, his adored brother, his hero, was truly gone. No more visits home from college. No more visits home -- period. Texas was too far away for anything except very infrequent visits. Letters would have to suffice. For Edmund meant to keep in touch.

---

[8]J.B. Hamilton to Charles Folger, Washington, D.C. , August 9, 1882, Office letters, Marine Hospital Service XXXVIII, 3; Charles Folger to H.F. French, New York City, August 10, 1882, MHS Letters and Reports Received, (March 6, 1882 -- September 18, 1883), 185; Circular, "Compliance with Local Health Laws," Washington, D. C., August 11, 1882, *ibid.*,186.

Chapter XV
The Year of the Hawk

-1883-

Jerome finally pulled himself together after the loss of his beloved wife. The hawk in him came to the fore. He gathered information systematically and used it to attempt to better the delivery of safe medicine and humane care to the people of his State.

On alcoholism

At the 1882 annual Association meeting held in Mobile, the subject of prohibition was brought forward. A committee, composed of Drs. Peter Bryce, A. J. Reese, James T. Searcy, William H. Anderson, and William H. Johnston had presented its report, undertaking to show:

(1) That alcohol is not a beneficent or harmless luxury.

(2) That alcohol is not a food.

(3) That alcohol even as a medicine is of very questionable value,

and should be prescribed only with the utmost caution.[1]

The Committee had then put forth a resolution stating that because of the deleterious effect of alcohol on both body and mind when used indiscriminately, even producing, the committee felt, idiocy in descendants. The members favored "judicious measures or efficient legislation" which would ban alcohol.

There had followed much animated discussion, and Cochran, as Senior Censor, felt that the arguments were too partisan and one-sided -- a part of the truth and not the whole truth; ...." He later wrote of the incident: "I was, therefore, for the second time, under the disagreeable necessity of obstructing the action of the Association in regard to a matter in which, to many of its members, its duty seemed to be, not only clearly evident, but almost imperative. In the meantime, the Association was too much hurried by pressure of pending business, and I was not sufficiently prepared, whatever may have been the case with other members, for the full discussion which the importance of the subject demanded. I, therefore, moved that the further consideration of the whole matter should be again laid over; and this motion was agreed to on my promise to present my views upon it in writing at our next meeting...."[2]

In this 1883 presentation, Cochran finished his review of the facts, then went on to tell the Association of his subsequent findings and conclusions.

As in past papers and arguments, Cochran researched thoroughly, then proceeded to produce accounts of other eminent physicians on their researches and findings. At one point in his answer to The Alcohol Question, he recalled the words of his fellow physicians in requesting the Association's approval in calling for prohibition. In their presentation to the Medical Association they

---

[1]The Appendix of Medical Papers, "The Alcohol Question," *Transactions of MASA*, p. 359.

[2]*Ibid.*, p. 361.

stated:

"Statistics in abundance, which we have not space for here...conspire to show...the habitual use of alcoholic beverages is the most fruitful of all causes of sickness...the duration of life is inversely proportioned to the amount of alcohol consumed." He wrote of this: "I am a little ashamed to be obliged to confess my ignorance of these abundant statistics, and of the notorious facts which they so victoriously establish; but all the same it is true that if there are such facts and statistics in existence, they have never come to my knowledge."[3]

Being a past master of making such presentations, Cochran probably paused and looked around, allowing his audience to realize that he had actually admitted he didn't know something! When he judged his timing to be correct, he would have continued:

"Now these are some of the ways in which the so-called statistics that are adduced to prove the agency of alcohol in the production of diseases amongst moderate drinkers have been evolved. The more we study the question the more we find that all these imposing arrays of figures -- imposing at least in latitudinal and longitudinal extension -- are at the best the offspring of ingenious guess work, and as far removed from the reasonable probability of the accepted data of established science as the equator is from the poles. And yet it is upon such questionable data -- upon the testimony of tables of statistics constructed under the influence of preconceived opinions -- made to order -- that the temperance people base their demonstrations of the tremendous potency of the habitual moderate use of alcoholic beverages in the production of diseases.

"At the risk of being thought a little tedious, let us now examine a little more closely some of the statements quoted a little while ago from the report of the committee."

Cochran then proceeded to explain away the presentations. For example: of the statement that *the moderate use of alcohol is the most fruitful of all the causes of sickness* he wrote: "Can the

---

[3]*Ibid.* p. 365.

committee have appreciated the full force of these remarkable words? We know that in all the temperate and warm climates of the globe malaria comes up out of the swamps and low places armed with malignant powers, and that it strikes down its victims literally by millions. But not even malaria, according to our committee, is so prolific of diseases as alcohol moderately used...."

He then told the story of one time in Montgomery, a friend with whom he was walking pointed out a poor lady with severe spinal curvature. The friend told him that for years the woman had been a great opium eater, and then asked: "Do you suppose her opium eating had anything to do with bringing about the condition she is in?" "My instant reply was, that I thought it much more likely that the condition she was in afforded an explanation of the opium eating -- that it was almost certain that the appetite for opium had been provoked by the same organic changes that had resulted in the spinal deformity."

Cochran succinctly continued "... we can very often trace the genesis of the alcohol habit to some diseased condition of the system clamoring for relief. In a word, I am fully satisfied that the agency of alcoholic beverages, in the production both of physical and of psychical diseases, have been greatly overrated, and that it is far more frequently the case that some organic degeneracy leads to inebriety than it is that inebriety leads to organic degeneracy. ..."[4]

Of the premise that alcohol is a poison, Dr. Cochran wrote that if it were a poison, it is one well tolerated by the human body. "...A very wise physician whom I knew a long time ago, and who had a great horror of drunkenness, used to say: 'No, they don't die. They waste their substance, become burthen [sic] their families, dishonor our common human nature, and still persist in living on. If they only had the grace to die and get out of the way it wouldn't so much matter.' He also quoted Mr. John McElroy: "With very few exceptions, every one who goes to Perdition by the Alcohol route, would reach that destination by some other highway if the Alcohol

---

[4]*Ibid.*, p. 373.

line were not running. ...People who have done much in the way of reforming drunkards have been astonished to find how little real manhood remained after eliminating whisky from the equation. They have supposed the manhood to be only obscured, and have been disheartened to find how frequently it happens to be demonstrated that there was never enough of it to pay for the trouble of 'saving the victim of intemperance.'"

Realizing that the Committee, in giving their report and request, quoted many writers, Cochran proceeded to agree with some things these writers had to say, but mostly he debunked them, giving profoundly insightful and dramatic reasons for doing so. He gave chemical analyses, the regular and uninvolved use by various races and countries of wine, etc, on the physiological, psychological and sociological influences of the beverages. He described the various alcoholic beverages of wines, beers and brandies and their alcoholic and other content.

He then wrote:[5] "Medical men are more in the habit of discussing diseases and their remedies, than of elaborating arguments in regard to social and dietetic problems not falling directly with the domain of medical practice. Hence it happens that while every medical treatise on the multiform diseases that flesh is heir to, bristles with testimonies of the value of alcoholic liquors as medicinal agents, the problem of their use as beverages in health, while it has not by any means been neglected, has received much less attention."

Cochran then quoted recent literature on the subject published in the *Contemporary Review* of 1878 by several physicians: Drs. William B. Carpenter, G.W. Balfour, Charles Murchison, James Risdon Bennett, Charles Bland Radcliffe, Joseph Kidd, A.B. Garrod, R. Brudenell Carter, Albert J. Bernays, Sir James Paget, Dr. Orpheus Everts, and James F. Johnston, Esq.

From his defense of moderation and his condemnation of using half truths in prohibitionist propagandizing, Cochran moved on to

---

[5]*Ibid.*, p. 389.

the prevention of drunkenness by writing:[6]

"The individual and social evils growing out of the excessive use of alcoholic beverages are many and great. About this there is no question." He then stated unequivocally that, "I must be allowed to give expression to my own deliberate conviction, that they have been greatly exaggerated by the intemperate advocates of temperance." He agreed that legislative suppression of the sale of alcohol was wise. But he astutely recognized that "The only question of practical importance in regard to this matter is to determine in what way and to what extent the State may be able to interfere for the regulation of the traffic in alcoholic liquors without transcending the boundaries of wise and prudent legislation."

In his inimitable way, Cochran then proceeded to outline just how he thought the above might be accomplished. First he stated the obvious-- that "There are two methods, and only two, by which the prevention of drunkenness can be accomplished. One of these methods is to place all alcoholic beverages beyond the reach of those who would use them to excess; and the other is to place all persons who are disposed to alcoholic excess under such restraint as will prevent them from indulging their intemperate inclinations. In plainer language, either the drink must be kept away from the drunkards, or else the drunkards must be kept away from the drink. Either device, if thoroughly enforced, would accomplish the desired result; I say if thoroughly enforced, and this qualification is a most important one; because every practical statesman will recognize at once, and without the aid of elaborate argument, that the thorough enforcement of either method, at least in our American communities, is absolutely impossible."

He went on to recall various trials of prohibition and how they failed. Cochran came up with a completely valid and viable solution when he suggested that "the State need have no scruple about taxing them at rates as will bring in to the State, to the counties, and the towns, the largest possible revenues. ...not for the

---

[6]*Ibid.*, pp. 409-10

purpose of ... suppression of liquor traffic ... but to put the liquor laws into execution and enforcing them.

"It is right to make the liquor-seller responsible for the way in which he makes use of his privileges, it is also right that the liquor-drinker should be made responsible for the way in which he uses his privileges. ...In the execution of this part of the scheme[,] the rules for restraining drunkards of their liberty might be largely modeled upon those in regard to the commitment of the insane; and at the same time there would be a similar need for hospitals and reformatories, which would have to be supplied out of the fund already mentioned." He gave to the group as a model, that of Dr. Everts, Superintendent of the Cincinnati Sanitarium: 'AN ACT FOR THE PREVENTION OF DRUNKENNESS, AND THE PROTECTION OF THE INFIRM.'"

As a result of Cochran's stand on the "Alcohol Question," no action was taken by the Board of Health or the Medical Association of the State of Alabama. The earnest physicians Dr. Searcy, Dr. Bryce and the others might have become offended by Cochran's remarks. But there is no record of any malice shown toward him by any of the doctors who favored prohibition.

Today [1997] Alabama law has Cochran's suggested solutions on the books.

On the use of Quinine

In 1882, as the executive officer of the State Board of Health, Jerome Cochran was interested in the chief cause of sickness in the state -- the group of febrile diseases believed to be caused by the swamp miasma, or malaria. In this group he included: intermittent, remittent, hemorrhagic, pernicious, and other fevers. Quinine, a bitter substance taken from the bark of the cinchona tree, was first used by the Andes Indians of South America to treat malaria and other diseases. The Andes mountains was the only place these trees grew before the Spanish immigrated in the 1500's. Later, the trees were transplanted to other areas, principally Java, an island off the coast of Indonesia that favors cinchona's growth.

In the early 1600's, quinine began to be utilized more and more around the world. Everyone agreed that quinine worked miraculous cures in most of these cases of febrile diseases caused by malaria. Some doctors even believed quinine was capable of curing or helping in the treatment of practically all diseases.

Today [1997] it is known also to help with dysrhythmia of the heart, and nocturnal leg cramps if the patient doesn't have contraindicating diseases. But the side effects involving all body systems can be disastrous if not monitored carefully. In malaria, it interferes with the DNA of the parasite causing the disease.[7] To the patient, it is given by mouth or intravenously, metabolized by the liver and excreted by the kidneys.

Cochran wanted to know how the drug was being used, what the proper doses were thought to be, and what side effects, toxic manifestations, and idiosyncrasies the practicing physicians of the State were encountering. Like the true researcher that he was, he tried to be as objective as possible. With these thoughts in mind, he decided to collect and collate the opinions and practices in regard to this important agent of the medical profession of the State. He issued one thousand copies of the following letter:[8]

"Dear Doctor,

I have been appointed by the president of the State Medical Association to prepare a Report on the Therapeutic Uses of Quinine in Alabama.

In the preparation of a report of this sort, I shall have to depend in a large measure upon the aid given me by members of the medical profession.

I shall therefore be very greatly obliged to you if you will favor me with the facts and results of your experience in the uses of this remedy. For convenience of subsequent comparison, I suggest the presentation of what you may have to say under the following heads

---

[7]Linda Skidmore-Roth, R.N., M.S.N., N.P., "Quinine Sulfate," *Mosby's Nursing Drug Reference,* The C.V. Mosby Company, St. Louis, 1988, p.717.

[8]"The Therapeutic Uses of Quinine in Alabama," *Transactions of M.A.S.A. 1883,* pp. 266-345.

1. The uses of quinine in malarial fevers -- intermittent, remittent, hemorrhagic, pernicious, etc.

2. The uses of quinine in other malarial maladies -- such as dysenteries, neuralgias, bilious colic, etc.

3. The uses of quinine in the continued fevers, and the quasi continued fevers -- such as typhoid fever, typho-malarial fever (so called), mountain fever, gastric remittent fever of children, continued malarial fever (so called), etc.

4. The uses of quinine in various zymotic diseases -- such as yellow fever, dengue, septicemia, diphtheria, cerebro-spinal fever, small-pox, measles, scarlet fever, etc.

5. The uses of quinine in rheumatism, pneumonia, bronchitis, pleurisy, and other phlegmasiae; and in other diseases that I have not mentioned by name.

6. The uses of quinineother phlegmasiae;. The physiological reactions of quinine as a tonic and restorative. Curious idiosyncrasies in regard to quinine. Doses, intervals, and methods of administration.

7. I would like to give as complete a catalogue as possible of papers by Alabama physicians in which the uses of quinine are discussed. To this end I beg that all who have files of medical periodicals -- especially of periodicals published before the war -- will look them over and furnish me the titles of such papers, names of authors, and names and dates of the periodicals in which they appeared.

"It is not expected that every one will go through the programme here indicated; but it is hoped that every physician into whose hands this circular letter may fall will be able and willing, out of his own experience, to furnish some facts, or principles, or cases, in connection with the uses and abuses of quinine that will be worthy of preservation. The shortest notes will be thankfully received, and will not be overlooked on account of their brevity. Every fact or opinion made use of will be duly credited to the author of it. My object is to give a complete résumé of the opinions and usages of the doctors of Alabama in regard to the most important of all the agents of our materia medica -- the most important certainly, in all southern climates, if not the most important without any sort of qualification; and I venture to hope that such a general response will be made to my appeal as will enable me to present a report that will be of permanent value.

"Answers should be sent in as soon as possible -- say within the next six weeks."

Out of the 1,000 circular letters sent out by Cochran, 44 Alabama physicians responded. By the beginning of 1883 he was ready to study them and formulate his conclusions. Their answers varied in strength and style and in the character and value of the information they contained. Some were practically worthless, but some of them showed that their authors were familiar with the most advanced speculations in regard to the powers and properties of the antimalarial drug. Some of the responses showed skill and inge-nuity in the practical applications of it for the cure of disease. All of the responses were useful to the theme of the paper, and all gave evidence of the qualifications of the doctors engaged in the practice of medicine in Alabama. He therefore published all of them arranged in alphabetical order of the names of the writers.

The following are excerpts from some of the more interesting replies: [9]

One of the longer reports was that of Dr. J.C. Abernethy of Birmingham. He was both wordy and he used such words as 'emunctories,' (excretory organs) 'diaphoretics,' (agents that cause perspiration) 'pedeluvia,' (foot baths) etc. He presumed, to his best knowledge of the day, to explain the action of quinine:

"How does quinine relieve engorgement and congestion? And you see more or less of this in every malarial attack -- say that it is simple engorgement of the spleen or liver. By exciting the muscular fibre and vaso-motor nerves, and driving on the stagnant blood into the general circulation, thereby restoring the equilibrium of the circulation, and then its antidotal powers coming in play at the same time, there is nothing for the emunctories to do but rid the system of any lingering poison that may be left behind in the system."

---

[9]*Ibid.*

Notice Abernethy's treatment of hemorrhagic fever, a condition which carries a very high mortality even in this enlightened twentieth century:

"But quinine is indispensable in the treatment of malarial hemorrhagic fever. The course I pursued was somewhat after this style: Called to see a man, middle aged; had been having chills and fevers for weeks and probably months; had a severe one yesterday evening; a very high fever succeeded, with an intense icteroid hue of skin; pokeberry juice urine; not secreted very rapidly, and but very little desire to void it; more than likely a most horrible nausea and retching, etc., with bowels constipated (usually). First move on the chess board is to move the bowels, a decided mercurial purgative; combine the mercury with any other brisk purgative; when the bowels are sufficiently acted upon, the nausea ceases. Begin now with large doses of some preparation of iron, and combine with it quinine in moderate doses, say five grains every three or four hours; keep the patient quiet with morphine hyperdermically [sic], lemonade drinks, warm foot baths, milk punch; keep the bowels open with some mild purgative; never give but the one dose of calomel spoken of above, unless imperatively required, but keep up the iron and quinine for several days; iron in as large doses as the stomach will bear, and quinine in doses sufficient to arouse the system and not depress it. If the nausea can be controlled so that the medicines can be taken into the stomach, this course of treatment will save the great majority of such cases."

Most of Cochran's correspondents felt that quinine was harmful rather than helpful in the treatment of this condition. But Abernethy continues: "The objection by some physicians to the use of quinine in this peculiar condition is caused by an improper use of the drug, in too large doses, and trying to force it into a stomach that positively refuses to receive it."

Dr. A.G. Clopton of Scottsboro, wrote of his area that it had been a "malarious county for more than a quarter of a century." He made these observations:

"I am far from believing that because one lives in a malarious district he cannot have any other than a malarious trouble. I have found many diseased people living in malarious districts whose troubles could not be attributable to that cause. My observations and experience is that quinine is the most misused of all medicines we have. I have known of some bad results by reason of its misapplication. I give one striking illustration. I was called to see a young lady, an only daughter, the pride and idol of the family, of full habit and rather robust. Her physician claimed to be too unwell to go after waiting on her twelve days. So, on the 13th I went and found her with the pathognomonic evidences of typhoid fever (enteric of Wood). After a careful examination, I told her father it was almost a hopeless case. I did not think it possible for her to live. I was told she was given first calomel, followed by oil and turpentine, and quinine was given her continuously every two hours for eleven days, she having taken more than three ounces. I think I never saw the nervous system so disturbed in any case that I had met before. She died on the 16th day, an exceeding hard death."

Dr. D.M.A. Dansby, of Rehoboth, related some interesting experiences:

"I settled in a place called South Boston...in Marengo county. ...About this time a large number of wealthy planters from Virginia and other parts were buying and settling those rich black lands, and the lands were soon cleared and thousands of acres were put in cultivation. Each summer brought with it numerous cases of fever of nearly every type from malarial poisoning, and many were the new made graves frightening to a young physician as I was. There were old doctors there, and I asked their manner of treating those fevers. I was constantly told the only reliable treatment was purging by mercurials and oil, reducing the heart's action as much as possible by the lancet, and after the fever was broken to give tonics, as quinine, bark, etc.; their patients died all around. I have been differently taught, and when I began to get some practice I pursued a different plan. Most of the fevers this and two or three years after, were of a congestive character. I gave calomel, oil, etc., continually, and from the beginning I gave quinine and stimulants freely; at the same time I used external means, as mustard poultices, red pepper, and in fact any and everything that would excite the surface. My object was to bring out the fluids and relieve the congested viscera. My mode of administering quinine was three grains at intervals of three hours to adults, and when it was rejected, I blistered over the region of the stomach, which generally relieved that organ, and the quinine would be retained. ...I have never administered quinine in those large doses that some do. ...In giving such large doses it produces, in many cases, a very disagreeable sensation in the head, that I think it is well to avoid. ...In the malarial hemorrhage fever, that we have often prevailing in the southern part of the State, I am of the opinion that quinine does a real injury."

Dr. Dansbury had discontinued the practice of bleeding patients. He had begun the practice of treating early with small but appropriate doses of quinine. He had discovered the danger in giving quinine in hemorrhagic malarial fever, and his other remedies probably did little harm.

Dr. J. R. Hoffman, of Athens used quinine hypodermically. He administered it as follows:

"Quinine, two and one-half drachms; hydrochloric acid, fifty minims; distilled water, four and one-half drachms[10] -- mix. Dose, five to twenty drops. Five to twenty minims, for hypodermic use, gives rise to a little smarting, with some swelling and redness of surrounding tissue, but I have never seen it followed by an abscess."

Dr. George E. Kumpe, of Leighton, [the physician who supported Dr. Cochran's plan for the reorganization of the Medical Association of the State of Alabama when he was President of that association] wrote of hypodermic administration of quinine:

"I invariably adopt, namely, first, to have my solution as near as possible neutral and well filtered; and secondly, to thoroughly wash out the syringe with warm water immediately after administering a dose...a failure of which will permit the evaporation of what remains in the needle of the syringe and its consequent recrystalization, and hence the easy introduction of quinine crystals, which is thought to be the chief cause of abscesses." "...In the great dysentery epidemic

---

[10]Drachms = teaspoonfuls; minims = drops.

of 1852, the administration of quinine at an early state of the disease was of immense value in assisting promptly in relieving all the symptoms and favoring convalescence, and I am fully convinced that much of the fatality of that epidemic was due to the malarial factor in it."

Dr. Kumpe's practice was in the Tennessee Valley where malaria was quite prevalent. He was probably right in his assumption that, in using quinine early in the disease, the malaria was cured and the patient had a better chance of recovering from the dysentery. I [John Morris] suspect that many of Dr. Kumpe's cures with quinine were really cures of underlying malaria.

In his "Analysis of Testimony" Cochran was astute. [It is a testimony of his mental powers, and the document shows intimately the working of his great mind. The conclusions, therefore are presented *in toto*.]

"In the therapeutic value of quinine in the more common forms of malarial fevers -- that is to say, in intermittents and remittents -- there is no diversity of opinion amongst my correspondents, all of them regarding   "In the therapeutic value of quinine in the more common forms of malarial fevers. There is some diversity, however, in regard to the methods of administration.   In intermittents of whatever type, the common practice is to wait for the subsidence of the febrile stage, and to give the quinine during intermission; but this rule, which I myself believe to be a wise one, is not always observed. The quantity of quinine considered necessary varies considerably ... at about fifteen grains as the minimum, and about sixty grains as the maximum; but in the large majority of cases and with a large majority of practitioners the quantity preferred ranges from twenty to thirty grains during a single paroxysmal period, whether longer or shorter.

"...Many skillful practitioners still favor the old custom of emptying the bowels, depleting the portal circle,[11] reducing

---

[11]The circulation of blood from the enteric capillaries through the hepatic portal vein through the liver to the hepatic vein to the inferior vena cava to the heart.

inflammatory complications, when they exist, by mercurial purgatives, blisters, and other antiphlogistic remedies,[12] and waiting for a remission before the exhibition of the quinine. The drift of professional opinion, however, in Alabama, seems to be in favor of depending upon the quinine as the leading remedy in every stage of the fever, giving it in full doses during the height of the fever as an antipyretic; and during the remissions, also in full doses as an antiperiodic to prevent the return of the fever.

"...It is in regard to hemorrhagic malarial fever, that the greatest diversity of opinion is found to prevail. This disease is attended with too much danger to admit of timid treatment, and its malarial origin being conceded, it was the most natural thing in the world to reach the *a priori* conclusion that the energetic administration of the great anti-malarial remedy was the proper way to combat its ravages. Soon after the war, when this form of disease prevailed very extensively in many parts of the State almost or perhaps altogether, all of our physicians adopted the quinine treatment. It was soon found, however, that under this treatment the mortality was discouragingly great. It was also found that after the subsidence of the hematuria even a moderate dose of quinine was often sufficient to reestablish it. The consequence has been that the efficacy of the quinine in this disease has become a matter of very grave question.

"There is a very general agreement as to the value of quinine in neuralgias, particularly those characterized by intermissions or remissions. The testimony is more conflicting in regard to its use in dysenteries, although the majority of my correspondents speak of it in favorable terms. Several of them have found it more decidedly efficacious in autumnal and winter dysentery than in those occurring in the spring. Can it be that autumnal dysenteries are more decidedly malarial?

"There is another group of fevers, believed to be of malarial origin:

---

[12]Antiphlogistic = anti fever.

"The uses of quinine in the continued fevers, and the quasi continued fevers, such as typhoid fever, typho-malarial fever (so called), mountain fever, gastric remittent fever of children, continued malarial fever (so-called), etc.

"Under this head, the testimonies received relate almost exclusively to typhoid fever, typho-malarial fever, and continued malarial fever; and a good deal of confusion grows out of the fact that these names are not always, or even generally used, to designate clearly differentiated diseases. Before the war, for several years epidemics of undoubtedly genuine typhoid fever was very little, if at all benefitted by the use of quinine, although the abortive quinine treatment of Fenner was tried by many of them. During the last four or five years, a continued fever has presented itself in various sections of the State, and more especially in the northern and mountainous portions of it, about the nosological position of which there has been much difference of opinion. So far as I know, although there have been many deaths occasioned by this fever, there have been no post mortem examinations made to clear up the diagnosis. It has been indifferently called by some typhoid fever, by some typho-malarial fever, and by some continued malarial fever. Most of the testimonies here given relate to this fever, though a few of my correspondents undertake to distinguish between typhoid and typho-malarial, or continued malarial fever, the last two designations being regarded as synonymous.

"It is admitted, to begin with, that none of these fevers can be cut short by quinine, in whatever way it may be used. (However some of the correspondents used it and claimed success in all of them).

"There is very general agreement that quinine is a valuable remedy in rheumatism, although no special details are given; this perhaps for the reason that its exhibition in this disease has been almost entirely superseded by salicylic acid and its salts. In pneumonia, and especially in asthenic pneumonia, its value seems to be universally recognized. It is mentioned with some favor in bronchitis. In pleurisy it seems not to have acted so well. It is favorably mentioned as a restorative and expectorant in phthisis; and as almost specific in spasmodic croup....

"The evidence here collected entirely disproves the presumption that quinine can cause abortions or premature labor, when administered during pregnancy.

"Toxological effects, unconnected with idiosyncrasies, have been very rarely observed, and have manifested themselves mostly in the shape of temporary deafness, temporary impairment of vision and nervous erethism[13]-- conditions rarely if ever permanent, Idiosyncrasies to the influence of quinine, while not notably numerous, are not sufficiently rare to be ranked as curiosities."

As Cochran found out, quinine and calomel were used on every febrile disease encountered by the physicians of that day. His research indicated, in a rough way, which conditions were amenable to the therapy, which it did not help and in which it was contraindicated. He had found that over half of the illness in Mobile was due to diseases attributed to the malarial miasma. Certainly most of these were due to the various plasmodia [not yet discovered] and were amenable to quinine therapy. Some patients were ill from other causes superimposed on malaria. Some pregnant women, thought to have puerperal sepsis, had malaria. It was particularly useful to find that quinine would not cause premature labor or abortion.

Quinine was of no help in infectious disease, and aspirin, newly arrived on the scene, was superior to quinine in the treatment of arthritis. Quinine is still used as a later resort in the treatment of night cramps in elderly people. From this study it was found that large doses of quinine were not necessary in the treatment of any of these diseases. This study opened the eyes of the Alabama doctors.

On prisoner maltreatment

In spite of his many official and non-official activities, Cochran remained the humanitarian. Seeing how badly prisoners were treated, he worked out concrete statistics to reveal just how bad the situation was.

---

[13]Erethism = excessive irritability or sensitivity to stimuli.

Birmingham was a mining community. In a letter to the Editor, *The Sunday Chronicle*, Birmingham, Alabama, August 12, 1883, he stated: "If the people of Alabama intend to support the penitentiary system of the State as a reformatory institution to which is attached the double purpose of humane infliction of punishment for crime, they must demand the execution of the laws framed to fulfill that purpose." He understood the agreement made between the State and the criminal: that the criminal, in return for his life, "accepts disgrace, and hard labor for a specified season," after which "his freedom shall be restored to him, exclusive of the right of suffrage." Now he asked: "...is the state faithful or is it shockingly faithless to its pledge when it permits the sanitary conditions of the convicts to display the statistics I have gathered?" His statistics showed that in two of the mines that worked prisoners, the death rate was more than 300 persons per 1,000 per annum. He quoted, "The United States census reports the average rate in 1879, to have been 18 to the 1,000 in the entire population." These miners were blacks, who were known to be susceptible to tuberculosis.

"...We give full credit to reported improvement, and to the promise of further improvement in the management of the mining convicts, but humanity cannot endure the calculating policy of the delays which unnecessarily attend, and have attended the execution of those improvements. There can be no excuse for delay in furnishing tepid water and dry towels, none in supplying clean and dry beds, none the withholding men from hard work when absolute rest is essential to health and life." He urged the editor to: "Let the people of Alabama know that[,] beside death by hanging[,] their laws provide death by prolonged and outrageous neglect of prison masters in the management of defenseless men who have the solemn guarantee of the sovereign law of the state for the protection of their limbs and lives."

In this regard, he also wrote other articles, spoke and wrote in medical circles, in the legislature cohd in private circles. He was finally able to interest Dr. J.B. Gaston, president of the State Medical Association. That gentleman became active in promoting a program to prevent mistreatment of state prisoners.

On the health of children

Cochran was also very interested in the health of school children. Under his leadership, the State Department of Health suggested a health education program for public schools. Schools would be required to conduct systematic physical exercises; to provide adequate ventilation, suitable desks and lighting arrangements; proper recreation; smallpox vaccination [which recommendation was ignored until 1906 when many children died of smallpox]; wholesome school lunches; place sanitary supervision of all schools, public and private, under the supervision of local boards of health; to test the vision of all school children; and to require all schools to teach physiology and hygiene.

On the topic of abortion

His love for children, and his total commitment to the Catholic faith, is evident in his opinion of abortion. But thoroughness and honesty were immediately noted in his written word, bringing out a clarity that was most pleasant. Regardless of his personal feelings or opinion, Cochran could be nothing less than candid. In "The Omnibus Discussion," he joined a number of other physicians in expressing his views, but always keeping at the forefront his innate sense of legal and moral codes. He wrote:[14]

"...the final decision of the question now under discussion ... namely of the production of abortion to the relief of the un-controllable vomiting of pregnancy ... depends upon the previous determination of two primary questions. One of these is the purely moral and psychological question as to the moral right of the physician to destroy, under any circumstances, and for any purpose whatever, the life of the foetus. The other is the ...question proper, as to whether upon purely medical...the sacrifice of the foetus ever becomes necessary. ...I am very emphatically of the opinion that this question is of such character and importance as to need more thorough and explicit attention than has so far been accorded to it.

---

[14]"The Omnibus Discussion," *Transactions of MASA, 1883,* pp. 68-75.

"...the difficulty, namely, that we have no absolute standard of morals. On the contrary, the laws of moral obligation, like all other laws of nature, and of human nature, are, unquestionably, provisional, tentative, liable in the onward march of human and social evolution to modification and change. What is demonstrably right in one century may be demonstrably wrong in another. What is perfectly innocent in one country, amongst one race of people in one stage of advancing civilization, may be atrociously criminal in another country, in another people, in another civilization. And not only so; but even in the same age, and the same nation, we find different classes of the community widely separated from one another in regard to many questions of moral obligation as the results of differences of religious and scientific training. There are, it is true, certain great central principles in practical ethics about which all civilized communities are virtually in agreement. But in the practical application of even these central principles to the complex exigencies of social, and political, and religious conduct conflicting interpretations gain currency and lead to different estimates of the moral quality of identically the same acts. Take, for example, that familiar precept of the decalogue, 'Thou shalt not kill'. Everywhere amongst civilized nations the binding obligation of this rule is admitted in general terms without question. But in practice it is subjected to many qualifications. The organized community acting under the authority of the State may kill their enemies in war. Under the operation of the laws of the land the individual offender who has maliciously killed his neighbor may forfeit his right to live. And the individual citizen may take the life of his assailant in necessary self-defense.

"In the absence then of a moral code of absolute and universal authority, what are we to do? To this question there can be but one answer. Every man may do with a good conscience whatever is not in contravention of the laws of the land and the recognized customs of the community in which he lives."

Dr. Cochran proceeded to define the rule of the Catholic Church and of the members of that church, that *all cases* of abortion are morally wrong. He then proceeded to call to mind that the medical profession "in recent times" ..."it is allowable to destroy the ... child to save the mother..." He then wrote: "...who can estimate the value of the foetus? He might develop into a great statesman or a great soldier, the pride and ornament of his country... It seems to me that the only safe ground to take in a question like this is, that every human life is altogether beyond all price, so that human lives can not be coolly weighed against one another in calculating expediency. I have no words of censure for those who in good faith and with consciences void of offense have reached conclusions different from mine; but for myself, I am free to say that in these cases, under no circumstances whatever could I be induced to play the double role, first of judge and jury to condemn, and then of executioner to destroy. So much for the moral question.

"As to the medical question, if the moral question could be hid away out of sight, I am willing to admit that there are cases in which the production of abortion in the interests of the mother is justifiable. ...after making all allowances there can be no doubt that there is a small residuum of cases, indeed, in which she will die any how whether she is relieved of the foetus or not. This melancholy possibility is one of the inheritances of feminine humanity.

"These cases divide themselves into two classes. First, those in which the foetus has reached the stage of viability, that is to say, about the seventh month of pregnancy, when the induction of parturition is designated as premature delivery." Cochran counseled the use of surgery to attempt to save both lives.

"The second class consists of those cases in which the foetus has not reached a stage of development that will allow extra-uterine life."

However, Cochran cautioned: "...That where the aggregate advantages of a procedure so fraught with danger and responsibility as this is are at all doubtful, a wise conservatism most emphatically counsels non-interference."

He then resumed the discussion of the case that had been brought before the Association: whether abortion is a valid treatment for morbid nausea and vomiting of pregnancy.

"I think it tolerably certain, although I know of no definite statistics to appeal to, that a larger percentage of deaths have occurred in cases where interference has been practiced than in cases where interference has not been practiced; but the evident reply to this statement is, that interference is never resorted to except in the most extreme cases, and that in these cases, as a rule, it is delayed until the patients are too much enfeebled to bear the additional shock. There is no doubt some truth in this explanation; and here emerges one of the special embarrassments which confront the physician in the management of these cases. As a conscientious man he cannot advise abortion until it is quite certain that all other remedies have failed, and if it is done then it must be done under the most unfavorable circumstances and with the probability staring him in the face that instead of saving the life of his patient he may in fact accelerate the approach of death. This is truly a dreadful dilemma, and one from which it is impossible to escape.

"The danger in these cases comes from the inability of the patient to retain, digest, and assimilate food. Other pathological factors count for something, but the principal cause of the nervous prostration, the principal cause of death in these cases -- if indeed these cases ever result in death -- is inanition.[15] When the vomiting makes it impossible to feed the patient by stomach we resort to rectal alimentation; and it has been asserted that rectal alimentation properly managed may always be depended upon to bring the woman safely through her trouble."

At this point, Cochran's wry sense of humor surfaced to lighten the dreadful topic under discussion. His next sentence stated: "Cases, however, have been reported here today in which the rectum rejected everything that was put into it as persistently as the stomach did -- uncontrollable rectal vomiting, if such an expression is allowable."

He then proceeded to give a completely anatomic, chemical and medical breakdown of the condition, then wrote: "...the only cases,

---

[15]See Glossary

therefore, that need be despaired of, are those in which rectal alimentation is impracticable because nutritive injections cannot be retained long enough to be absorbed; and the number of these [cases] must be small indeed.

"I conclude, therefore, that a majority, and perhaps a large majority of the cases in which artificial abortion has been resorted to for the relief of the mother -- including craniotomy in contracted pelvis -- might be treated with more favorable results by other methods; and when I say at least half of the cases, I think I am stating the proportion very moderately. To my mind this slaughter of the innocents is dreadful beyond all possibility of expression. On June 2, the quarantine powers of The National Board of Health were officially ended, given to the Marine Hospital Service by Congress. Congress, however, did not repeal the law that created the NBH for 10 more years. Therefore, it continued to fight for its existence in Congress, never winning, ever sliding into obscurity as the MHS quietly gathered momentum and gradually assumed authority over national quarantine. And so went 1883. Dr. Cochran was once again a forceful leader in the State.

Chapter XVI
Never too Old to Learn

-1884-

In 1884 Dr. Cochran was President of the Mobile Medical Society. He remained active in the American Medical Association. He remained as County Health Officer of Mobile and also as State Health Officer. He continued as Senior Censor of the Alabama Medical Association, and was named Grand Senior Counsellor, a position which he held for the rest of his life. And, not one to sit on his laurels, he constantly evaluated, and worked to update any procedure or design he determined to need revision.

At that annual meeting of the Association in Selma, April 8 - 12th, Cochran -- forever desiring to better the Association -- offered three amendments to the Constitution:[1]

"(1) That the first clause of Article 22 of the Constitution, which is in the words following, to-wit: 'The President shall be elected for one year;' shall be amended as to read as follows: 'The President shall be elected for three years.'

(2) That the second clause of Article 22 of the Constitution, which

---

[1]Amendments to the Constitution, *Transactions of MASA*, 1884, pp. 62-64.

is in the words following, to-wit: 'the Vice-Presidents for one year;' shall be so amended as to read as follows: 'the Vice-Presidents for two years, but in such way that only one vacancy will occur annually by expiration of official term.'

(3) That the Constitution shall be amended by striking out from the end of Article 30, the words, 'The same person shall not be eligible for the presidency for two successive terms.'

In offering these amendments Cochran emphasized: "I entertain an almost superstitious respect for our existing constitution; and I desire to insist with all the emphasis I am master of, that not even the slightest change should ever be made in it without the most earnest consideration." He felt that, at that time, there were not enough able men of commanding capacity to fill the office of President in an efficient manner, and that the president should not be a mere figurehead, but a wise leader and disciplinarian. He told the Association that he was "quite willing also to wait, not simply one year, as the constitution itself requires, before demanding the vote, but to wait two, three, or even five years, until times and circumstances and wider experiences than we have heretofore had, have convinced the Association that the proposed changes ought to be made." He concluded with "...I want the members of the Association to think about [these amendments]." They did, and heeded -- at least after consideration and discussion. Today's by-laws reflect that far-sighted consideration in that the president remains in office for three years as follows: as president-elect, then as president, then as immediate past president. They learn, they do, they advise.

Cochran, bothered greatly by the 1883 epidemic fever in Brewton, [seven miles north of the Florida State Line, in the approximate center of southern Alabama] and *totally unafraid to let his peers know that his own understanding of a subject was limited,* admitted that[2] "I had for many years been familiar with yellow

---

[2] Jerome Cochran, "Hemorrhagic Malarial Fever," *Transactions of MASA,* 1884, pp. 495-506.

fever, and to me it seemed perfectly clear that the fever at Brewton was yellow fever. The physicians of Brewton had been for many years familiar with hemorrhagic malarial fever, and they asserted with persistent emphasis that the Brewton fever was hemorrhagic malarial fever. At that time I had no circumstantial and critical knowledge of hemorrhagic malarial fever, having in all my professional life seen only one case of it. I had read in a casual way the papers which had been published with regard to it in the Transactions of the State Medical Association, and had on several occasions heard it discussed during the annual sessions of said Association. But all this had given me only a vague general knowledge of the malady, and not that minute, definite and circumstantial information of the concourse and succession of symptoms which is needed for purposes of diagnosis in the presence of an emergency such as that which confronted me at Brewton.

"As a consequence of this embarrassing experience, I made up my mind to make as careful a study of hemorrhagic malarial fever as I could, with the special object in view of establishing the data upon which any medical man of ordinary skill might be able with confidence and certainty to discriminate this said hemorrhagic malarial fever from specific yellow fever." Having had a successful response to his 1883 letter to the physicians requesting their input on the uses of quinine, on January 22, therefore, he wrote another letter and sent it to 1000 physicians in the state asking for their help.

"Dear Doctor -- With a view to the preparation of a paper for the approaching session of the State Medical Association, I am anxious to obtain all the information Alabama physicians are able to give me in regard to hemorrhagic malarial fever in its several varieties. If you have ever treated any cases of this disease, no matter how small the number, please furnish me as promptly as possible with a full and circumstantial account of your experience, arranged under the following: "THE HEMAGASTRIC OR HEMATEMESIC: ...THE HEMATURIC FORM."

Cochran asked for the number of cases, recoveries, deaths, full clinical histories including symptoms of the several stages, the treatment, especially the use of quinine, the "natural history" of the disease, and the physician's differential diagnosis from yellow fever. Of the last he wrote: "This is important. Note, therefore, as carefully as possible, the points of resemblance and the points of difference."

In the letter he requested: "...Above all, please forward reports promptly, as the session of the Association is near at hand."

Forty-five responses came in. He stated, as he read the paper in April, "To all of these I desire to express my sincere thanks for the trouble that they have taken to oblige me, and to assist me in the solution of an important medical problem. ... My own lack of clinical acquaintance with the disease makes it impossible for me to undertake to estimate the comparative values of the statements and opinions of these forty-five witnesses, and I therefore publish their several communications in full, so as to do full justice to all of them."

The letters were quite revealing of the way each doctor practiced medicine. They are clear and intelligent. Most of them show the ineffectiveness of quinine, some of the practitioners observed that quinine seemed to precipitate the condition.[3] Nearly all of the correspondents gave the case histories as follows:

 * Preceded by several attacks of malaria, usually over a period of two or three years; with or without control by quinine;

 * Hematuria. Microscopic examination -- rarely done -- revealed much hemoglobin, substances interpreted as the cellular carcasses, and rare whole red blood corpuscles.

 * Rigors and chills followed by remittent and/or intermittent fevers. Quinine seems to have been effective in the latter.

 * Headache.

 * Pain in epigastrium and over liver, spleen and kidneys.

 * Jaundice, going to bronze, comes on with the initial chill, deepens rapidly in intensity, diminishes in protracted cases, and may disappear completely after death.

---

[3]Modern observations seem to confirm this and some observers feel that a type of immune reaction is involved. This has not been confirmed. No antibodies have been found by modern techniques.

 * Vomiting, comes on early in the attack, is quite nauseating, is yellow to green, to port wine, or "poke berry juice" color, to black, to coffee ground. The black vomit looks the same as that in yellow fever.
 * Constipated or melanotic or port wine stools.
 * Post mortem findings are substantially the same as found in other malarial disease.

In his paper, Cochran gave a tabular statement of reported cases, by physician. He stated: "This table gives us an aggregate of forty-one reporters; six hundred and forty-two cases; four hundred and eighty-four recoveries; and one hundred and fifty-eight deaths. The percentage of deaths to cases, therefore, is 24.60; or, in round numbers, one-fourth of the cases died and three-fourths of them recovered. Five of my correspondents fail to give the number of cases and the number of deaths in their practice; and, therefore, their names do not appear in the foregoing table."

From the physicians' accounts, Cochran was able to lucidly put forward seventeen points about the disease. *[Because this is so indicative of his life's work, it is placed here almost in toto rather than in an appendix.]*

"(1) That hemorrhagic malarial fever originates only in malarial regions, although the morbilic paroxysm may occur after the removal of the subject of it to a healthy locality.

(2) That the poison which causes hemorrhagic malarial fever is the same as that which causes ordinary intermittent and remittents.

(3) That hemorrhagic malarial fever may manifest itself in three forms -- intermittent, remittent, and congestive, to which may be added a fourth form, namely, the quasi-continued.

(4) That the congestive form of the malady is almost necessarily fatal under all forms of treatment; the remittent form extremely dangerous, with the deaths in excess of the recoveries; the intermittent form less dangerous than the two others just mentioned, with the recoveries in excess of the deaths; while the quasi-continued form is the result of inflammatory visceral complications.

(5) That Negroes and mulattoes are comparatively exempt from

the disease in any of its forms, being indeed less susceptible to this fever than to yellow fever; and the rate of mortality amongst them is very much less than the rate of mortality amongst whites.

(6) That in the immense majority of cases it attacks persons who have a malarial cachexia, and a history of chronic chills. But in a small minority it attacks persons who, while they have been much exposed to malarial influences, have still remained apparently as well as usual up to the moment of the malignant outbreak.

(7) That one attack affords no guarantee of immunity against another -- the same person often suffering successive attacks in successive seasons, and even in the same season.

(8) That the paroxysms usually commence with a chill, which is often of protracted duration, which occurs frequently during the afternoon or night, and which is accompanied or speedily followed by troublesome bilious vomiting, by hemorrhagic urine, and by icteroid discoloration of the eyes and skin.

(9) That the febrile reaction, as marked by the temperature and the pulse rate, is not usually of very high grade. But there seem to be exceptions to this rule in the intermittent and remittent forms, and especially in the quasi-continued form.

(10) That while the fever continues the skin is apt to be harsh and dry, although this rule is not universal, and that the occurrence of free, and even of profuse, diaphoresis is a symptom of favorable omen.

(11) That the bowels are usually constipated, the portal circulation obstructed, the liver congested and torpid, and the whole system deluged with bile; and that free bilious purging seems always to afford some measure of relief.

(12) That the bilious vomiting makes its appearance early in the attack, is attended with distressing nausea, and is usually copious and persistent, the vomited matters ranging through many shades of color -- yellow, black, green, and even blue.

(13) That the hemorrhagic urine usually comes on with the initial chill, and always in an early stage of the paroxysm; is at first very profuse; diminishes and often disappears in the remissions and intermissions of the fever, and is often suppressed towards the

termination of fatal cases.

(14) That the icteroid discoloration usually comes on with the initial chill; deepens very rapidly in intensity; may grow less marked towards the end of protracted cases; and often disappears completely after death.

(15) That a comparatively small number of cases are marked by the occurrence of black vomit not distinguishable from the black vomit of yellow fever.

(16) That this black vomit, when it occurs at all, almost always occurs at the beginning of the attack, and is always accompanied by haematuria, the haematuria showing itself first.

(17) That the more obvious post mortem appearances in hemorrhagic malarial fever are substantially the same as are found in other malarial diseases, namely: Liver enlarged and congested, and of dark bronze or slate color; bile abundant in gall bladder and alimentary canal; spleen enlarged and congested."

Cochran admitted that what he was really looking for was whether the black vomit of hemorrhagic malarial fever was truly blood as in the black vomit of yellow fever. That differential diagnosis, he felt, was the telling point of the whole study. What he found was the rarity of the haematemesic form - only 14 out of 599 cases. He found, too "that those of my correspondents who have practiced in the most intensely malarial sections of the State, and who have seen the largest number of cases and the most malignant types have not seen the haematemesic form at all; and some of them distinctly take the position that the so-called black vomit of hemorrhagic malarial fever is altered bile, and not, like the black vomit of yellow fever, altered blood."

But, like the devil's advocate that he was, Cochran went on to explain: "I am, however, inclined to believe that we may sometimes have in hemorrhagic malarial fever gastric hemorrhages; and these hemorrhages mixed with the gastric acids, would furnish a black hemorrhagic vomit, and if this was ejected unmixed with bile, we might have black vomit very much like that of yellow fever."   He, therefore, pointed out the following:

"PROBLEMS IN HEMORRHAGIC MALARIAL FEVER:
(1) To determine by chemical and microscopical examination
whether the so-called black vomit of hemorrhagic malarial fever is
a true hematemesis; or whether it is altered bile instead of altered
blood.

(2) To determine the true therapeutic value of quinine in
hemorrhagic malarial fever; that is to say, whether it could be
beneficially used in any of the several stages of the malady; and if
so, under what limitations as to doses and times and circumstances
of administration.

(3) To determine whether hemorrhagic malarial fever is caused by
the same morbid poison that gives rise to less ordinary intermittent
and remittents; or whether it is produced by a poison *sui generis*,
allied perhaps to the ordinary malarial poison, but not specifically
the same.

(4) To determine whether the hemorrhagic malarial fever of
Alabama is, or is not, identical with the melanuric fever of
Beranger-Ferand, and other French writers."

True to his purpose, he addressed the burning need to understand
how to treat this malady. And true to his nature, he researched
everything he could find printed, either in America, South America,
or Europe. Having thus learned from his colleagues and the printed
works of others, he added his own deductions in order to clarify and
consolidate the knowledge and make it available to the medical
profession:

"(1) There is virtually unanimity of opinion as to the
superabundance of bile, the congestion of the liver, the engorgement
of the portal circle, and the constipation of the bowels; and there is
also virtual unanimity of opinion as to the beneficial influence of
purgatives, especially of mercurial purgatives. The methods of
administration vary. Some give small doses of calomel, or of
calomel in some of the usual combinations of it with other drugs,
every few hours until the bowels are freely moved and the portal
and hepatic congestion relieved. Others give larger doses at less
frequent intervals; and a few advocate the administration of
enormous doses, thirty, forty, and even seventy grains. For myself

I should prefer moderate and repeated doses, until the accomplishment of the end aimed at.

(2) The disease seems to be always attended by very distressing nausea and copious, frequent, and protracted bilious vomiting. It is of course impossible to arrest nausea and emesis as long as there is bile in the stomach. My correspondents say very little about the management of these symptoms except as to what is indirectly accomplished through the influence of purgation. The indication, however, is very clear, the stomach ought to be emptied of all the bile that finds its way into it through the duodenum. It is hardly necessary to administer emetic medicines; but copious draughts of warm water and of warm teas would probably be found to be useful.

(3) A dry, harsh skin is another common symptom, mentioned again and again by my correspondents; and in such cases sweating is always mentioned as giving more or less relief. This may be induced by the external application of heat by any of the usual methods; and will be favored by the ingestion of hot drinks as just mentioned in connection with another indication. Very little mention is made as to the use of diaphoretic drugs. One very remarkable case is related to where the patient seems to have been snatched from the very mouth of the grave by the hypodermic exhibition of two doses of jaborandi.[4]

(4) It does not seem to be settled whether or not it is desirable to address remedies directly to the kidneys; but all attempts to check the haematuria by the agency of astringents and styptic have proven certainly unavailing, and perhaps mischievous.

(5) As this disease has been almost universally regarded as of malarial origin, it was very natural that our physicians should have felt that quinine was the very sheet anchor in the treatment of this as of other malarial maladies; and for a long time, and even now, the general rule was to give quinine in liberal and frequent doses. It was, however, very soon observed that quinine exercised far less control over this disease than over our ordinary intermittent and

---

[4]Jaborandi see Glossary.

remittent fevers. It was also observed that it often increased the flow of bloody urine; and even reestablished it again after it had ceased. Strangest of all, it was observed that in many cases the chills came on while the patients were thoroughly under the influence of quinine. ...In the treatment of this most dangerous of malarial maladies quinine, the great anti-malarial remedy, has lost ground..."

Cochran ended the study with the summation of Dr. R.S. Williams, of Mount Meigs, Montgomery County:

"I will conclude by recapitulating, that hemorrhagic malarial fever is confined to localities; that one attack does not afford immunity from other attacks; that it rarely, if ever, commences *de novo* that only a seeming black vomit attends some of the fatal cases; also, that the vomiting is mostly confined to the early stage of this disease, and always attended with nausea; that I have never seen a case in a pure African; that among the whites it is more frequent among blondes, and has no respect for sex or age; that it is unknown in cities where there has been no exposures to malaria. The disease is always preceded by previous malarial attacks; that the discoloration of the skin is more marked in the early stages of the disease, and diminished after death; that most fatal cases die from uremia, and die from the seventh to the tenth day after attack; that the congestive types are nearly always fatal, by or before the termination of the fourth day; that quinine, while it may, as a curative of malarial fevers, lessens the number of attacks of hemorrhagic malarial fever, it ceases to be a curative after the haematuria becomes continually established, and is according to my experience, positively injurious, and lessens the chances of recovery; that I have seen repeatedly after the urine had cleared up, that the administration of quinine was followed by a return of haematuria; that I have never seen quinine suspend the diurnal paroxysm of hemorrhagic malarial fever that attends haematuria; that I have seen the remedies that we would prescribe in non-malarial haematuria, lessen the hemorrhage and apparently have good effect. As you [Dr. Cochran] have intimated that you would publish my views on hemorrhagic malarial fever, I have tried to write this so as not to be misunderstood. These views I have entertained for over thirty years, and have yet to regret that I acted on them."

DIFFERENTIAL DIAGNOSIS

Malarial Haematuria	Yellow Fever
1. Attacks only those who have been in some malarial region for a long time, having been emaciated by frequent attacks of chills and fever, producing enlarged liver and spleen.	1. Attacks most commonly strangers. Healthy persons are as subject as those who are anemic. Those who have been in infected districts for a long time are not as apt to be attacked as newcomers.
2. Having once had an attack renders a person more liable to a subsequent one, and if the party remains in the same locality is almost certain to have a second or third attack.	2. One attack generally gives an immunity from a subsequent one, if the party remains in the same locality.
3. Malarial haematuria is not infectious or contagious.	3. Yellow fever is slightly contagious.
4. Malarial Hemorrhagic fever usually occurs in localities where there are causes for malaria, without reference to distance from the sea or large rivers.	4. Yellow fever rarely prevails many miles from the sea, or some large river.
5. Malarial haematuria frequently develops in mid winter.	5. Yellow fever never develops after a heavy frost.

Charles Louis Alphonse Laveran (1845-1922), a French Army surgeon, in 1880 discovered the parasite that causes malaria, and in 1884 became convinced that mosquitoes played an important part in spreading the disease. But this was not general knowledge in Alabama at that time.

[How sad the pitiful little armamentarium with which our predecessors attempted to make war on this great killer. Their leading drugs were: iron, strychnine, iodine, digitalis, atropine, Dover's powders, Norwood's tincture of veratrum viride, ergot, bromide, bismuth subnitrate, morphine, chloralhydrate, sugar of lead. Some wag has said of the calomel dosage: "The patients took so much mercury they were six inches taller in summer than in winter."]

-1885-

More and more of Cochran's work centered from Montgomery and he found himself having to spend more time there. While there, he stayed at the Madison House. Since the last time the census of Mobile showed Cochran's residence and working address to be in that city, it is presumed that sometime in that year, before the census was taken, to remain close to his family and still be able to do his work as State Health Officer, Cochran, now aged 53, moved Ina Lou, now aged 25, and Edmund Collins, now 16, from their home at Saint Francis Street, Mobile, to 404 Dexter Avenue, Montgomery, Alabama. The new residence was only a few yards from the State Health Offices in the State House. There were congenial neighbors: Marcus Herman lived at 400 on one side and Susie White at 406 on the other side.[5]

The Montgomery City Board of Health consisted of some of the finest doctors in the State. Dr. J.B. Gaston was its chairman. He had joined Dr. Cochran in the fight for prisoners' rights. Other doctors were: J.S. Weatherly, still a friend in spite of differences on

---

[5] *Montgomery City Directory.*

the type of public health legislation for Alabama; B.J. Baldwin, a past president of the American Medical Association; R.F. Michel, a past president and charter member of the Medical Association of the State of Alabama since before its revival in 1868; S.D. Selye, whose wife was secretary to the Board of Directors of the Montgomery Infirmary.

Cochran and his family attended Father D. Savage's Masses at St. Peter's Roman Catholic Church on the corner of Lawrence and Adams Streets, the only Catholic Church in Montgomery at the time.

It is significant that, in his contributed section to the Memorial Record of Alabama, published in 1893 by Brant & Fuller, Madison Wisconsin, Cochran mentioned, with no little enthusiasm, the Montgomery Social Medical Club. "It consists of ten members, and was organized in 1872. During the twenty years of its existence it has been an important factor in promoting and maintaining that harmony and high ethical tone which so remarkably characterizes the medical profession of Montgomery. During the cooler half of the year it holds meetings every two weeks in succession at the houses of the members. These meetings are purely social, all medical discussions being forbidden. At each meeting there is a supper and much social conversation. The members attend in full dress." The fact that he mentioned the Society at all -- much less with such speaking knowledge, allows us to assume he became one of the ten members.

The 1880's were crowded with significant medical innovations. Besides Laveran discovering the malarial parasite, in 1880 Robert Koch (1843-1910) a German physician, demonstrated the technique for growing germs on solid media (gelatin), making possible their isolation and identification by this method. Also in 1880 Edwin Klebs, another German physician, discovered diphtheria germs, Robert Koch isolated the cholera bacillus, and Pasteur (1822-1895) of France discovered a chicken cholera vaccine. In 1881 Gehlensen cultured streptococcus from erysipelas, and Pasteur produced a vaccine against anthrax. In 1882 Robert Koch discovered the tubercle bacillus. In 1884 William Henry Welch moved to Baltimore and established his bacteriology laboratory there. In 1884 Karl S. R. Credé (1819-1892) a German obstetrician and gynecologist, showed that by using 2% silver nitrate in the conjunctival sacs of newborn infants he could prevent a high percent of neonatal blindness. In 1884 German physician Arthur Nicolaier (1862-1934) discovered the tetanus bacillus.

In 1885 Pasteur devised a rabies vaccine to cure hydrophobia. In 1889 Von Mehring and Minkowske proved that the pancreas secretes insulin, preventing diabetes.

On the growth of technology: in 1880 Thomas Edison and J.W. Swan independently devised the first practical electric lights. In 1882 Thomas Edison designed the first hydroelectric plant in Appleton, Wisconsin. In 1883 English scientist Sir Joseph Swan produced a synthetic fiber. In 1884 the great French engineer, Ferdinand de Lesseps finished the Suez Canal and was in Panama. That year, Dr. William Crawford Gorgas was promoted to Captain in the United States Army Medical Corps.

One can only imagine the reading, self-teaching, and learning delight of Jerome Cochran.

-1886-

At the annual Association meeting in Anniston, April 13-16, Cochran entered the Omnibus Discussion on at least two subjects. Through his words, recorded by the Secretary of the Association, we see Dr. Cochran at his most authoritarian -- his sharpest. We see one of the rare glimpses of humor that allow his associates to see the all-too-human side of him, that of which his biographer of 1880 describes: "This mask to strong passions, while it serves to conceal deep emotions, has the disadvantage of concealing, also[,] the silent revelations, if not the very existence of those fine feelings of sympathy, friendship, and genial sociability which, on fit occasions, break forth as through a rift in a cloud, to the delight of his friends, and to the surprise of those accustomed to regard him as little more than an intellectual machine."

On the subject of excessive use of antiseptics in midwifery, i.e.

the practice of antiseptic irrigation two or three times a day by the mother in order to prevent puerperal maladies, Cochran had this to say: "I want to say a few words in regard to this matter, because I think they ought to be said by somebody. I have been surprised to see the extremes to which some of our authorities -- and some of them very high authorities, too -- are disposed to push the use of antiseptics in midwifery. It may be that in certain maternity hospitals, contaminated by long use, or in certain crowded and unhealthy quarters of large cities, the more frequent use of antiseptics as a precaution to ward off the onset of infectious puerperal maladies is demanded. This, as I say, may be. But I am very certain that in Alabama, whether in our cities and towns, or in our country neighborhoods, in an immense majority of our cases, no antiseptic interference is needed. The proof of this is overwhelming. Our doctors and midwives have been practicing midwifery for several generations, and in many hundreds of thousands of cases without antiseptic precautions, and the cases that have been complicated with infectious puerperal diseases have been very rare indeed." His stated opinion was that "In the natural woman, labor is a purely physiological process, and nature is able to manage it very well with very little interference on the part of the midwife, and usually the less the interference the better for both mother and child."

On the subject of quarantine, the imp residing in Dr. Cochran was revealed, perhaps because he was an expert on the subject and was able to fully relax in his discussion. "I claim to know something about quarantine, at least in its relations to yellow fever. I have been in one way or another associated with yellow fever in every epidemic that has occurred in the South since 1855. I have been, too, somewhat extensively associated with quarantines and quarantine work, both by land and sea. I have enforced quarantines against others, and I have had quarantines enforced against me. I have been inside of quarantines, and outside of quarantines. I have been detained for weeks at quarantine lines, and I have managed to slip through quarantine lines, in violation of the quarantine regulations. And, besides all this, I have written somewhat extensively on the subject..." He proceeded to briefly outline his beliefs: "I undertook to predict that the quarantine of the future would be a purely local quarantine; that, except under special circumstances, we would cease to ward off yellow fever by an expensive surveillance of travel and commercial intercourse, and by the detention of vessels from yellow fever ports, and trust to our ability to restrict its spread in any community after it had manifested its presence by the occurrence of cases in the community. ...Let us oppose the beginnings. When a case of yellow fever occurs in a town let the health authorities take possession of the house in which it has found lodgment [sic], and let them make all intercourse with that house impossible, except under such precautions as are known to be safe. Do this, and I believe that the infection may be confined to its original limits."

-1887-

In his paper on The Value of Vital and Mortuary Statistics, read before the Association's annual meeting in Tuscaloosa, during the second week in April, Cochran again put forth his ideas and his reasoning, this time in a compiled and forceful delivery, spoken as the State's Public Health Officer,[6] but subtitled as Senior Censor and Grand Senior Counsellor of the Medical Association of the State of Alabama. This paper was originally written when he was a resident of Mobile, and thus he left the heading as such: by Jerome Cochran, M.D., of Mobile, Senior Censor and Grand Senior Counsellor of the Medical Association of the State of Alabama. The wording, the passion, the dedicated cry for the careful and systematic accrual of births, diseases, and deaths of the people of the State of Alabama is profound. That Cochran had been trying for some years to get the physicians of the state, through the offices of county health officers, to comply with his directive as State Health Officer to record these statistics, is evidenced in previous works. But he was largely

---

[6]Jerome Cochran, "The Value of Vital and Mortuary Statistics," *Transactions of MASA*, 1887, pp. 337-350.

ignored. The system, apparently, was not ready for this dedicated compilation. For, as Cochran recognized, *it costs money to gather and record this information with the degree of accuracy needed.*

Now, he led them again to consider the importance of this effort. The following is the first paragraph, and it shows clearly Cochran's gift for painting a graphic picture with his words, and also shows the extent of his reading:

"Perhaps there is hardly anything else in the shape of a printed book that to the ordinary reader is less entertaining or less instructive than a volume of statistics, with its innumerable numerical details, its aggregates, its averages, its percentages, and its long rows of puzzling figures stretching in serried ranks and files up and down and across the crowded pages. And yet to the trained expert who knows how to make use of them, such volumes grow luminous with suggestions which involve the progress and prosperity of men and nations. They have stories to tell more wonderful than those that embellish the pages of *Gulliver* or of the *Arabian Nights' Entertainments.* They have lessons to teach which command the attention and influence the conduct of all classes and professions -- merchants, manufacturers, mechanics, statesmen, soldiers. In a word, the domain of statistics has become almost universal, and includes the whole world of human enterprise."

He went on to say, most emphatically, and in a challenging manner: "They are indispensable factors in the development of nations and the progress of civilizations."

He told them of England's success since 1838. He quoted America's own Dr. Stanford E. Chaille, of New Orleans, in Chaille's lucid address to the American Medical Association in 1879 on this same subject:

"...If a human being is much more valuable to the state than is a bale of cotton, then the statistics of the human crop would prove much more valuable than the statistics of the crop. ...Ignored by the average American legislator, their practical utility has been recognized by Napoleon and Theirs, by Bismarck and Cavour, by Gladstone and Disraeli; and their establishment has become a test of the degree of civilization reached by a people and their rulers."

Of the cost of compiling data, Cochran reiterated: "What do we mean when we speak of the value of vital and mortuary statistics? Ordinarily when we speak of the value of anything we mean how much money is it worth.... But it is only commonplace things that admit of this sort of valuation; and there are many things not commonplace to which this method of estimating values is highly inapplicable. How would any one go about to estimate the money value of the Sermon on the Mount? or of the binomial theorem? or of one of Shakespeare's immortal dramas? or of the chemical law of Avogadro? or of one of Beethoven's symphonies? Such things are simply above all price in money or in money's worth.

"...If your child is in danger you don't stop to count the cost of saving him, but pay eagerly all the money you can get. So should it be with the state when the lives of her children are at stake -- when the mothers and fathers of the land, the young men and maidens and the innocent children, like the tender grass and the bearded grain, go down before the reaper whose name is death."

Cochran ended his paper and his plea with the following: "Man subdues nature. ...Given adequate knowledge and adequate means, and it is not to be doubted that the ravages of disease may be largely mitigated; that the generation of indigenous endemics may be prevented by the drainage and purification of their breeding places; and that even the great pestilences may be checked in their destructive migrations. It is the great mission of public hygiene to furnish this adequate knowledge; and, as we have seen, vital and mortuary statistics furnish the foundation stones upon which the edifice of public hygiene has been constructed."

-1888-1891-

Dr. Cochran continued his vast and multifaceted work.

-1891-

On July 22, his daughter Ina Lou, at age 31, died. By this time, Edmund Collins was 22 and had moved to Houston, Texas to work with Jerome Bowling. Both led active lives and Jerome Bowling had begun his family. Dr. Cochran was now quite alone and it devolved upon him to transport the casket to Mobile and the family plot. The boys probably made it in time for the funeral.

A few weeks later Dr. Cochran came down with an illness that was diagnosed as locomotor ataxia. He slowly, painfully recovered most of his functions from this illness and again resumed his tasks.

Cochran continued to work hard for his State, his Association, his Country, the American Medical Association, and for his "family," the people of the State.

His plan for medical organization did not stop at the state level. He believed that the State Medical Association should tie in with the American Medical Association and, as the State Association related to the State Government, the A.M.A. should relate to the Federal Government. He served as an official delegate to the American Medical Association for many years.

The leadership of the A.M.A. saw the wisdom of Cochran's plans. In a great demonstration of confidence in him, they appointed him Chairman of a Special Committee to petition the United States Congress to create a Department of Public Health with cabinet status and a Secretary of Public Health. The committee was authorized at the 1891 annual meeting. Through various reports of the Committee, one gets the tenor of Cochran's firm views.

Excerpted from "Report of the Committee Appointed by the American Medical Association to Act in Conjunction with a Committee of The American Public Health Association":

"...A portion of your Committee believed, and still believes, that no lessor office than that of Secretary of Public Health in the Cabinet of the President should be encouraged, but as it was impossible to convince the members of these two Committees that such course was the only advisable one to pursue, the following resolution was submitted and adopted by the American Public Health Association as a compromise between the two factions of the joint Committees:

"Resolved: That the American Public Health Association again urges upon Congress the necessity of the appointment of some officer with general sanitary authority in connection with the

National Government;

That functions of such an authority are of sufficient importance to demand the exclusive attention of the best instructed sanitarian;

That such authority should be enabled from time to time, and under proper regulations, to secure the advice and cooperation of the State Boards of Health.

Respectfully submitted

U.O.B. Wingate,
James H. Parkinson,
Jerome Cochran"

-1892-1894-

To the Congress of the United States, Dr. Jerome Cochran presented the following from Alabama:

"Resolved: That the Medical Association of the State of Alabama, which is also the State Board of Health, is earnestly in favor of the passage of the bill now pending in Congress, to establish a Department of Public Health, and recommends said bill to the favorable consideration and support of the members of Congress, Senators and Representatives from Alabama.

Resolved: That we believe the bill would be materially improved by the insertion of an additional clause in the following words: "He shall once in every year, call to meet in the city of Washington, a conference of State Boards of Health, to be composed of one delegate from every State Board of Health in the United States, and to be for the purpose of discussing questions of public health, and for concerting plans of sanitary administration."

On motion of Dr. C. Denison, Colorado, the report was received, the addition proposed by Alabama accepted, the resignation of Dr. Conegys as Chairman accepted, and Cochran appointed Chairman.[7] He was now in a position to do for his Country what he had done for Alabama.

---

[7]*Journal of the American Medical Association, Vol. 22,* Jan - June 23, 1894, p. 594.

-1895-1896-

Dr. Jerome Cochran, chairman of the committee working to create the position of Secretary of Public Health, reported to the Congress as follows:

"1. ...facilities for doing the important work entrusted to us have been strictly limited by want of funds.

2. ...Communication to the officers of State and other medical societies and associations urging them to appeal to the members of their respective organizations to write to their members of Congress requesting them to give their support and votes in aid of the passage of our bill. ...very few responses. Articles in medical and sanitary periodicals ...attracted more or less favorable responses.

3. ...In December, some members of the committee visited Washington City for the purpose of ascertaining just what could be done toward pushing our enterprise to a successful result. ...all agreed that it would be impossible to accomplish anything during the continuance of the LIII Congress."

After explaining the amount of effort and cost involved in the endeavor the Committee states: "It is for the Association to say whether it is prepared for an effort of this magnitude.

"To this end we had prepared a resolution recommending an appropriation, but as this object has been accomplished by the action of the Association on the recommendation of the Section on medicine, it is not necessary to offer this resolution.

"All of which is respectfully submitted.

(Signed by the Committee)"

On motion, the report was received.[8]

-1896-

As in every annual meeting of the State Association, he not only

---

[8]*Journal of the American Medical Association, May 18, Vol. 24,* Jan. -June 1895, p. 763.

read his reports as Senior Censor and as Public Health Officer, he read a scientific paper. This year, in Montgomery, April 21-24, Dr. Cochran, now 64, as Grand Senior Life Counsellor and Senior Censor, had been asked to "write a report on Recent Progress in Hygiene." [9] He thought to write about tuberculosis, but "when I looked over the schedule of regular reporters, I found to my dismay that..." this assignment had already been given to another. He, therefore, spoke about sources of contamination of the earth or soil, of the air, and of water. Under each heading, he listed all diseases known to be found in each area, and why sanitation was so necessary, to the health of the populace.

Of soil contamination and sanitation, he said: "Let the earth in the neighborhood of human habitations be kept scrupulously clean, and let the sub-soil be carefully drained to a depth of several feet."

Of contamination in air, he said: "...it carried for short distances the germs of measles, scarlet fever, and small pox, and for short distances -- for distances of a few yards -- I do not question the assumption. ...in the neighborhood of human habitations and other localities, it often contains innumerable millions of many species of microscopic organisms.

"The discussion of atmospheric germs makes a very important chapter in sanitary science. A few years ago it was the fashion to believe that the atmosphere everywhere, except in some uninhabited regions, was swarming with pathogenic bacteria. This belief led to the adoption for the performance of surgical operations the closed chamber with the air in it saturated with carbolic acid spray. ...We have learned for the most part the germs that infect surgical wounds are carried by soiled instruments, soiled hands and soiled dressings, and not by the atmosphere."

Of water contamination Cochran was most prolific. After a frightening dissertation on the horrors of "Filth enough, one would think, to make water an unfashionable beverage" he proceeded to

---

[9]Jerome Cochran, "Recent Progress in Hygiene," *Transactions of MASA* 1895, p. 280-290.

say: "Infected water is far more to be dreaded as a carrier of diseases than infected air or infected soils. It is then far more important, as a dictate of common decency, that the water used in human habitations shall not be made foul by miscellaneous mud and slush and by the products of animal and vegetable decomposition; and it is important as a sanitary precaution that drinking water shall not contain the microscopic germs of communicable diseases. ...And every industrial establishment from which there is an outflow of foul water should be required to purify such outflow."

-May 5, 1896-

Pushing his own health beyond limits, Cochran never ceased his battle for high public health standards. As the Chairman of the Committee appointed by the American Medical Association to act in conjunction with a committee of The American Public Health Association, he reported that, "The bill which was prepared for presentation to Congress was extremely crude and indefinite in its provisions, and gave this proposed high official [himself] very little important work to do. It was, indeed, found to be so defective that last year the effort to have it enacted into law was abandoned."

In the meantime, the Marine Hospital Service, which in 1890 had already been invested with some important health functions, was by the Act of 1893 converted into a National Health Department "with very large and far-reaching powers and abundant means. ...It seems to us to be a fundamental proposition that we shall have but one National Department of Public Health. This being conceded, one of three courses remain open to us:[10]

1. We may devise and advocate a plan to deprive the Marine-Hospital Service of its public health functions, and for the establishment of an entirely new department;

2. We may accept the Marine-Hospital Service just as it stands as a department sufficient for our present use or;

---

[10]Marine Hospitals were originally for seafaring persons. Since many diseases brought into the Country were first seen at the Marine Hospitals, they naturally figured highly as public health agencies.

3. We may endeavor to improve the Marine-Hospital Service and make it a more satisfactory National Health Department than it now is.

"...In arranging any scheme of national public health supervision it would seem desirable that nothing should be done to discredit and weaken the various State Boards of Health. But that contrariwise the effort should be to strengthen the State organizations, and to foster and facilitate their further evolution. If this principle is conceded it is at once made evident that the National Department of Public Health should act in and through the State Boards of Health, in cooperation and harmony with them, and not outside of them and independent of them. If the national Department acts within the States independently of the State Boards, and assumes the work that ought to devolve upon the State Boards then the State Boards become comparatively useless institutions and will fall into disfavor. Some of the State Boards are still weak institutions, and any rivalry between them and the National Department in state work would doom them to speedy destruction. In this direction it would seem that additional legislation is needed, and the simplest plan to reach the desired reconciliation would embrace two provisions:

1. That the National Department should act within the States by and through and in cooperation with the State Boards.

2. That the head of the National Department should call annually to meet in the city of Washington an Advisory Council to be composed of one representative from every State Board of Health. This would bring about mutual understanding and cooperation and reciprocity of action, and would virtually constitute a great central school of public hygiene.

"Such a scheme as this would probably command the approval and support of the national Conference of State Boards of Health, which conference is quite as deeply interested in movements of this character as is the American Medical Association.

"As the conclusion of the whole argument, we recommend that we be authorized to draw up a new bill along the lines we have indicated, and that we be authorized to invite the cooperation of the Conference of State Boards of Health and of the American Public

Health Association in our endeavor to have the proposed bill enacted into law.

"All of which is respectfully submitted.
          JEROME COCHRAN, M.D., Chairman Committee."

"In answer to the above:
DR. HIBBERD -- I move that the report of the Committee be accepted, the plan outlined adopted, the Committee continued and enlarged by the appointment of a member from each State. Seconded.

The report was then adopted."[11]

In a letter to the editor of the *Journal of the American Medical Association,* Dr. Cochran indicated that he had been ill for several weeks but that he had made some progress in enlarging the committee.

This was, however, not to be continued. For in a few short weeks -- on August 17, 1896 -- He died. The cause of death was reported as Bright's disease.

He was laid to rest in the family plot in the Roman Catholic Cemetery of Mobile, the last occupant to be interred in this plot. At last he was reunited with his beloved wife, Sarah Jane, and the six children who had preceded him. In life, Jerome had been separated from them much of the time due to his efforts to provide a longer and happier life for *all* people. Their bodies interred in one plot, their souls would be united for all eternity.

As the mourners turned away and began to dry their eyes and recompose themselves, a faint wisp of fresh air was noted. There was no longer a "miasma of malaria." The man in the grave had dissipated it. There was no longer the "odor of diphtheria," or of erysipelas; the air was fresh, the water was sweet, sewers drained well, garbage was hauled away frequently, ships came and went.

---

[11] *Journal of the American Medical Association,* May 16, Vol 26, Jan.- June, 1896 pp. 988-9.

Life was indeed sweet. In another year Mobile would have its last epidemic of yellow fever, three years before the mode of transmission was known and the disease became eradicated in Cuba, six years before the last epidemic in New Orleans. The mourners prayed that Dr. Cochran had found peace.

EPILOGUE

"And now, Dear Doctor, let me say, that though you have not met me often, scarcely sufficient to know or locate me, yet I know of you long and well. Let me repeat to you what I have said to others: that Alabama owes to you, and to you alone, a debt of gratitude, both the professional and the lay, for the high position you have caused her to assume in the *medicolegal* niche of fame. Yea, not only Alabama, but the whole Union, should sing and are singing your praises for the advanced position you have caused the profession to occupy, which is alike beneficial to the public as well as the brotherhood; and when you die (which God grant may be far in the future) the shaft which marks the spot, and points heavenward, should bear the inscription —
"To the Father of Legalized Medicine!"

> \- Dr. J. C. Nicholson
> Mt. Meigs, Montgomery County, 1884

The above was added to his response to Cochran's call for information of hemorrhagic malarial fever, and, as promised by Dr. Cochran to all those answering the call, it was published *in toto*. It expressed vividly the sentiments of most of the physicians of the time. Perhaps, even had Cochran wished to strike it from the record, the Secretary of the Association — whose job it was to have the Transactions published — did not see fit to leave it out.

At Selma's April meeting of the State Medical Association in 1897, an evening memorial service was held. There were many eulogies. Dr. George Augustus Ketchum, in his eighties, and one of the original founders of the prewar Medical Association of the State of Alabama, co-founder of the Medical College of Alabama and currently serving as Dean, had known Cochran longer and more intimately than anyone. He gave one of his finest addresses.

The Hon. A. L. Mcleod, a prominent attorney, was invited to the service and delivered an impassioned tribute using the following words: "The people of Alabama owe a debt of gratitude to the memory of Jerome Cochran that would bankrupt them to pay."

Rev. A. J. Dickenson, a distinguished minister, said this: "To this broad, liberal public servant I pay my humble tribute in behalf of my fellow pastors, for well did he realize in his work the maxim wherein is fulfilled all the sociology of the law and the prophets, namely, 'thou shalt love thy neighbor as thyself.'"

Dr. Jacob Huggins seemed to sum up the feelings of the doctors best:

"The next Counsellor to pass through the Vale of Shadows was Jerome Cochran, a grand Senior Life Counsellor, and a man whose name, for a quarter of a century, has been a house-hold word among the physicians of Alabama, —a man at whose feet many of us have been accustomed to sit, like Saul at the feet of Gamaliel, to receive wise counsels, and to catch some sparks from the scintillations of his genius; a man whose distinction was not confined to the narrow limits of his own state but extended to the remotest bounds of our Great Republic. It was my good fortune to have known Dr Cochran for 28 years.

I first met him in March, 1868, when twenty physicians assembled in this beautiful city to reorganize the Medical Association of Alabama. The writer was present during the entire session, and well remembers the part played by Dr. Cochran at this first session of our Association. The same zeal, the same indomitable energy, that has since characterized him in the work of building up and perfecting our organization, was displayed by him from day to day, and plainly foreshadowed the great work he would probably perform in bringing up the association to the present high position it occupies in the eyes of the medical world. Since that time, having been thrown with him at our annual reunions and often holding official relations with him, which necessarily create a certain degree of intimacy, the writer can say, in estimating his character and talents that Dr. Cochran was, from an intelligent standpoint, one of the most remarkable men it has been his great privilege and pleasure to meet. The modest recital of his great work in connection with the Medical Association of Alabama, and his other labors in the field of medicine, will be given in a somewhat imperfect and concise manner. To do justice to his great genius, and to properly estimate his work in lifting the medical profession from the vale of ignorance to a high plane of intelligence, would require the mental accomplishments and vigorous pen of a McCaulay.

"...By his work, we are now practicing medicine under the finest system of medical legislation in the world. Dr. Cochran was the author of the new constitution of the Medical Association of Alabama that gave it the power to govern the profession of the state. He drew the act 'To Establish the State Board of Health,' which was passed in 1875, constituting the Medical Association of the State of Alabama, the County Medical Societies, the State Board of Censors. ...Holding towards Dr. Cochran feelings of admiration and gratitude for the work he has done for the Medical Association, and entertaining for him personally sentiments of almost filial affection, lest I might be considered partial in my estimation of his work and character, I will take the liberty of quoting the opinion of others. In an obituary notice of Dr. Cochran's death, The Journal of the American Medical Association, among other complimentary things, has this to say of him: 'Dr. Cochran was one of the most active Health Officers of the United States, and a man of phenomenal energy. His long and faithful service to his state, is such, that it can not be overestimated, or excluded from the history of its progress. He had his 'quips and oddities.' What genius has not? But take him all in all, we shall not see his like. His friends, his state, his country and the Association, have suffered a great loss. In the 'Memorial History of Alabama' his biographer speaks thus of him: 'Intellectually, Dr. Cochran was of the most imposing proportions, and was unquestionably one of the most learned men of the South. Nature had endowed him with the capacities of a great scholar. His untiring energy had accumulated a vast amount of information, which his almost matchless memory enabled him to retain, a fine command of language, a chaste and luminous style, aptness of philosophical speculation, large powers of analysis, a self-control which has never disturbed, and self-reliance based on a consciousness of strength, gave him absolute command of his resources, and rendered him at once, an able writer, an instructive and interesting talker, and a consummate master of debate. His pursuit of an object was untiring, and his zeal in whatever he undertook, approached enthusiasm as nearly as his stoical temperament permitted. In debate, his concentration on the matter in hand, and his obliviousness of collateral results, unfortunately betrayed him at times into securing disregard of the feelings of those who opposed his plans. He was firm almost to obstinacy, and unselfish almost to the verge of improvidence. He has been known to persevere in his convictions in regard to important professional interests, and struggle for their ascendance, notwithstanding it involved the alienation of friends, and the sacrifice of private interest with which he could ill afford to part. The great aim of his life in Alabama, was the organization of the medical profession and its investment with legal powers and functions honorable to itself and useful to the state. In this field his great ability gave him an ascendancy and influence in the public counsels of the medical profession which no other man has ever attained.'

"...His was a record that any society can point to with pride. The people of Alabama owe Dr. Cochran a debt of gratitude which can scarcely be estimated, and could they see and appreciate it as this Medical Association does, a monument would be erected to him whose pinnacle would reach to the clouds. But the people of Alabama are not the only beneficiaries of his great work. The reputation of the medical laws of Alabama have extended to distant lands, and our worthy secretary informs me that he has on his letter files, letters from South America, Europe and Australia, seeking information in regard to certain features of our medical system. This is a compliment that should create a feeling of pride in the heart of every member of this association. The last years of Dr. Cochran's life showed the true character of the man. Though in feeble health for several years prior to his death, still his ambition to render faithful service to his profession, to the Association showed no diminution in his almost Herculean labors. Those who attended the last meeting of our Association will remember his feeble condition, and will also remember how nobly he stood at his post and went through the role of his official duties. About four years ago he had an attack of what was supposed to be locomotor ataxia, from which he partially recovered. About a year or more prior to his death, that insidious complaint, Bright's disease[1] began its attack on his constitution, and day by day it encroached nearer and nearer the citadel of life. Yet he would not lessen up on his work. Like a true soldier, he remained at his post of duty. At the close of our last session he took his bed, yet in a very short time the bugle call to duty again sounded, and he rose from his couch, and went to Atlanta, to attend a meeting of the American Medical Association, and came within a few votes, I learn, of being elected president. Again in June, he went to Chicago, against the protests of his physician, to attend a 'Conference of the State Boards of Health.' After his return, on the kind invitation of Dr. Moody, and the advice of his physician, he went to Bailey Springs to rest and test the virtues of those noted waters. Here he remained but a few weeks, and there being no perceptible improvement in his condition, he returned to Montgomery, and on August the 17th, 1896, his great spirit threw off its mortal tenements and winged its flight to realms beyond the stars. In his departure, a great light has been taken from

---

[1]Bright's disease=nonsupperative nephritis with albuminuria and edema; corresponding to the stages of glomerulonephritis now termed acute, subacute, and chronic.

the Counsels of our Association, one that added to its lustre year by year. To say that he will be greatly missed, but feebly expresses the feelings of all who knew his worth. He was a tower of strength to our organization and one upon which we have leaned with confidence for many years. The impress of his noble character will long abide with us, as a fragrant memory of benevolent deeds and faithful duty."[2]

Dr. William Henry Sanders (1838-1918) of Montgomery became Dr. Cochran's successor as State Health Officer. He served from 1896 to 1917. He continued Cochran's quarantine and epidemic control programs. He administered a public health education program and one for health among state prisoners. He promoted sanitary engineering and stimulated interest in county health work. Unlike Cochran, Dr. Sanders was not bashful about asking the State Legislature for funds. In 1902 the annual appropriation was increased to $4,000; by 1911 it was increased to $25,000. He used the increased appropriation to open a pathological and bacteriological laboratory and to appoint a full-time registrar of vital statistics.

At the 1897 annual meeting of the Association, Dr. Barckley Wallace Toole of Talladega, President and Senior Counsellor of the Association, in the Annual Message of the President, stated a firm belief that: "I have dwelt upon the character and the benefits to the profession and to the people of the organization under which we exist to-day, and the importance of sustaining it. If the views thus announced are true, then, as we recognize that it was, to a very large degree, the conception of one man, and developed by him into a strong and symmetrical body, it is proper and just that his name and memory should be preserved; and an enduring memorial be given by the members of that profession, which he did so much to advance, and place upon a plane worthy of its name and aims.

---

[2]Jacob Huggins , M.D.," Eulogy to Dr. Jerome Cochran," *Transactions of MASA, 1897,* pp. 287-94.

Believing that a *great work has been done*, it is but just and commendable that the name and philanthropic deeds of the man, whose brain evolved the system, and then with a will and an energy which was phenomenal, and a spirit which discouragement only made stronger, developed the plan, till now it stands forth as the best of all medical organizations, I recommend that measures be taken at this session to erect a suitable monument to Jerome Cochran, to be placed in one of our cities;..."[3]

At the annual meeting of the Association in Birmingham, April 19-22, 1898, the board of censors recommended that the location of the proposed monument to Dr. Cochran be changed from Selma to Montgomery. "...a far more suitable place in the State for the erection of the proposed monument is in [sic] the Capitol grounds at Montgomery."[4]

In the 1900 annual meeting the monument was again discussed. It was reported that both houses of the General Assembly, in the 1898-99 session, granted the privilege of erecting the monument either in the Capitol building or on the grounds. It was recommended that a full length bronze statue, upon a granite pedestal be commissioned, at an estimated cost of five thousand dollars. To raise this amount, it was decided that the county societies could voluntarily contribute fifteen hundred dollars annually, or by a pro-rated scale according to their numerical strength and financial ability. It was estimated that this could take three years. The report was unanimously adopted, and the committee was instructed to proceed as early as practicable.[5] The committee consisted of Drs. W. H. Sanders, Benjamin J. Baldwin,

---

[3] Barcklay Wallace Toole, M.D. "The Annual Message of the President," *Transactions of MASA, 1897,* p. 34.

[4] John Clark Le Grand, M.D., "The Annual Report of the Senior Vice President," *Transactions of MASA,* 1898, p. 91.

[5] Report of the Committee on Cochran Monument, *Transactions of MASA,* 1900, pp.138-9.

and J. B. Gaston.

The collection of money apparently could not meet the estimated cost [which probably kept going up.] In 1914 WWI intervened. No monument was ever erected.

Dr. Luther Leonidas Hill was President of the Medical Association of Alabama in 1898. He was a fine innovative surgeon, the first to suture a lacerated heart. Dr. Hill is best remembered as the father of United States Senator Lister Hill. The latter was the most knowledgeable lawmaker of either House of Congress regarding the mid-twentieth century health needs of the American people. During his 1898 Message of the President to the Association Dr. Hill proposed:

"We have been under the necessity of mourning the loss of the organizer of this great Association, Dr. Jerome Cochran, and to show the high esteem, veneration and respect with which we cherish his memory I recommend that the future presidents of this Association appoint some eminent medical man, either in Alabama or from a distance, to deliver an address pertaining to medicine, to be known as the 'Jerome Cochran Oration.' This, if possible, should be the first medical paper read."[6]

The Association passed this recommendation. It is given each year at the annual meeting. The first lecture was given by one of Alabama's most illustrious physicians — one who had felt the barbs of Cochran's sarcasm as they opposed each other on "The Alcohol Question," yet who remained Cochran's steadfast friend. It was he who gave the paper the lasting title: The "Jerome Cochran Lecture." His subtitle for that year: "What is Insanity?"

After Cochran's death, his committee on setting up a workable National Department of Public Health seems to have collapsed and no further work was done on the project. One can but speculate on the arrangement of the cooperative venture of Medicine and

---

[6]Luther Leonidas Hill, M.D., "The Annual Message of the President," *Transactions of MASA, 1898*, pp. 20-21.

Government the genius of Cochran might have worked out. This author [Dr. John Morris] feels sure that the Department would be as far separated from politics as possible. The Secretary of Health would be chosen from the highest leadership of the American Medical Association on merit alone without regard to vote-getting or payment for past support. During America's entire history we have been invaded by hostile armies only twice: in the War of 1812 when the Canadians burned Washington; and when the British invaded New Orleans. We have been invaded by disease constantly. Death due to disease is far more likely than death by hostile armies. Cochran was aware of these facts. I think he would have insisted that the Department of Health and the Public Health Service be taken as seriously as the War Department or the State Department.

Nothing more was done about it for another half century, until the present system was set up when President Dwight David Eisenhower appointed Oveta Culp Hobby the first Secretary of Health. Is the present system working? I think Dr. Cochran would have demanded more input by the medical profession. I think it would have been a more viable office with more authority and leadership by the best qualified physicians and health professionals, regardless of political pull or color coordination.

Thus Dr. Jerome Cochran led the medical profession forward. He indicated the paths the profession should follow. He delineated the problems medicine faced at his time and the directions that should be followed in the future. He pointed out the sins of the medical colleges, anticipating the Flexner Committee; he pointed out the value of medical statistics, vital and mortuary; he lauded facts and investigation, and condemned ill-conceived therapeutics that had no rationality; he advised doctors to assert themselves and insist on making all decisions regarding medicine, even governmental decisions. He led the profession up to the twentieth century as Moses led the "Children of Israel" to the promised land, and like Moses, he was not allowed to see the glorious revolution in medicine of the twentieth century except in his prolific imagination which at times seemed to approach the clairvoyant.

The tapestry he wove remains strong and bright, a pattern followed throughout the world. But unfortunately, his name today is all but forgotten.

THE LEGACY

1. A well organized, cohesive, professional medical association with legal and legislative functions.

2. A health department run by experts and with the backing of the medical profession, fully organized, ready for the great changes to come.

3. Strong laws governing the medical profession; the establishment of the boards of medical examiners.

4. Improved medical education. Cochran made the medical colleges more selective as to entrance and graduation of doctors of medicine. (If the Medical College at Mobile had not shown some value, reflecting this goading, it would have been closed completely by the Flexner Committee in 1910. As it was, the Medical College became a first rate two year school, moved onto the campus of the University of Alabama at Tuscaloosa, and later expanded to become the Medical College of Alabama at Birmingham and subsequently the university of Alabama School of Medicine.

5. Improved medical writing: 1st. By providing a first class, well financed (by the state) journal. 2nd. By encouraging members of the Association to write up their cases in the journal. 3rd. By setting a good example with his own writing.

6. Introduced the concept of objectivity in his medical case studies and in his other researches.

7. Introduced the technique of collecting the experiences of a group of doctors on one subject, and studying the results for common denominators. He hoped, in this way, to find the truth. In publishing the experiences of his contemporary physicians, he gave us a marvelous insight into the practice of late nineteenth century Alabama doctors.

8. Led the State and County Health Departments in draining swamps and stagnant water, diminishing the pestilence of the malaria that had destroyed so many Alabama settlements, including at least one State Capitol City (Cahaba).

9. Made and enforced quarantine laws, practically eradicating yellow fever in Mobile, Alabama. (The last epidemic in Mobile was in 1898, two years after Doctor Cochran's death.)

10. Introduced control of the Aedes aegypti mosquito (before he knew that he was doing so) by the use of chlorine gas and burning sulfur as fumigants in ships, houses etc. This was thirty years before Aedes aegypti was found, in 1900 to be the vector of yellow fever.

11. Sought a healthy water supply for the state and its cities and counties and all its citizens.

12. Asked for good vital and mortuary statistics and registration of births and deaths.

13. Introduced laws requiring smallpox vaccination for all school children. The law was passed in 1905, nine years after Dr. Cochran's death.

14. Worked for sanitary facilities for black State convicts. He gave statistics to prove that working in damp mines increased their mortality rate by more than ten fold. He believed that, if the crime committed did not merit the death penalty, that penalty should not be inflicted through the agency of filthy and unsanitary conditions that the prisoner could not control.

15. Led in convincing the surrounding southern states to be honest with each other and share information about quarantinable diseases within their borders. Formerly the various states, and particularly Louisiana, would make every effort to conceal these diseases, especially yellow fever, within their borders.

16. A leader in the Public Health Movement nationally. He was a charter member of the American Public Health Association, which became a powerful force in Public Health in America.

17. As chairman of The National Congress's Subcommittee of Experts on cholera and yellow fever, Cochran wrote the "best treatise on yellow fever ever written"[1]

18. Worked with the American Medical Association and the American Public Health Association to persuade Congress to create a Department of Public Health, with Cabinet status. Cochran died before this could be completed, and a half century later, President Dwight D. Eisenhower created the position and appointed Oveta Culp Hobby as the first Secretary of Health, Education and Welfare.

19. Promoted garbage pickup and filth control, diminishing the spread of typhoid and other enteric fevers.

20. Advised proper ventilation and diminished crowding of housing for the control of pulmonary phthisis (tuberculosis), and other lung diseases.

21. Advised against polluting Alabama's waters: streams, lakes, and ponds. Entirely too much of Alabama's generous water supply has been contaminated with chemicals and sewage. Cochran's advice in this realm has gone virtually unheeded.

22. Jerome Cochran's suggestions, advice and orders were not carried out as well as he would have liked, but they were able to reduce deaths and increase the lifespan of Alabamians a decade or more by the turn of the century. Near the beginning of the twenty-

---

[1]William H. Anderson, " Doctor Jerome Cochran of Alabama," *Representative Men of the South* Philadelphia, Charles Robson & Co. 1880. P. 17.

first century, smallpox is eradicated completely. Yellow fever no longer exists in Alabama. Diphtheria is a rarity. Typhoid fever is rare and quite curable. Tuberculosis had declined greatly, but it seems to be increasing in a form resistant to antibiotics, due to the increasing number of immune compromised patients.

If Dr. Cochran's advice on quarantine and isolation had been carried out today, the AIDS epidemic would be over. As it is, the cases seem to be increasing daily. World wide, this epidemic has reached cataclysmic proportions, and no real relief is in sight!

I have fought a good fight,
I have finished my course,
I have kept the faith.
—II Timothy 4: 7

GLOSSARY

Acetabulum. The socket on each side of the pelvic girdle for the head of the femur.

Actinon. A sea anemone.

Aides Egypt mosquito. This carrier of the yellow fever virus doesn't ordinarily fly more than 200 yards from its breeding area; but it is easy to see how it could be blown a half mile or so in the flat area of Mobile and its environs. The mosquito lives as an adult for only 20-30 days. The female can lay up to 3,000 eggs. These eggs will not hatch in cold weather. When the insect bites an infected person, the yellow fever virus goes through an incubation period of about nine days. It then becomes virulent and remains so for the remainder of the mosquito's lifetime.

Ague. Layman's term for malaria.

Albumen. A protein substance having certain properties, such as solubility in water, precipitability in strong acids, etc.

Alimentary. Pertaining to the digestive tract.

American Public Health Association. The national association founded in 1872 to define and promote public health on a broad national basis. Dr. Jerome Cochran was one of the founders, a charter member.

Amino acid. Organic acids containing the NH2 radical and having certain chemical properties. They enter into the composition of all proteins.

Amoeba. A genus of one celled animals, a protozoan of the class Rhizopoda.

Amphioxus. A primitive fish-like animal belonging to the subphylum Cephalochorda of the Chordata.

Anabolism. The aggregate of constructive processes comprised in metabolism.

Anaesthesia. Loss of feeling or sensitivity. The name given by Dr. Oliver Wendel Holmes to the state of consciousness rendered by ether in the original demonstration by Dr. Morton.

Analogous. Similar in function.

Archenteron. The cavity within the endoderm of a gastrula. It communicates with the exterior.

Aristotle. The most famous of the Greek naturalist philosophers, who lived 384-322 B.C.

Artery. A blood vessel conducting blood from the heart.

Artificial parthenogenesis. The artificial stimulation of an egg to develop without fertilization.

Asexual. Not involving germ cells nor fusion of nuclei; said of reproduction, or an individual employing such a mode of reproduction.

Assimilation. The conversion of digested foods and other raw materials into protoplasmic substances.

Autonomic nervous system. Same as sympathetic and parasympathetic nervous system.

Bilious colic. Abdominal pain accompanied by the passage of bile or of vomiting bile.

Biogenetic law. The doctrine that animals in their embryonic development repeat the evolutionary history of the race. (Haekel's Law).

Blastocele. The hollow interior of a blastula.

Blastula. An early developmental stage, consisting of a hollow ball of cells.

Botanico Medical College of Memphis. Newly chartered in 1846. Their treatment was with herbs and plant products. They did not use calomel or phlebotomy.

Budding. The division of an organism into unequal parts.

Cachectic, cachexia. A profound state of constitutional disorder, ill health, malnutrition and weakness.

Carbolic acid. Phenol. A disinfectant introduced as a spray in the operative field by Lord Joseph Lister 1867.

Cardiac. Pertaining to or near the heart.

Catabolism. The aggregate of destructive processes comprised in metabolism.

Catarrh. Name for inflammation of mucus membranes, especially of nose and throat.

Caudal. Belonging to the tail.

Cell doctrine. The theory that all animals and plants are composed of similar units of structure called cells.

Central nervous system. The brain and spinal cord.

Cerebrospinal fever. Inflammation of the cerebrum and spinal cord, usually by virus or bacteria. (Modern term is cerebro spinal meningitis).

Cervical. Pertaining to the neck.

Chitin. A horny substance forming the outside skeleton of insects and many other animal parts.

Cholera. An acute infectious disease caused by Vibrio cholerae, characterized by severe nausea, vomiting, diarrhea, dehydration, cramps, collapse.

Cleavage. The division or segmentation of an egg.

Coelenterata. The phylum to which Hydra, the hydroids, jellyfishes belong.

Coelom. The true body cavity, a cavity within the mesoderm on the walls of which the principal reproductive organs are located.

Coloid. A mixture in which particles greater in size than molecules are held in suspension in a liquid.

Colony. A group of individuals of the same species organically connected with each other.

Comparative anatomy. The study and comparison made between the anatomical structures of various groups of animals notably the mamalians.

Conjugation. The meeting of two cells for exchange of nuclear material or for complete fusion.

Consumption. Common name for tuberculosis.

Cryptogam. Any of the lower plants that have no true flowers but propagate by spores.

Curare. A substance used by South American natives as arrow poison. It acts by paralysing the motor end plates of nerves. Used in research and in clinical medicine and surgery.

Cyst. Any enveloping structure, usually a secreted membrane.

Cytology. The science which deals with the structure of cells.

Cytoplasm. The protoplasm of a cell exclusive of the nucleus.

Darwin, Charles. (1809-1882). Wide acceptance of the theory of evolution dates from the time of Charles Darwin. He brought together so many facts indicating evolution , together with a theory to account for the facts, which was so plausible that all thinking people were forced to adopt his views.

Deglutition. The act of swallowing.

Dichogamy. The maturing of the male and female germ cells of a hermaphrodite at different times, thus preventing self-fertilizing.

Dioecious. Having the male and female organs in separate individuals.

Diploblastic. Composed of two cell layers.

Division of labor. Distribution of functions among cells, or organs or individuals.

Dorsal. Pertaining to the back ; hence, usually upper.

Dujardin, Felix. French naturalist 1801-1860. Early described protoplasm in lower animals and called it sarcode.

Dysentery. Inflammation of the intestine, especially the colon, with abdominal pain, frequent bowel movements containing blood.

Ectoderm. The outer layer of cells of a gastrula, or the representative of this layer in later stages.

Ehrlich, Paul. (1854-1915), German physician and bacteriologist. Introduced staining techniques for dried blood films. Discovered the first chemotherapeutic agent, salvarsan.

Embryo. An undeveloped animal while still in the egg membrane or in the maternal uterus.

Endemic. Pertaining to or prevalent in a particular region or location.

Endoderm. The inner layer of cells of a grastrula, or the representative of this layer in later stages.

Entomology. The zoology of insects.

Epilepsy. A disease characterized by one or more of the following symptoms: paroxysmal loss of, or impairment of consciousness, involuntary excess or cessation of muscular activity, psychic or sensory disturbances. ·

Epithelium. A layer of cells at the surface of a tissue or organ, or lining a cavity.

Erysipelas. A contagious, infectious disease of skin and subcutaneous tissue, marked by swelling and redness, usually caused by beta hemolytic streptococcus.

Etiological agent. Causative factor, as trauma, or germ, etc.

Fever. Intermittent. Fever coming in paroxysms at three (tertian) or four (quartan) day intervals, as malarial fever. Remittent fever, showing shorter remissions daily, as typhoid fever.

Fistula. An abnormal tract or connection of one hollow viscus with another or to the surface of the skin.

Flexner, Abraham. (1866-1959). As a member of the Carnegie Foundation for the Advancement of Teaching, he was commissioned to research and write *MEDICAL EDUCATION IN THE UNITED STATES AND CANADA*. This study was published in 1910 and was influential in the ultimate reformation of American medical education.

Fomites. Any substance other than foods that may harbor and transmit infectious disease.

Freud, Sigmund. The late Viennese Psychiatrist, originator of the doctrine of psychoanalysis. Chief work was with *the Subconscious, Basic Insecurity, The Neuroses.*

Galen. Famous Greek physician and anatomist, born about 130 A. D. His writings were long the highest authority in medical science.

Gamete. A germ cell, or other cell which fuses with a second cell in reproduction.

Gastrula. That stage in the ontogenetic development of the animal that corresponds to the animals known as coelenterata.

General paresis. Central nervous system infection with Treponema palidum, the microorganism that causes the clinical disease, syphilis. The clinical phenomena of G.P. is that of dementia and generalized muscular weakness. G.P. usually comes on years after the initial infection.

Germ cell. A cell capable of reproduction, or of sharing in reproduction, as contrasted with the somatic or body cells which are sterile.

Habital state. Predisposition or bodily temperament.

Haeckel, Ernst Heinrich. A German Naturalist. Postulated that an individual, in developing from the ovum, goes through the same changes as did the species in going from the lower to the higher forms of life. "Ontogeny recapitulates phylogeny"

Harvey, William. (1578-1657). An English physician and

physiologist who first described the circulation of blood in humans and animals. Wrote, De *Motu Cardis et Sanguinous in Animalibus.*

Hematocele or haematocele. An effusion of blood into a cavity.

Hemolysis. The liberation of hemoglobin from the red blood cells in solution.

Hermaphrodite. An organism possessing both male and female organs. Also (adjective). Possessing the organs of both sexes.

Hexiology. The science of the relation of animals and plants to their environment.

Histology. The science which deals with the structure of tissues.

Homology. Similarity of origin in evolution and hence in the embryo; applied to organs that arise in the same way.

Hooke, Robert. (1635-1703). English natural philosopher and mathematician.

Huxley, Thomas Henry. (1825-1895). Spread Darwin's theory of evolution by his forceful lectures to biologists and to laymen.

Hydra. A small tubular freshwater animal with tentacles and stinging organs, belonging to the phylum Coelenterata. Two species are common H. oligactis, and H. viridissima.

Hydranth. A Hydra-like, tentacle-bearing member of a hydroid colony.

Hygiene. The science of health and its preservation.

Hysterectomy. The operation of removal of the uterus.

Inanition. The condition that results from lack of food and water; lack of vitality and vigor; lethargy.

Incision. A cut or wound.

Jaborandi. A pilocarpine drug extracted from either the leaves of South American shrubs or a Brazilian pepper root.

Kékulé, von Stradonitz, Friedrich August. (1829-1896). German Chemist who established the ring structure of benzine and postulated atomic bonds of which carbon had four. These concepts are essential to the understanding of organic chemistry.

Koch, Robert (1843-1910). German Bacteriologist (Father of bacteriology). Invented methods for isolating and identifying bacteria. Discovered the tubercle bacillus. Awarded the Nobel Prize in 1905.

Larva. A free-living developmental stage of an animal in which certain adult organs are still lacking or in which organs are present that are lacking in the adult.

Leeuwenhoek, Antonius van (1632-1723). Dutch naturalist and microscopist.

Ligation. The application of a ligature, as placing a thread or wire around a vessel and tying it.

Ligature. A thread or wire for tying a vessel.

Lister, Lord Joseph (1827-1912). English surgeon, the father of antiseptic surgery (1867).

Lumbar. Pertaining to the region of the back below the ribs and above the sacrum.

Lymph. A clear fluid containing colorless cells found in lymph vessels. It is essentially blood without its red cells and somewhat diluted.

Malpighi, Marcello (1628-1694). Italian anatomist, founder of microscopic anatomy.

Malthus, Thomas Robert (1766-1834). English political economist, author (1803) of "Essay on Population."

Mammal. A class of vertebrates having hairy bodies, producing young within the body of the mother, and nourishing them after birth with milk secreted by the mother.

Marine Hospitals. Established in 1798 to service seamen. Their medical officers were often the first to diagnose such contagious diseases as yellow fever, cholera and smallpox, which were being imported into the United States. In the great epidemics, the marine hospitals were called on to help treat those patients. Therefore they became the public health hospitals.

Materia medica. That branch of medical study that deals with drugs, their sources, uses and preparations.

Medical jurisprudence. The application of the principles of law and justice as they relate to the practice of medicine and the relations of physicians to each other and to society in general.

Medusa (pl., Medusae). A jellyfish, the free-swimming member of many hydroid species.

Mendel, Gregor (1822-1884). Austrian monk and plant breeder, founder of modern genetics; author of "Mendel's Law" of heredity .

Mesentery. A double sheet of tissue, continuous with the peritoneum, which supports an organ (such as the intestine) from the body wall.

Metabolism. The sum total of the chemical processes going on in protoplasm.

Metagenesis. The occurrence of two or more forms of individual in the same species, one or more of which reproduce asexually and one of which reproduces sexually.

Metamorphosis. The transformation of a larva into an adult.

Metazoon. An animal composed of many cells.

Meyer, Adolph. The first professor of Psychiatry at the Johns Hopkins School of Medicine. Founder of the Mental Health Move ment in America.

Mithridatium. Named for Mithridates, an ancient king of Pontus. It was a mixture of many known poisons, to be taken in small quantities over a period of time to make one immune to the poisons.

Mitosis. Cell division involving the formation of chromosomes, spindle fibers, etc. (karyokinesis).

Morula. The cleaving ovum during the phase when it forms a solid or mulberry like mass.

Neuralgia. Pain from an irritated nerve.

Neuron. A nerve cell.

Olfactory. Pertaining to the sense of smell.

Ontogeny. The complete developmental history of the individual organism.

Oogenesis. The maturation of female germ cells.

Optic nerve. The nerve of sight.

Organism. Any organized body of living economy. A living plant or animal.

Ovariectomy. Surgical removal of the ovary, usually due to disease, such as cyst formation and enlargement.

Paedogenesis (or pedegenesis). Sexual maturity in an animal otherwise immature; the capability possessed by some species of reproducing while in the larval condition.

Palliative. Affording relief but not cure.

Paroxysm. A sudden recurrence; intensification of symptoms.

Parthenogenesis. The development of an egg without fertilization.

Pasteur, Louis (1822-1895). French chemist and bacteriologist Founded the science of microbiology. Developed the technique of vaccinating with attenuated organisms. His discoveries embrace the entire field of microbial activity.

Pelagic. Pertaining to the open water of a lake or ocean, not near the shore nor far below the surface.

Phlebotomy. Opening a vein and removing blood. The old barber surgeons would do this by placing a bowl with a notch in the brim shaped to receive the patient's arm below the elbow. When in place the vein in the elbow was opened by a quick thrust of a lancet, a sharp pointed blade made for that purpose.

Phylogeny. The complete developmental history of a race or group of animals.

Physiognomist. One who studies the facial configuration and expressions to determine the moral and mental traits of the person.

Physiology. The branch of biology which deals with the functions of animals and plants, and the processes going on in them.

Placenta. A vascular tissue dove-tailing into the wall of the uterus on one side and connected with the umbilical cord on the other, thus forming an intimate nutritive connection between the embryo and the mother in viviparous animals.

Plague, bubonic plague, black death. An acute

infectious disease that occurred in epidemic form throughout Europe from ancient times through the seventeenth century.

Plasmodium. The naked mass of protoplasm containing many nuclei, formed by the fusion of many ameboid cells in the Myxomycetes.

Plato (ca.427-347B.C.). A Greek philosopher, Pupil of Socrates and teacher of Aristotle.

Polymorphism. Occurring in many or several forms.

Polyp. One of the feeding individuals of a hydroid or coral colony or simple related form.

Preceptor. A teacher. Used in medical education, it is a senior doctor who takes private students or interns or residents into his office and allows the juniors to observe and work with him on his patients. Usually writing histories etc. It is a time honored method of teaching, much used in the nineteenth century and frequently employed today.

Prophylaxis. The prevention of disease.

Protozoa. One-celled animals. The phylum comprising the one-celled animals, including colonial forms in which the cells of the colony are, at least potentially, all alike.

Pulmonary consumption, pulmonary pthisis.
Pulmonary Tuberculosis.

Purkinge, Jan Evangelista (1787-1869). Bohemian physiologist in the University of Prague.

Pyemia. *(G. Pyon* pus+*haima* blood) infection in which multiple abscesses occur.

Race. A group of individuals having certain characteristics in common because of common ancestry.

Raphé. A ridge or furrow that marks the union of the halves of symmetrical parts.

Regeneration. The production of lost parts by organisms.

Reticulum. A network.

Sarcode. The term first applied to protoplasm by Felix Dujardin.

Schleiden, Matthias (1804-1881). A German botanist, to whom is often attributed a share in the establishment of the cell-theory.

Schwann, Theodor (1810-1882). German physiologist and anatomist, founder of cell theory.

Seton. A skein of silk drawn through a wound to make a fistula.

Smallpox (variola). An acute infectious disease caused by a virus, Borreliota variolae. High mortality. The virus is now almost extinct. Not related to *BIG POX*, a name that referred to syphilis in the early years.

Specific. A drug used for one specific disease. Quinine is a specific for malaria.

Sphincter. A ringlike muscle that closes an orifice.

Spontaneous generation. Same as abiogenesis or "de novo generation".

Steapsin. The fat splitting enzyme of the pancreatic fluid.

Surrogate. A substance used as a substitute for another.

Synapse. The point of contact of two neurones.

Taxis. An orientation of an organism with reference to a stimulus.

Telluric. Pertaining to the earth, or coming from the earth.

Tentacles. Arm-like projections from hydroids, Bryozoa, Nautilus, and other animals.

Therapeutics. The science of healing.

Theriaca. A potion consisting of cut up body parts of 60 to 70 poisonous snakes, frogs, spiders, scorpions, etc. Usually macerated in honey as a vehicle. Taken by mouth, it was supposed to cure the effects of animal poisons. Since illness was presumed to be due to poison, it became used as a shot-gun remedy.

Thompsonians. Followers of Samuel Thompson, who advocated the use of herbal medicines instead of traditional therapies. The herbal medicine movement grew from 1800-1860.

Tincture. An alcoholic solution of a chemical substance.

Tropism. A response of an organism to a stimulus.

Typhoid fever. Infectious disease, frequently coming in epidemics, caused by Salmonella typhosa

Typhus fever (Gaol fever).   An infectious disease frequently transmitted by mice and mice fleas. There are many strains of typhus caused by several strains of Rickettsia.

Unisexual. Involving but one sex, the female; applied to parthenogenetic reproduction.

Ureter. The tube through which urine is conducted from the kidney to the bladder.

Urethra. The passage through which urine is discharged from the bladder.

Urogenital system or genitourinary system. A group of organs concerned with both excretion and reproduction in vertebrates.

Uterus. A modified portion of the Fallopian tube in which the eggs undergo at least part of their development.

Vagina. The passage leading from the uterus to the exterior in many animals. The female copulatory organ.

Vaginal dilator. A device for stretching the vaginal sphincter muscles.

Vaginismus. Painful spasm of the vagina due to local hyperesthesia.

Vagus. Tenth cranial nerve.

Vein. A vessel that conveys blood from the capillary bed to the heart.

Ventricle. The large muscular chambers of the heart that propel blood through the main arteries and connecting vessels.

Ventral. Pertaining to the belly, usually, lower.

Virchow, Rudolf (1821-1902). A German pathologist and physiologist.

Woodworth, John M. Appointed by the President, he was the first Director of the Marine Hospital Service.

Zygote. A cell or individual produced by the fusion of two cells or their nuclei in the process of sexual reproduction.

Zymotic maladies. Any infectious or contagious disease.

BIBLIOGRAPHY—A ARTICLES

"Alabama's Famous Health Officer Passes After a Long Illness." *The Birmingham Age Herald.,* Birmingham, Aug. 18, 1896.

Brace, C. Loring, Ph.D. "The Ethnology of Josiah Clark Nott." *Bull N.Y. Accad. Med.* Vol 50, No.4, April 1974. Pp. 509-528.

Cannon, D.L. "Jerome Cochran, The South's First Gift to Public Health." *Southern Medical Journal.* 29:1187, 1936.

Carmichael, Emmett B. "Early Alabama Physicians." *J.M.A. Alabama Vol. 28,* No.3.

——. "Jerome Cochran: The Guiding Genius in Public Health Legislation in Alabama." *The American Surgeon. Vol. 25, No.6,* June, 1959.

Cochran, J. "The Medical Profession." *Memorial Record of Alabama Vol. 2,* Chap.VIII: p. 107. Madison , Wisconsin: Brant and Fuller, 1893.

——. "Report of the Committee Appointed by the American Medical Association to Act in Conjunction with a Committee of   the American Public Health Association." *J.A.M.A.,* 22: 954, 1894.

——. (Chairman of Committee). "Report of the Committee on Department of Public Health." *J.A.M.A.,* 26:988, 1896.

——. "Address on Medical Education." *Tranactions of the Medical Association of the State of Alabama,* 1870, pp. 171-78.

——. "Public Hygiene." *Transactions of the Medical Association of the State of Alabama.* 1876, pp. 18-27.

——. "Yellow Fever & Its Cause." *Transactions of the Medical Association of the State of Alabama,* 1873, pp. 129-57.

——. "The Yellow Fever Epidemic of 1873." *Transactions of the Medical Association of the State of Alabama,* 1874, pp. 112-174.

——. "The White Blood-Corpuscle in Health & Disease." *Transactions of the Medical Association of the State of Alabama* 1874, pp. 204-255.

——. "The Theory and Practice of Quarantine." *Transactions of the Medical Association of the State of Alabama,* 1880, pp. 336-385.

——. "Sketches of Yellow Fever on the Gulf Coast of Florida." *Transactions of the Medical Association of the State of Alabama.*1881,   pp. 451-487.

——. "The Therapeutic Uses of Quinine in Alabama." *Transactions of the Medical Association of the State of Alabama.* 1883, pp. 266-345.

——. "The Alcohol Question," *Transactions of the Medical Association of the State of Alabama.* 1883, pp .358-423.

——. "Hemorrhagic Malarial Fever." *Transactions of the Medical Association of the State of Alabama.* 1884, pp. 495-615.

——. "The Value of Vital and Mortuary Statistics." *Transactions of the Medical Association of the State of Alabama.* 1887, pp. 335-359.

——. "The Medical Profession." *Memorial Record of Alabama,* Vol. 2 pp. 107-140.

Cochran, Dr. Jerome, "Obituary." *Mobile Daily Register. August* 18, 1896.

Cochran, Jerome to NBH, Memphis, Tennessee, August 10, 1879, NBH Correspondence, Inspectors Report 1644; Cochran to NBH, New Orleans , Louisiana , September 6, 1879, *ibid.* 2162.

Cochran, S. Vadah. Personal Correspondence October, 1993.

——. Personal Correspondence, Dec. 23, 1993.

"Conclusions of the Board of Experts ," New York *Times,* January 31, 1879, pp. 21, 23, 26.

Deupree, J.G.(Professor University of Mississippi). "First Mississippi Cavalry." *Publication of the Mississippi Historical Society IV, pp.* 47-61.

Gill, D.G. "The Father of Alabama's Department of Health."*Journal of the Alabama State Medical Association.* 18:53, 1948.

Gregg, Mary. *Genealogy of the Cochran Family of Marshall County, Mississippi.* Typewritten Manuscript.

Hudgins, Jacob. "Memorial Service to Dr. Cochran." *Transactions of the Medical Association of the State of Alabama.* 1897, pp. 287-294.

"Insurance Man Dies Tuesday." (Jerome Bowling Cochran). *The Houston Post.* Wed., July 2, 1924.

Johnston John, to NBH, Memphis, Tennessee, August 13, 1879, NBH Correspondence , State Report 1581; J.D. Plunkett to NBH Nashville, Tennessee, August 11, 1879, *ibid,* 1489.

Mitchell, R. W. to NBH, Memphis, Tennessee, July 18, 1879, NBH Correspodence Undesignated Communication 816; Mitchell to NBH, Memphis Tennessee, August 2, ibid 1334; NBH to J. D. Plunkett [in Nashville], Washington, D. C. , August 6, 1879, Letters I, 299-90.

"Mobilian Became Alabama's First State Health Officer." *Mobile Press,* Jan. 15, 1947.

Morris, John T. "Josiah Clark Nott and the Heroic Age of Alabama Medicine." *Alabama Medicine, Vol. 62, No.7.* January, 1993.

——. "Beyond the River." *Alabama Medicine. Vol.63, No. 1.* July 1993.

——. "Alabama Quartet." *Alabama Medicine, Vol. 62, No. 4* Oct.. 1992.

Minutes of the Executive Committee, National Board of Health, I, 1, April 2, 1879, pp. 4-5, RG 90, National Archives.

NBH Bulletin, I (1879-80), Supplement 2, NBH Annual Report, 1879, p. 4-5.

NBH to Mitchell, Washington D.C., August 21, 1879, Letters I, 376-7.

"Near Invalid Fathered Alabama Public Health." *The Birmingham News,* May 13, 1951.

New Orleans *Picayune*, November 23, 1878.

"Obituary of Cochran J." *Journal. of the American Medical Association, 27:448,* 1896.

"Reorganization of the Ala. State Med. Ass'n." *The Selma Times &*

Messenger, Selma, AL. March 4,5,6, 1868.

Resolution of the Sanitary Council of the MississippiValley to Congress, May 5, 1879, House Select Committee on Epidemic Disease, 46 Congress, First Session. HR 46A-H26., National Archives.

Riggs, Benjamin A. "Annual Oration." *Transactions of MASA.* April 1878. p. 172.

Rodning, Charles B. "Medical College of Alabama in Mobile: Legacy of J.C. Nott." *Birmingham: Journal. of the Southern Medical Association, Vol. 82, No. 1,* Jan. 1989, pp. .53-63.

TRANSACTIONS OF THE MEDICAL ASSOCIATION OF THE STATE OF ALABAMA, 1860-1900.

"Yellow Fever Heroes." *Journal of the Medical Association of the State of Alabama., 1:168,* Oct. 1931.

BIBLIOGRAPHY—B BOOKS

Anderson, William H. "Doctor Jerome Cochran of Alabama" *Representative Men of the South.* Philadelphia, Penn.: Charles Robson and Company. 1880.

Atkinson, W.B. *Physicians and Surgeons of the United States,* Philadelphia, Penn.: Charles Robson & Co. 1878, p. 228.

Baker, Rachel. *The First Woman Doctor*, New York: Messner, 1944.

Bloom, Khaled J. *The Mississippi Valley's Great Yellow Fever Epidemic of 1878.* Baton Rouge: Louisiana State University Press. 1993.

Bruton, Peter W. *The National Board of Health.* Vol. I, II. Ph. D. Dissertation. University of Maryland. 1974.

Bordley & Harvey, *Two Centuries of American Medicine.* Philadelphia, London, Toronto: W.B. Saunders Co. 1976.

"Constitution and Bylaws." *MASA Pictorial Membership Roster.* 1996. pp. 387-400.

Cumming, Kate. *The Journal of a Confederate Nurse.* Baton Rouge: Louisiana State University Press. 1959.

Cumming, Kate. *A Journal of Hospital Life in the Confederate Army of Tennessee.* Louisville, KY: John P. Morton & Co. 156 West Main Street. 1866.

Cunningham, H. H. *Doctors in Gray: The Confederate Medical Service.* Gloucester, Mass.: Louisiana State University Press. Peter Smith. 1970.

Deupree, J.G. "The Capture of Holly Springs Dec. 20, 1862" *Vol. IV. Oxford, Miss.: Miss. Historical Soc. Publications.* 1901.

Eichold, Samuel. *History of Medicine, Vol. I* (Senior Elective) U.S.A. Med. Univ of South Alabama, College of Medicine. Self Published. 1987.

Evans, Gen., C.A. *Confederate Military History, Vol. XII* Secaucus, N.J. 07904: Blue and Gray Press. 1899.

Ferguson, Kitty. *Stephen Hawking, Quest for a Theory of Everything.* New York. Bantam Books. August,1992.

Fleming, Donald. *William H. Welch and the Rise of Modern Medicine.* Edited by Oscar Handlin. Boston: Little, Brown and Company, 1954.

Fleming, Walter L. *Civil War and Reconstruction in Alabama.* Cleveland: Arthur H. Clark Co. 1911.

Foote, Shelby. Vol. 1 *The Civil War, a Narrative. Fredericksburg to Meridian.* 3 vols. New York, N.Y. U.S.A.: Vintage Bks. Div. of Random House. 1986.

Garrison, Fielding H. *An Introduction to the History of Medicine.* Philadelphia and London: W. B. Saunders Co. 1914.

Hamilton, Virginia Van der Veer. *Alabama, A History.* New York, London: W.W. Norton & Company. 1984.

Hamilton, William B. *Holly Springs, Mississippi to the Year 1878.* Holly Springs, Miss.: Marshall County Historical Society. 1984.

Harris, Joel Chandler. *Life of Henry W. Grady, Including His Writings and Speeches.* New York: Cassell Publishing Company. 1890.

Hawking, Stephen W. *A Brief History of Time.* A Bantam Book. April, 1988.

Hippocrates & Galen. *Hippocratic Writing and On the Natural Faculties by Galen.* Chicago, London, Toronto, Geneva: Encyclopedia Britannica, Inc. William Benton, Publisher. 1952.

Holly, Howard L. *The History of Medicine in Alabama.* P.O. Box 2877, University, Alabama 35486: The University of Alabama Press. 1982.

Humphreys Margaret. *Yellow Fever and the South.* Ph. D. Disseration. Harvard. 1983. New Brunswick, N. J. Rutgers University Press.1992.

Johnston, Mary Tabb. *Amelia Gayle Gorgas, A Biography.* University, Alabama: The University of Alabama Press. 1978.

Jones, Francis Arthur. *Thomas Alva Edison.* New York: Thomas Y. Crowell & Co. 1908.

Kelly & Burrage Obit. *Dictionary of American Medical Biography.* New York, N.Y.: D. Appleton & Co. 1928.

Kelly, H.A. *A Cyclopedia of American Medical Biography.* Philadelphia, Penn.: W.B. Saunders Co. 1912.

Martin, David G., *The Shiloh Campaign.* New York: Fairfax Press. 1987.

McNeill, William H., *Plagues and People.* Montecello Editions, New York: History Book Club. 1976.

McSherry, Frank Jr. *Civil War Women.* New York, N.Y.: Touchstone: Simon & Schuster. 1990.

Memorial Record of Alabama. Vol. I. Philadelphia, PA: Charles Robson & Co. 1880.

Memorial Record of Alabama. Vol II. Madison, Wisconsin: Brant & Fuller. 1893.

Miller, J. *Moving the Wounded: Litters, Cacolets & Ambulance, Wagons.* P.O. Box 2243, Ft. Collins, CO 80523: The Old Army Press. 1979.

Mobile City Directory. 1874.

Montgomery County Directory. 1885.

Mosby's Nursing Drug Reference. St. Louis: The C.V. Mosby Company . 1988.

Owen, Thomas McAdory. *History of Alabama and Dictionary of Alabama Biography.* Vol. 3. Chicago. S.J. Clark Publishing Company. 1921.

Packard, F.R. *History of Medicine in the United States.* New York, N.Y.: Paul B. Hoeber, Inc. 1931 p. 829.

Pryor, Elizabeth Brown. *Clara Barton, Professional Angel.* Philadelphia.: University of Pennsylvania Press. 1993.

Record, James. *A Dream Come True, The Story of Madison County.* Huntsville, Alabama: James Record, Publisher. 1970.

Reynolds Historical Lectures 1980-1997. Edited by Marion G. McGuinn, Curator of the Reynolds Historical Library. Birmingham: The University of Alabama at Birmingham. 1993.

Rogers, Ward, Atkins and Flynt. *Alabama: The History of a Deep*

South State. Tuscaloosa and London: The University of Alabama Press. 1994.

Rowland, Dunbar. *History of Mississippi, The Heart of the South.* Chicago-Jackson: The S.J. Clarke Publishing Co. 1925.

Sanders, W. H., M.D. State of Health Officer. The History, Philosophy, and Fruits of Medical Organization in Alabama. Read before MASA at its annual meeting in 1914. : 1914.

Selwyn-Brown. *The Physician Throughout the Ages.* New York, N.Y.: Capehart-Brown Co., Inc. 1928.

Shryock, Richard H. *Medicine in America, Historical Essays.* Baltimore, Maryland: Johns Hopkins Press. 1966.

Steiner, Paul E. *Medical Military Portraits.* : 1968.

Stone, R.F. *Biography of Eminent American Physicians and Surgeons.* Indianapolis, Indiana: Carlon & Hollenbeck. 1894.

War of Rebellion: A Composite of Official Records, Union & Confederate. Washington, D.C.: Government Printing Office. 1886.

Watson, I.A. *Physicians & Surgeons of America.* Concord, N.H.: Republican Press Association. 1896.

United States Census 1840.

United States Census 1850—1870.

BIBLIOGRAPHY — C OTHER REFERENCES

Correspondence:
Cochran, S. Vadah. Personal Correspondence with Dr. John
    Morris, October, 1993.
Cochran, S. Vadah. Personal Correspondence with Dr. John
    Morris, December, 1993.
Letter from Dr. F.A. Ross, President of MASA, to Dr. Cochran
    Transactions of MASA. 1871. p. 14.
Letter from Dr. Cochran to Dr. Ross. *Transactions of MASA*.
    1871. pp. 14-15.

Genealogy:
Gregg, Mary Owen Sapp. *Genealogy of the Cochran Families
    of Marshall County, Mississippi.*

Newspaper Articles:
Mobile Daily Register: "Obituary." Dr. Jerome Cochran.
    Mobile, Alabama. August 18, 1896.
Mobile Press: "Mobilian Became Alabama's First State
    Health Officer." Article on Dr. J. C. Nott.
    Mobile, Alabama. January 15, 1947.
New Orleans Picayune: November 23, 1878.
New York *Times*: "Conclusions of the Board of Experts."
    January 31, 1879. pp. 21, 23, 26.
New York *Times*: Other articles pertinent to the National
    Board of Health as referred to in this biography:
    June 20-25, 1879; July 11, 1879.
The Birmingham Age Herald: "Alabama's Famous Health
    Officer Passes After a Long Illness." Article on
    Dr. Jerome Cochran. Birmingham, Alabama.
    August 18, 1896.
The Birmingham News: "Near Invalid Fathered Alabama Public
    Health." Article on Dr. Jerome Cochran. Birmingham,
    Alabama. May 13, 1951

The Houston Post: "Insurance Man Dies Tuesday." Obituary
    of Jerome Bowling Cochran. Houston, Texas.
    July 2, 1924.
The Selma Times & Messenger: "Reorganization of the Alabama
    State Medical Association." Selma, Alabama.
    March 4,5,6, 1868.

Records:
Congressional Records of the United States. National
    Archives and Record Service.
    1. Resolution of the Sanitary Council of the
       Mississippi Valley to Congress: House Select
       Committee on Epidemic Disease. 46th Congress,
       First Session, HR 46-H26. May 5, 1879.
    2. Resolution of the City of Montgomery, Alabama
       to Congress: House Select Committee on Epidemic
       Disease. 46th Congress, Second Session, HR16A-H26.
       May 24, 1880.
Marine Hospital Service XXXVIII: Letters 1882-83; Circular -
    "Compliance with Local Health Laws," Washington, D.C.
    1882.
Military Annals of Mississippi, Compiled by J. C. Rietti of
    the 10th Regiment, Jackson, Mississippi, Washington
    Guards, Organized at Holly Springs, Mississippi,
    May 10, 1861, for home protection.
National Board of Health 1879-1893. National Archives and
    Record Service. Record Group 90: Bulletin;
    Minutes April, 1879 - July, 1882; Letters I,
    Letters II, Undesignated correspondence -
    subdivided into 37 different subject headings.
    Found as looseleaf collections, and unbound
    manuscripts. Also preserved on microfilm reel #753.

APPENDIX # 1A

After careful consideration of the whole subject we are of the opinion that the Association should accept the provisions of the bill in the form in which it passed the General Assembly.

A copy of the bill in this form is here subjoined:

AN ACT TO ESTABLISH BOARDS OF HEALTH IN THE STATE OF ALABAMA.

SECTION 1. *Be it enacted by the General Assembly of the State of Alabama,* That the Medical Association of the State of Alabama, organized in accordance with the provisions of the Constitution, which was adopted by said Association at its annual meeting, in the city of Tuscaloosa, in March, 1873, be and is hereby constituted the Board of Health of the State of Alabama.

SECTION 2. *Be it further enacted,* That the Board of Health of the State of Alabama, thus established, shall take cognizance of the interests of health and life among the people of the State; shall investigate the causes and means of prevention of endemic and of epidemic diseases; shall investigate the influences of localities and employments upon the public health; shall from time to time make to the General Assembly such suggestions as to legislative action as in their judgment may seem advisable; and shall be, in all ways, the medical advisors of the State.

SECTION 3. *Be it further enacted,* That such Board of Health of Alabama shall make to the Governor for transmission to the General Assembly an annual report of their investigations and transactions; of which annual report there shall be annually published, as other reports transmitted through the Governor to the General Assembly, a sufficient number of copies for distribution among the members of the General Assembly, and the members of the Board of Health of the State of Alabama, and such additional numbers as may be deemed advisable for the purpose of exchanging for the reports of similar Associations in other States.

SECTION 4. *Be it further enacted,* That the County Medical Societies, in affiliation with the Medical Association of the State of Alabama, and organized in accordance with the provisions of the Constitution of the said Association, as described in the first section of this act, be and are hereby constituted Boards of Health for their respective counties; and, as such, shall be under the general direction of the Board of Health of the State of Alabama, created by the first section of this act.

SECTION 5. *Be it further enacted,* That the County Boards of Health, thus established, shall have only advisory powers, and shall be conducted without expense to the State or to their respective counties, except under the conditions provided for under the sixth section of this act, which here follows:

SECTION 6. *Be it further enacted,* That the competent legal authorities of any county in this State, or of any incorporated town or city of any such county, shall, whenever in their judgment it becomes expedient to do so, proceed to invest the Board of Health of the county, with such executive powers and duties for the promotion of the public health, and under such rules and stipulations as shall be agreed upon between the two parties.

SECTION 7. *Be it further enacted,* That in any such agreement, as is contemplated in section six of this act, the right to elect or appoint the officers and servants employed in the administration of the sanitary regulations so agreed upon shall, in all cases, be reserved to the Board of Health; and further, that all questions relating to salaries, appropriations, and expenditures, shall be reserved to the legal authorities of the county, town, or city, as the case may be.

SECTION 8. *Be it further enacted,* That no Board of Health, or advisory, or executive medical body of any name or kind for the exercise of public health functions, shall be established by authority of law in any county, town, or city of this State, except such as are contemplated by the provisions of this act, the object of this prohibition being to secure a uniform system of sanitary supervision throughout the State. But nothing in this article shall be so construed as to prevent any of the Boards of Health created by section four of this act from accepting and executing any special powers that may be granted them by the General Assembly of the State; *Provided,* That this act may be changed, modified, or repealed at any time, at the pleasure of the General Assembly of this State.

Approved February 19th, 1875.

STATE OF ALABAMA,   }
OFFICE OF SECRETARY OF STATE. }

I, R. K. Boyd, Secretary of State of the State of Alabama, do hereby certify that the foregoing act entitled An act to establish Boards of Health in the State of Alabama, approved February 19th, 1875, is a true and correct copy of the original now on file in this office.

Given under my hand and the Great Seal of the State, affixed at Montgomery, this 15th day of April, A. D., one thousand eight hundred and seventy-five, and of the independence of the United States of America the ninety-ninth year.

(Signed)

R. K. BOYD,
Secretary of State.

In order to facilitate the action of the Association in reference to this matter we have prepared the following resolutions, and respectfully recommend their adoption:

Resolved, That the Medical Association of the State of Alabama hereby accept for themselves and for the County Medical Societies under their jurisdiction the provisions of an act entitled An act to establish Boards of Health in the State of Alabama, and approved by the Governor on the 19th day of February, A. D. 1875; and will endeavor to discharge the duties assigned to them in said act in good and with earnest purpose, to be of service to the people of Alabama.

Resolved further, That a copy of these resolutions, properly certified by the President and the Secretary of the Association, be transmitted to the Governor of the State.

If the Association, in accordance with our recommendation, should accept the terms of agreement authorized by the State, then at once several questions of practical importance present themselves for solution.

We must decide, for example, whether we ought to expect the State to defray the expenses of publishing the Transactions of our present session; and whether the Transactions of our present session should be designated in its subordinate title as the report of the State Board of Health.

We are unhesitatingly of the opinion that both of these questions must be answered in the negative—that the Association does not, in fact, become the State Board of Health until it has made formal acceptance of the terms of agreement and notified the State accordingly.

Still further, if we accept the terms and undertake to discharge the functions of the Board of Health of the State, we must proceed to what specific duties the discharge of these functions devolves upon us, and what special action is necessary for their execution. In other words, we must decide what we are to do, and how we are to do it.

3

APPENDIX # 1B

ACTS

OF THE

GENERAL ASSEMBLY OF ALABAMA,

PASSED AT THE

SESSION OF 1876-7,

HELD IN

THE CITY OF MONTGOMERY,

COMMENCING 3D MONDAY IN NOVEMBER, 1876.

GEO. S. HOUSTON, Governor.
R. W. COBB, President of the Senate.
N. N. CLEMENTS, Speaker of the House.

MONTGOMERY, ALA.:
BARRETT & BROWN, STATE PRINTERS.
1877.

No. 63.] '   AN ACT   [s. b. 199.

To regulate the practice of medicine in the State of Alabama.

Practice of irregular system of medicine prohibited.

SECTION 1. *Be it enacted by the General Assembly of Alabama,* That no person except those proposing to practice some irregular system of medicine, shall be permitted to practice medicine in any of its branches or departments as a profession and means of livelihood, in this State, without having obtained a certificate of qualification from some authorized board of medical examiners, as hereinafter provided.

Dipl'ma or certificate of qualifications required.

SEC. 2. *Be it further enacted,* That no person shall be permitted to practice any irregular system of medicine in any of its branches or departments as a profession or means of livelihood, in this State, without having obtained a diploma or certificate of qualification in anatomy, physiology, chemistry and the mechanism of labor, from some authorized board of medical examiners, as hereinafter provided.

Const'tution of boards of medical examiners.

SEC. 3. *Be it further enacted,* That the board of censors of the Medical Association of the State of Alabama, organized according to the constitution of the said Medical Association of the State of Alabama, which was adopted at its annual meeting, at the city of Tuscaloosa, in March, 1873, and the boards of censors of the several county medical societies, which are in affiliation with the said Medical Association of the State of Alabama, and organized in accordance with the provisions of the constitution just mentioned, be and are hereby constituted the authorized board of medical examiners referred to in the first section of this act.

Standard of qualifications determined by State medical association.

SEC. 4. *Be it further enacted,* That the standard of qualifications required of persons desiring to practice medicine in this State, together with the rules for the government of the authorized boards of medical examiners, shall be such as may be determined, from time to time, by the said Medical Association of the State of Alabama, in accordance with the provisions of its said constitution of 1873.

Dipl'ma or certificate officially endors'd under county seal by probate judge.

SEC. 5. *Be it further enacted,* That every diploma or certificate of qualification authorizing any person to practice medicine in this State, which shall be issued by any authorized board of medical examiners, shall be presented to the probate judge of the county in which said person resides, who shall officially endorse the same and seal it with the seal of the county, and who shall also cause a full and fair copy of the same to be made in a well bound book, to be kept for that purpose, and called the register of licensed practitioners of medicine, and for this service he shall be entitled to a fee of one dollar; *Provided*, That said Medical Association, nor any board of censors in affiliation with it, shall be allowed to charge any fee for any diploma or certificate of qualification which may be granted by it.

SEC. 6. *Be it further enacted*, That any person practicing medicine in this State in violation of any of the provisions of this act, shall be guilty of a misdemeanor, and upon conviction thereof before any court having competent jurisdiction, shall be fined in the sum of not more than one hundred for every such offense, and if the fine so imposed be not immediately paid, said person shall be imprisoned in the county jail for not more than one year for every such offense.

SEC. 7. *Be it further enacted*, That all persons who shall be legally engaged in the practice of medicine in any county of this State before the organization of the board of medical examiners in said county, all persons who at any time have been legally engaged in the practice of medicine in this State, and who are now authorized to practice medicine in this State, shall be entitled to the certificate of the board of medical examiners and to be inscribed in the register of licensed practitioners of medicine without examination as to qualification.

SEC. 8. *Be it further enacted*, That the provisions of this act shall take effect in any county of this State whenever the board of medical examiners for said county shall have been organized, as hereinbefore provided, and the fact of such organization officially communicated to the probate judge of said county by the board of censors of the Medical Association of the State.

SEC. 9. *Be it further enacted*, That none of the provisions of this act shall apply to females who now are or may hereafter be engaged in the practice of midwifery; *Provided*, Said females practice no other branch of or department of medicine.

SEC. 10. *Be it further enacted*, That all laws and parts of laws in conflict with the provisions of this act be and

6

the same are hereby repealed, and this act shall be in
force from and after its passage.
Approved February 9, 1877.

APPENDIX #1C

REPORT OF THE SENIOR CENSOR ON THE ROLL OF COUNSELLORS.

At the Annual Session of the Association in Tuscaloosa, last year, a resolution was adopted in the terms following, namely :

Resolved, That in order to determine the composition of the House of Counsellors, Dr. Jerome Cochran, as Senior Censor of the Association, be requested to address a Circular Letter to all who are now eligible for permanent membership under the old Constitution, explaining the conditions upon which they may become Counsellors under the new Constitution. All who elect to accept the position of Counsellor to forward their names to the Senior Censor for registration on the Roll of Counsellors ; and to forward to Dr. W. C. Jackson, the Treasurer of the Association, the fees for the current year, if not already paid.

I have now to report that I have complied with the instructions of this resolution, and that the following named gentlemen have signified to me their willingness to accept the position of Counsellor, with its duties and responsibilities, namely :

Dr. WILLIAM HENRY ANDERSON, Mobile.

Dr. J. S. BANKSON, Stevenson.

Dr. HENRY W. BASSETT, Huntsville.

Dr. WILLIAM D. BIZZELL, Gainesville.

Dr. PETER BRYCE, Tuscaloosa.

Dr. J. P. BURKE, Meridionville.

Dr. JEROME COCHRAN, Mobile.

Dr. WILLIAM C. CROSS, Cherokee.

Dr. CALVIN A. CROW, Moulton.

Dr. JOHN J. DEMENT, Huntsville.

Dr. WILLIAM DESPREZ, Tuscumbia.

Dr. LOUIS W. DESPREZ, Russellville.

Dr. EDMOND H. FOURNIER, Mobile.

Dr. EDMUND PENDLETON GAINES, Mobile

Dr. JOHN TAYLOR GILMORE, Mobile.

Dr. RHETT GOODE, Mobile.

Dr. JAMES GUILD, Tuscaloosa.

Dr. WILLIAM HESTER, Tuscaloosa.

Dr. Samuel Henry Hill, Carrolton.

Dr. Wyatt Hollingsworth, Mobile.

Dr. Walter Clarke Jackson, Montgomery.

Dr. Robert D. Jackson, Selma.

Dr. William A. Johnson, Uniontown.

Dr. John David Johnson, Livingston.

Dr. Mortimer H. Jordan, Birmingham.

Dr. George A. Ketchum, Mobile.

Dr. George Ernest Kumpe, Leighton.

Dr. James Kyle, Florence.

Dr. John Little, Jr., Tuscaloosa.

Dr. Albert Gallatin Mabry, Selma.

Dr. Nicholas P. Marlowe, Tuscaloosa.

Dr. Adam Alexander McKittrick, Evergreen.

Dr. John B. McMillan, Evergreen.

Dr. Edward Davies McDaniel, Camden.

Dr. Richard Fraser Michel, Montgomery.

Dr. Gratz A. Moses, Mobile.

Dr. Goronwy Owen, Mobile.

Dr. Francis M. Peterson, Greensboro.

Dr. A. J. Reese, Mobile.

Dr. Benjamin Hogan Riggs, Selma.

Dr. Frank Armstrong Ross, Mobile.

Dr. Lewis H. Sadler, Leighton.

Dr. Edward Armisted Semple, Montgomery.

Dr. Samuel Parrish Smith, Prattville.

Dr. Thomas O. Summers, Jr., Greensboro.

Dr. Caleb Toxey, Mobile.

Dr. Job Sobiesky Weatherly, Montgomery.

Dr. Robert Dickens Webb, Livingston.

This makes in all a list of forty-eight names.

The Publishing Committee are mistaken, along with the Treasurer, as to the accidental omission from the roll of the names of Dr. R. Searcy, and Dr. G. M. Arnold. I made the omissions intentionally. Dr. Searcy declined to accept the position, and Dr. Arnold had removed to the city of New York before the roll was prepared. There is a mistake in the name of Dr. Hill, of Carrollton, in the published Roll. The correct initials are S. H., for Samuel Henry, not S. F.

I may add that I took a great deal of trouble in the discharge of the duty

APPENDIX # 2 The Genealogy of the Cochran Family of Marshall County, Mississippi.

For centuries the Cochrans have thrived in Northern Ireland and Scotland, some having attained high positions of leadership. They had adapted well to the climate and politics of that region until they tangled with Oliver Cromwell. The drastic and cruel policies of Cromwell caused permanent hatred on the part of the Irish for the Englishmen. North Ireland supported James II in the battle of the Boyne River in 1690. After this battle proved to be a fiasco and Ireland had become a "slave state", that hatred for the English continued. With further atrocities inflicted on the region by William of Orange, the situation in Northern Ireland became untenable, and we find many citizens of the region emigrating to America. In North Ireland and adjacent Scotland, the Cochrans had lived in the same region for centuries. In America they moved freely about the land, but continued to practice their clannish ways as far as possible. At about this time two brothers Cochran made their way to Philadelphia. One remained in Pennsylvania to establish the Northern branch of the Cochran family. The other moved into Virginia and his progeny has effectively covered the Southern States of America., benefitting themselves and the region. Among this southern progeny was Samuel Cochran, whose date of birth was probably before 1744. Samuel Cochran appears on the tax list of Cornwall Parish in 1764. Cornwall Parish was that area of Lunenburg County that was cut off to form Charlotte County, Virginia, in 1765. It is in Charlotte County that we find the first traces of Samuel Cochran. On July 10, 1766, he received a grant of 281 acres of land on Horn-snake Branch in Charlotte County.
So, sometime before Feb. 6, 1779. Samuel moved his family to Bedford County, Virginia, the next county westward from Charlotte county. There, on this date, James Davidson, Jr. obtained a license to marry Janet Cochrane (sic.), her parents, Samuel and Mary (or Marah) Cochran, giving their consent.. Surety was James Davidson, Sr. If Janet were the oldest child of Samuel and Mary , and if she were at least 15 years old at the time of her marriage, then her

father, Samuel, must have been not younger than 35 years old in 1779, therefore born not later than about 1744. On August 23, 1779, David Davidson received license to marry Elizabeth Cochran with consent of her father, Samuel Cochran. James Davidson was security.

Samuel Cochran cut his ties to Bedford County, Virginia on September 6, 1779, when he sold the 281 acres of land that he had received as a grant there in 1766. The buyer was Thomas Sowell. Mary, wife of Samuel Cochran relinquished her right of dower. The Samuel Cochran family was now firmly established in Charlotte County, but not for long. In 1781-1782 Campbell County, Virginia was formed from the eastern end of Charlotte County and Samuel and Mary Cochran's land fell into the new county. We know from Samuel's will that at the time of his death, he still owned land in Campbell County, Virginia. No further record of the land is available.

Little is known of the Cochran's activities during the American Revolutionary War. Several Cochrans are listed among the troops. We do know that Samuel's sympathies were with the American forces. On June 6, 1782, Samuel Cochran proved that he had provided rope during the Revolutionary War to Christopher Irvine, Commissary of Provisions, and this patriotic service established the eligibility of his descendants for membership in the Daughters of the American Revolution.

On the move again, by February 9, 1785, the family of Samuel Cochran had moved to Georgia. On that date, Samuel received a grant of 200 acres of land in Wilks County, Georgia. Samuel's family lived on this land , which fell into Oglethorpe County when it was created in 1793, until his death in either 1791 or 1792. He made his will in 1791, making bequests to his wife Marah (sic.) and to his children Elizabeth, Jennet, Thomas, John, Samuel, William, and Micajah. He nominated his son John and "my friend Benjamin Baldwin" to act with his wife as executors. Baldwin did not accept the trust, and in July of 1791 John Cochran and Mary (Marah) Cochran qualified as executors, with John MuckleRoy (or McElroy?) as their security.

In 1796, Mary, William and Samuel Cochran appeared on the tax lists of the new county, Oglethorpe. After that date Mary was no longer listed. Mary had either died or remarried. There is no record of remarriage. She probably died in 1796 or 1797. Apparently deaths were not as accountable as Marriages at this time in history. (Births were not registered until 1838 in New York City. Compilation of official mortality statistics did not begin until 1900. Death certificates did not come into general use in any part of America until 1915).

Samuel Cochran Jr. had apparently had enough travel. He is the only one of Samuel Cochran, Sr.'s family to make Georgia his permanent home. On the contrary, William Cochran, another son of Samuel Cochran, and the grandfather of Jerome Cochran, travelled considerably. He was born in Virginia February 20, 1774 and traveled to Georgia with his family . He married Elizabeth (Betsy) Owen (born July 24 or 28, 1783 in Georgia or Virginia; Died April 12, 1849 or 1859) . At first William and his wife, Betsy, apparently did not plan to move. On September 28, 1800, in Oglethorpe County, Robert Leverett and Polly , his wife, sold to William Cochran of Oglethorpe County, for $1,000.00, two hundred acres of land on Little River in Oglethorpe County. William and Betsy must have remained on this land at least until December 15, 1815, on which date they sold 214 acres on Little River to Parke Watson for $454.00. It seems likely that they continued to live in Oglethorpe County even after they sold the land, for in that county, on January 12, 1818, their daughter Nancy E. Cochran married Jabez King.

William and Betsy may have been in Jefferson County, Alabama on February 2, 1825 , when their son, Owen Cochran was married to Alpha Cochran, with Lynch Cochran as bondsman. (Who was this Lynch Cochran?). William and Betsy may not have attended the wedding , but they certainly lived in Jefferson County, Alabama for a while. There is a bill of sale dated September 6, 1826 and recorded in Fayette County, Tennessee, in which William Cochran of "the State of Alabama, Jefferson County ," sells a slave to Daniel Johnson of Fayette County. Apparently, by January 23, 1827,

William and Betsy had, migrated to Fayette County, Tennessee. On that date, William Cochran bought 500 acres of land in Fayette County from John Wallin, it being part of a former grant to Thomas and Robert King. Witnesses to the deed were Daniel Johnson, Lynch Cochran and William G. Cochran. William Cochran died shortly thereafter, late in 1827 or early in 1828 in Fayette County, Tennessee.

In January 1828, Owen Cochran came into Court and petitioned for administration papers on making bond in the amount of $6,000.00, with Augustus Cochran, Lynda Cochran and William Cochran as securities. On December 25, 1828 Owen J. Cochran, as administrator of the estate of William Cochran, deceased, made over to Augustine (Augustus) O. Cochran "for the consideration of the natural love and affection which he, the said William Cochran had for the said Augustine O. As also for the better support and livelihood of him the said Augustime" a certain tract of land in Fayette County, in the 11th Surveyor's District in Range 1 and Section 1, being part of a tract granted by the state of Tennessee to Thomas and Robert King. Witnesses were W. H. Cochran and Samuel T. Cochran. Just as with the land in Campbell County, Virginia, so with that in Fayette County, Tennessee - no record can be found to show how it passed out of the hands of the Cochrans. The 1836 tax list for Fayette County has been published in "Ansearchin'" News and at that time, Owen J. Cochran was still paying taxes on 300 acres "as administrator" and A. O. Cochran was taxed on one slave and "1 lot."

Augustus Owen Cochran (born October 3, 1805 in Oglethorpe County, Georgia; died April 19, 1877 in present day Pontotoc County, Oklahoma, and buried in Frisco Cemetery at Stonewall, Oklahoma), son of William Cochran and Elizabeth Owen, Married January 1, 1829, probably in Fayette County, Tennessee. Frances Bailey (born January 31, 1808 in Alabama; died January 20, 1893 in present day Pontotoc County, Oklahoma, and also buried in Frisco Cemetery). Frances Bailey's father was Benjamin Bailey, born in Jackson County, Arkansas died 1836. He was a veteran of the War of 1812. He married, in 1800, in Pendleton District, South

Carolina, to Pamella ("Milly") Baker (Born ca 1780; died 1856, in Claiborne Parish, Louisiana) She was the daughter of William and Elizabeth Baker.

Frances Bailey Cochran was the mother of ten children:

1. Elizabeth Owen Cochran (born February 25, 1830; died August 17, 1831).

2. Jerome (Hunter) Cochran (born December 4, 1831) Married Sarah Jane (Johnson) Collins.

3. William Lewis Cochran (born January 11, 1834) married (1) Jincy Bohannon; (2) Sarah (?) ; (3) Ella Redmon; (4) Effa B.

4. Augustus Owen Cochran (born March 19, 1838; died August 17, 1841)

5. Mary Susan Cochran (March 13, 1840) Married Barber.

6. Augustus Owen Cochran, Jr. (November 11, 1842) married Emma Leonie Rhodes.

7. Lynch Bailey Cochran (February 13, 1846) married (1) Susan Burris; (2) Viola Toole.

8. Eugene Cochran (born June 15, 1848; died in 1878 of yellow fever).

9. Ann Florence Cochran, twin of Eugene (born June 15, 1848; also died of yellow fever in 1878).

10. James Virgil Cochran (October28, 1851) married Jenny.

Daniel W. Head was one of the first settlers of Fayette County, Tennessee, at a time when the area was mostly in the hands of the Choctaw and Chickasaw Indians. Head, as the first gunsmith in the county, was fairly well off. His services were in demand because hunting was one of the chief means of procuring meat for the table at that time. In 1824, Daniel Head owned 60 1/2 acres of land situated just north of the south branch of Wolf River. The resourceful Head had established a ferry at this point for west-bound settlers to cross the river. The first road through the area, State Line Road, was cut in 1825, and in 1826 Head was appointed overseer to cut the road from "Head's Ferry" to Somerville. Moscow Tennessee was established the same year on part of Daniel W. Head's 60 1/2 acres. Horace Loomis opened a store in 1826 and Dr. Smith taught a school that year. On August 27, 1827 Daniel W. Head made the deed (reserving 1 acre for himself) for his 60 1/2 acres to the Town Company of Moscow. James Kimbrough, Nathaniel Ragland, Josiah Cotton, John Brown, and John Powell were the trustees. Owen Cochran opened the first hotel in town in 1827. This Owen Cochran was probably Jerome's uncle, the eldest son of William Cochran. He usually went by the name, "Owen" Jerome's father, Augustus Owen Cochran, usually went by the name "Augustus" or "A.O." At any rate, the Cochran's were among the original settlers of that region, and they worked to promote the area.

We do not know how long Owen Cochran operated the Moscow Hotel. It was sold to Dr. G. A. Renner, a graduate of Gotten (Göttingen?) University in Germany in 1845. Dr. Renner's plans were to accommodate invalids from a wide surrounding area. Augustus Owen Cochran had moved to Marshall County, Mississippi several years before this, and Owen Cochran had moved to Texas in the 1830's or early forties. While they lived in Moscow, on February 5, 1830 Elizabeth Owen was born. She was a frail child and lived only a little over a year. She died in August 1831. In December of 1831, the second child, and the first male child was born. This was Jerome. He too was frail and sickly. Moscow, lying between two river branches, as it does, with standing water and swampland, may have been an unhealthy place to live. The children may have been unduly exposed to infectious disease brought in by travellers to the hotel.. The Cochrans did not live in Moscow long after the birth of Jerome.

The above account of the Cochran genealogy is taken from "The Genealogy of the Cochran families of Northern Mississippi" by Mrs. Mary Gregg. The following is her brief autobiography:

I was born in Ouachita Parish, Louisiana, in 1924, the youngest of three children of Junius Eugene Sapp and his wife, Winfield Owen ("Winnie") Cochran. After graduating from Ouachita Parish

High School in 1941, I entered Northwest Louisiana Junior College, but married before graduating. My first husband, Lt. John. Wise was a pilot and was killed when his plane crashed in 1943. I remarried to Melvin Eugene Gregg, from whom I was later divorced. By him, I had two daughters, and I now have three grandsons.

I began genealogical research in 1972, and I still find it a fascinating undertaking. I have worked at it almost every day since 1972 except for about two years when I was working full time and attending college. Finally, 40 years after entering college, I received my A.B. degree from Memphis State University in December 1981.

A relative of my father's had done a great deal of work on that side of the family, so I began my research with my mother's Cochrans. Within about six months, I had learned as much as I know (or likely ever will know) about the ancestry of my Cochrans, but they are still one of my favorite families to research, and I have two file drawers of Cochran material, most of which concerns families that are unrelated to mine! Because of having accumulated all this material, I have had the pleasure of helping a great many people straighten out their Cochran lineage.

Mary Gregg

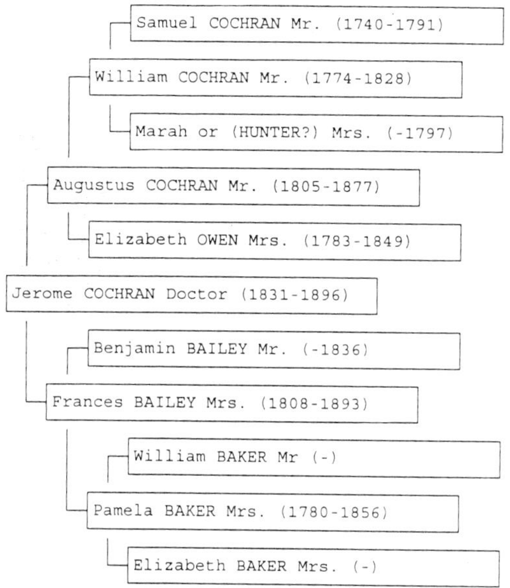


```
Jerome H. COCHRAN Doctor (1831-1896)
    ├────Augustine Schamyl COCHRAN Miss (1856-1869)
    ├────Louise Ina COCHRAN Miss (1860-1891)
    ├────Jerome Bowling COCHRAN Mr. (1863-1924)
    │       ├────Jerome COCHRAN Mr. (1884-)
    │       ├────Schamyl COCHRAN  Commander (1886-1967)
    │       │       ├────Margauet C. (COCHRAN) HAZARD Mrs. (-)
    │       │       └────Ina C. (COCHRAN) HUBARD Mrs. (-)
    │       ├────Walker COCHRAN  Commander (1892-1976)
    │       │       └────Mrs. Richard M. PAYNE Mrs (-)
    │       ├────Viola (COCHRAN)DUFFIE Mrs. (1894-)
    │       └────Irma (COCHRAN) SCHULZ Mrs. (1898-)
    ├────Mary Fooshea COCHRAN Miss (1867-1870)
    ├────Edmund  Collins COCHRAN Mr. (1869-1931)
    ├────Francis COCHRAN Master (1871-1871)
    ├────Lamoua B. COCHRAN Master (1872-1872)
    └────Louis COCHRAN Master (1875-1875)
```

APPENDIX #3

Artist, professor Vadah Cochran dies after long fight with cancer

Samuel Vadah Cochran, 76, of Holly Springs, died February 6, 1995, of cancer at Baptist Hospital in Memphis. A descendant of pioneer Marshall County families and the son of Samuel Vadah Cochran and Rita Binion, he was a graduate of Louisiana State University. He received a master's degree from the University of Wisconsin, and did postgraduate work at Yale University, University of Alabama, Florida State University, University of Mississippi and the University of North Carolina.

A person of many talents, he studied voice at Louisiana State and drama at Wisconsin. He taught drama and English for many years, first at Abraham Baldwin College in Georgia and then at the University of Memphis, from which he retired in 1983. He is remembered throughout the Mid-South for his performances with Theatre Memphis, most particularly for his roles as Alfred P. Dolittle in "My Fair Lady," and as Ben Franklin in "1776." He received an award from the Mississippi Arts Council for his writing in 1969.

Cochran was widely known and respected as a Mississippi artist.

He began studying art at the age of 15 under Netty Fant Thompson of Holly Springs. He later attended the Memphis Academy of Art and the Art Students League in New York, and studied under Glennray Tutor of Oxford.

"His lifelong interest in art flourished in the last fifteen years of his life, evidencing itself in many paintings of extraordinary artistic quality; the uncommon generosity he expressed through his talent and as a person will be long remembered and appreciated," Tutor said.

Cochran's work was the subject of several exhibits, most recently in June at the Jackson Mississippi Municipal Art Gallery. He leaves a lasting mark in Holly Springs in the beautiful murals he painted and in public and private collections in eight states. Throughout his life he worked for the preservation of the historic structures and the enhancement of the landscape of Holly Springs.

Cochran leaves his wife, Doris Sandusky Cochran; two step-children, Marie Sigman Moore of Holly Springs and Leslie B. Sigman of Ripley, Tenn.; and five grandchildren; a sister, Rita Binion Cochran Langus of Mobile, Ala., and two brothers, Deale Binion Cochran of Marietta, Ga., and James Clark Cochran of Holly Springs.

Services were held on Wednesday, February 8 at 11 a.m. at the First Presbyterian Church in Holly Springs, with burial in Hill Crest Cemetery. Thomas Funeral Home was in charge of arrangements.

Serving as pallbearers were Jack Wittjen, Dr. Robert E. Tyson, Edward Rather, Hugh H. Rather, Lanier Robison, Charles N. Dean, III, Hubert McAlexander and Glennray Tutor.

Honorary pallbearers were A. Q. Greer, Dudley Moore, Jr., Walker Hurdle, Dr. Al Hale, Dr. Dan Copeland, John D. Brown, Eugene Brown, Sr., Blanton Jones, Graham Miller, Billy Cupp, Norbert Barruel, C. C. Stephenson, S.B. Gresham and Dr. David Childers.

The family requests any memorials be made to the First Presbyterian Church of Holly Springs or the Marshall County Chapter of the American Cancer Society.

Julii 11ª }
A.D. 1864 } Eadem die undecima mensis Julii anno Domini millesimo octingentesimo sexagesimo quarto etiamque baptizavi juxta ritum SS. R. C. Ecclesiæ Susanam Rosam Jaafe, filiam legitimam Michaelis Jaafe et Susanæ Staggers – Infans jam quatuor circiter menses natus fuerat tempore Baptismi – Infantem de Fonte suscepit Patritius Jaafe – In cujus fidem subscripsi

Gulielmus F. McDonough –

Augusti 16ª
A.D. 1864 – Anno Domini millesimo octingentesimo sexagesimo quarto, die decima sexta mensis Augusti. Ego Gulielmus F. McDonough, Pastor hujus Ecclesiæ Stæ Joannis Baptistæ civitatis Tuscaloosæ baptizavi (sub conditione prius recepta abjuratione hæreseos et professione fidei) Josephum Davis Nicholson (adultum, novemdecim circiter annos natum) filium legitimum Andersonii et Jane Nicholson de Warren Co. Miss. – Patrini fuere Dr. Samuel Archinard et Martha L. Harris – In cujus facti testimonium propria manu

Subscripsi

Gulielmus F. McDonough –

Septembris 19ª }
A.D. 1864 } Anno Domini millesimo octingentesimo sexagesimo quarto die decima nona Septembris Ego Johannes Quinlan, Episcopus diœcesis ~~Stabaniensis~~ Mobiliensis (prius recepta professione fidei) baptizavi Hieronymum Cochran, filium legitimum Augusti et Franciscæ Cochran, neoconversumque ad fidem Catholicam. Sponsores fuere Rev. D. Gibbons et W. M. Easby Smith – In cujus facti testimonium propria manu

Subscripsi

+ Joannes, Epūs Mobiliensis

Sept. 23 - 1864
Anna Elizabeth
Boylan –   Die vigesima tertia Septembris A.D. millesimo octingentesimo sexagesimo quarto a Rmo Episcopo, Joanne Quinlan prius recepta professione fidei et abjuratione ... baptizata fuit Anna Elizabetha Boylan, neoconversa ad fidem

Augustus
Cochran
Dec 25ª
1864

Die vigesima quinta mensis Decembris anno Dñi mil-
lesimo octingentesimo sexagesimo quinto Ego infrascriptus
Baptizavi Augustum Cochran, filium legitimum Hieronymi
Cochran et Sarae I. Collins coniugii, adhibitis omnibus S.S.
Matris Ecclesiae ceremoniis. Puer tunc novem circiter annum
attigerat tempore Baptismi. — Sponsor fuit Frederica Walter

In cujus testimonium propria manu subscripsi
Gulm̃ I. McDonough —

Hieronymus B.
Cochran —
Dec 25ª 1864

Die vigesima quinta mensis Decembris anno Dñi millesimo octingentesimo sexagesimo quinto Ego infrascriptus
Hieronymum B. Cochran filium legitimum Hieronymi
Cochran et Sarae I. Collins baptizavi, adhibitis omnibus ceremoniis
requisitis. — Sponsor fuit Frederica Walter

In cujus testimonium propria manu subscripsi
Gul. I. McDonough. Past. Tusc.

McGuiness
Anna Agnes
et
Maria Joseph
Junii 13ª 1865

Die decima tertia mensis Junii anno Dñi millesimo octin-
gentesimo sexagesimo quinto Ego infrascriptus Tuscaloosae
Pastor, geminas sorores Annam Agnetem et Mariam Joseph
McGuiness, filias legitimas Georgii McGuiness et Hester Moore,
baptizavi adhibitis requisitis Ecclesiae ceremoniis. — Patrini Annae Agne-
tis fuere Thomas Rossiter et ... Winifreda Sponsores autem Mariae
Joseph fuere Ioannes Kehoe et Ioanna Costello. — In cujus fidem
Testatur

Guliel mũs I. McDonough. Past. Tusc

Cochran Louisa Jane
Junii 14ª 1865. —

Die decima septima mensis Junii anno Dñi
millesimo octingentesimo sexagesimo quinto Ego
infrascriptus Louisam Jane Cochran filiam legitimam Hieronymi Cochran et Sarae I. Collins, baptizavi, adhibitis ceremon-
niis necessariis. — Sponsor fuit Frederica Walter — In cujus
fidem propria manu subscripsi
Gulmũs I. McDonough. Past. Tuscal. —

Valedictory Address,
Dec. 17th, 1881 —

Gentlemen of the Mobile Medical
Society:

    I am very sorry to [have to] commence
my Valedictory Address with an apology
for having during the past year, been
able to discharge in [illegible]
the duties attaching to the presidential office.

    But it is well known [illegible]
that [illegible] duties as State [illegible]
have called me almost [illegible]
away from Mobile, so that [illegible]
possible for me [illegible]
frequently at your meetings, to give [illegible]
[illegible]
professional question [illegible]
[illegible] so [illegible] with [illegible]
[illegible]
Society, a [illegible]
machinery of the State [illegible]
[illegible] state of things has [illegible]
reasons. But I have all the [illegible]

comforted myself by the reflection that the Society has had in its vice president an officer quite as able to watch over its interests as I myself would have been under more fortunate circumstances; and I take advantage of this occasion to express to the vice president my most grateful acknowledgements for the cheerfulness with which he has seconded my efforts to serve you; and for the ability with which he has filled my place and supplied my deficiencies during my frequent absences.

I am glad to be able to congratulate the Society on the fact that its prosperity and usefulness during the past year have not fallen below the high standard which which for many years has marked the administrations of its successive presidents. When the several Annual Reports of the Secretary the Treasurer, the Board of Censors, the Board of Medical Examiners, and the Committee of Public Health, all

read at the first meeting in January,
& am sure that the exhibit will be one
that none of us will be ashamed of.
    The success of Societies like this depends
in large measure upon rules and
customs that would seem to many
to be of very small consequence. One
of the rules of this Society which has
contributed in my opinion very
greatly to our success is that which
prescribes weekly meetings, and
fixes those weekly meetings on
Saturday evenings. Would not any
other evening in the week serve our
purposes as well? I think not. It
seems to me to be the most natural
and proper thing in the world for
our doctors to get together on Saturday evening, and to wind up the
week's work by a general interchange
of views and discussion of cases;
and this going on from year to year
becomes a habit, so that we doctors
go to the medical society on Saturday
night, just as people generally go to

church on Sundays. I mention this
matter because on several occasions
it has been suggested that the night
for our meetings should be changed,
on the ground that some other
night would better suit the convenience of some of the younger
members of the Society. In my
judgment the argument is more
plausible than sound. I do not believe that the desired result would
be accomplished in that way.

It is a very strange fact, but it is
a fact, nevertheless, that the members of
our Society — and the same thing is true
of all other scientific organizations —
who are most constant in their attendance, who always have time to
write papers and to report cases,
and to discharge all other duties
imposed upon them are those who
are most heavily burthened with
practice, and with other public and
private business. A physician who
has twenty or thirty professional visits

to make every day always has time
to attend the meetings of the Society.
It is the young practitioner or the old
practitioner who has but little to do—
who is fortunate if he gets three or
four calls a day—who is always
too busy to come to the meetings—always too much pressed for time to
prepare himself to lead in a debate.
(start here) Now, I hope nobody will take offence
if I say that such excuses are not
simply paradoxical, but are in fact
misleading and untrue. It is not
want of time, but want of will that
keeps our younger men so generally
away the Society meetings. In this,
as in many other things, the old
maxim, Where there's a will, there's a
way, is full of suggestive wisdom.

It is perfectly true that members
have a constitutional right to stay
away from the meetings; and I would
not have it otherwise. A bad member is better than no member at all,
just as half a loaf is better than no bread.

But it would be better for the Society, if the meetings were always well attended; and I am sure that our meetings are always sufficiently interesting and instructive to make it worth while for all these younger members always to be on hand. They should remember that always, in the end, it is doctors that make the reputation of doctors—that no doctor can achieve any very large or very brilliant success amongst the people without the endorsement of his professional brethren. I hope I may be allowed to quote, without suspicion of irreverence, a very striking declaration of Holy Writ, "Seek first the kingdom of God, and his righteousness, and all these things shall be added unto you," these things—that is to say worldly honors and temporal successes. And so I say to every young man who desire to achieve success in the practice of medicine, Seek first to win the confidence and respect of the medical profession itself, and then popular confidence and popular patronage will come to you of themselves.

Every practicing physician will subscribe in general terms to the proposition, that a strict observance of the ancient ethics of the profession is necessary for the preservation of the profession's honor, dignity, and respectability. But I fear that a great many will make this subscription without appreciating the proposition in that thoroughgoing and emphatic fashion which its importance ought to command for it— In a word, I think I may venture to say—and I am very sorry that it is possible to say it— that a great many physicians admit the authority of the Ethics in words of disingenuous and equivocal meaning, and with many tacit modifications and reservations.

Now I do not hesitate to assert that the Ethics constitute the very soul and life blood of the profession—and that the abrogation of the Ethics means neither more nor less than the dissolution of all professional organization.

on the great West the ethics have become almost dead letters—and the profession of medicine has degenerated, almost completely, into a trade. At the recent session in Savannah of the American Public Health Association I had occasion to discuss this state of affairs with several distinguished western physicians; and I inquired of them if they were satisfied with the result. They emphatically and with one accord they said, No! that the resulting state of affairs was most dishonoring and calamitous—but that they were obliged to recognize established facts.

In our own State, as you all know, the State Medical Association and the County Medical Societies have been endeavoring for the last twelve years to vindicate the authority of the ethics in relation to professional charges, and in condemnation of all forms and fashions of contract practice. I am glad to be able to

y, and I say it with tolerably accurate knowledge of what is going on
in various sections of the State—
that our efforts in this direction
have been attended with a large
measure of success. But the whole
battle is not yet won. For example
in the coal mines and iron furnaces
about Birmingham the practice
of the employees is now done by
contract. I had occasion not long
ago to discuss this whole question
with the Jefferson county Medical
Society—And with the result that
the Society resolved to make war
against the evil practice, without
truce or favor, until it shall be
utterly suppressed. They have a
hard struggle before them. But if
they act with sufficient firmness,
resolution, and prudence they will
win the fight in the course of time.
On reference to this contract practice
the Mobile Medical Society has a record
of which we have good reason to be proud.

In all of its grosser forms contract practice in Mobile is a thing of the past. Nevertheless, I very much fear that the unholy and unprofessional leaven out of which the contract system sprang into mischievous activity in the beginning—that is to say the hankering after illegitimate loaves and fishes—is not even yet utterly dead and buried amongst us. It needs watching still. In the words of a famous outburst of patriotic eloquence, Perpetual vigilance is the price of liberty; and Josh Billings in his homely way clinches the nail when he adds, And of everything else that we've got and expect to keep.

Last Spring, feeling how important it was to push the war against medical contract to its utmost possible limits, I had the honor to present to this Society a set of resolutions condemning the appointment by the Board of Police Commissioners of a City Physician to treat the sick poor in their homes. To

my surprize—in the light of subsequent
events I cannot add—to my gratification the resolutions were adopted
by a large majority. I say "in the
light of subsequent events," because you
all know how the hour of trial came,
the Society was not brave enough to
stand squarely up to the high position it had assumed. It split hairs
in the way of compromises with a dexterity at least, that was admirable, and
I think made a mistake in doing
so.

Recently, in Atlanta, I have had
occasion to see a practical illustration of the evils and abuses that
may grow out of this system of
contract practice for the poor in
their own homes. In that city there
are six ward physicians paid by
the city to look after the poor. They
are paid from two hundred to four
hundred dollars each, and out of
these paltry salaries they are expected,
not only to give their medical services

to the poor of their respective districts, but to furnish them also with all the medicines they may stand in need of.

Of course, no honest and capable man could undertake to do such service for such pay. But Atlanta doctors are found who not only are willing to accept these appointments, but who enter into competition with one an other, and bring to bear all the political and personal influences they are able to command, to secure them. The testimony of the physicians of Atlanta generally is that the system is a cheat and a sham, and altogether mischievous and demoralizing.

There is one section in the Constitution
of the Society to which I desire to call
special attention, because I am afraid
that the members of the Society have
not always appreciated the just
measure of their duties and obligations
under its provision. The section I
have in mind is that which relates
to the duties of the Board of Censors,
acting in their three several capacities, namely, as a Board of Censors,
as a Board of Medical Examiners,
and as a Committee of Public
Health. In order that you may appreciate as fully as possible the
full scope and purpose of this
section I will read it, in extenso.

    x x x x x x x x x x x x x x x

Now I think that the Society has
no special reason to find fault
with the Board for the way in
which it has discharged its functions as a Board of Censors, and as a
Board of Medical Examiners. But
it does seem to me that neither the

APPENDIX #6

SCHEDULE OF JEROME COCHRAN LECTURES

1899 -- J.T. Searcy, Tuscaloosa -- What is Insanity?

1900 -- William Osler, Baltimore -- Not Present.

1901 -- William Osler, Baltimore -- Not Present.

1902 -- Nathan Bozeman, New York -- Declined.

1903 -- George H. Price, Nashville -- The History of Medicine.

1904 -- W.S. Thayer, Baltimore -- Cardiac and Vascular Complications of Typhoid Fever.

1905 -- Robert Abbe, New York -- The Problems of Surgery..

1906 -- Joseph Collins, New York -- Arteriosclerosis

1907 -- Nicholas Senn, Chicago -- Final Triumph of Scientific Medicine.

1908 -- E.L. Marechal, Mobile -- Absent.

1909 -- Lewellys F. Barker, Baltimore -- Clinical Methods of Cardiac Investigation.

1910 -- Frank S. Meara, New York -- Some Problems of Nutrition in Early Life.

1911 -- Rudolph Matas, New Orleans -- Inflammatory Tuberculosis.

1912 -- Maurice Richardson, Boston -- Elimination of Preventable Disasters from Surgery.

1913 -- L.L. Hill, Montgomery -- Surgical Complications and Sequelae of Typhoid Fever.

1914 -- Frank Smithies, Chicago -- Contributions of the Twentieth Century to the Better Understanding of Gastric Cancer.

1915 -- John B. Elliott, Jr., New Orleans -- Abscess of Liver.

1916 -- Howard A. Kelly, Baltimore -- Radium Therapy.

1917 -- William J. Mayo, Rochester -- Importance of Septic Infection in the Three Great Plagues.

1918 -- George I. Bushnell, Washington -- The Army in Relation to the Tuberculosis Problem.

1919 -- George W. Crile, Cleveland, Ohio -- Abdominal Surgery in Civil and Military Hospitals.

1920 -- Henry A. Christian, Boston -- Bright's Disease with Special Reference to its Treatment.

1921 -- J. Whitridge Williams, Baltimore -- A Critical Review of Twenty-One Year's Experience with Caesarean Section.
1922 -- Charles Mayo, Rochester, Minn. -- The Thyroid and its Diseases.
1923 -- James S. McLester, Birmingham -- Nutrition in its Newer Aspects.
1924 -- James S. Stone, Boston -- Abdominal Diagnosis in Children.
1925 -- H.A. Royster, Raleigh -- The Surgeon's Heritage and outlook.
1926 -- Stewart Roberts, Atlanta -- The Heart Muscle.
1927 -- G. Canby Robinson, Baltimore -- The Mechanism of Heart Failure and its Correction.
1928 -- John B. Deaver, Philadelphia -- Chronic Pancreatitis.
1929 -- Louis B. Wilson, Rochester , Minn. -- Some Suggestions for Improved Training of Medical Specialists.
1930 -- Walter E. Sistrunk, Dallas, Texas -- The Part That Surgical Anaesthesia Has Played in Medical Science.
1931 -- R.S. Cunningham, Nashville, Tennessee -- Studies on the Pathology of Tuberculosis and Syphilis.
1932 -- A. Benson Cannon, New York -- Prsctical Points and the Diagnosis and Treatment of So-Called Lymphoblastoma Group of Diseases.
1933 -- J. Shelton Horsely, Richmond -- Cancer of the Stomach and Colon.
1934 -- Russel L. Cecil, New York -- Present Trends in the Study of Rheumatic Fever and Rheumatoid Arthritis.
1935 -- George H. Semken, New York -- A Consideration of Tumors of the Breast.
1936 -- William D. Partlow, Tuscaloosa -- A Debt the World Owes Medical Science.
1937 -- Frank H. Lahey, Boston -- Carcinoma of the Colon and Rectum.
1938 -- T.M. McMillan, Philadelphia -- An Optimistic View of Some of the Problems of Heart Disease.
1939 -- George T. Pack, New York -- Recent Advances in the Radiation Therapy of Cancer.
1940 -- E.V. McCollum, Baltimore -- Some Contributions of Nutritional Research to Clinical Medicine.
1941 -- M.Y. Dabney, Birmingham --The Story of Breast Cancer.
1942 -- Harvey B. Stone, Baltimore -- Biliary Disease as Seen by a Surgeon.

1944 -- Tinsley R. Harrison, Dallas Texas -- The Value and Limitations of Laboratory Tests in the Practice of Medicine.

1945 -- Meeting Cancelled.

1946 -- Alton Ochsner, New Orleans -- The Influence of Serendipity on Medicine.

1947 -- Reginald Fitz, Boston -- The Early Characteristics of Certain Chronic Diseases.

1948 -- Andrew C. Ivey, Chicago -- The Gallbladder in Health and Disease.

1949 -- Max Thorek, Chicago -- Cholecystectomy its Technical variations.

1950 -- Paul D. White, Boston -- Historical Delays in the Application of Knowledge About the Heart.

1951 -- Emil Novak, Baltimore -- The Relation of Hormones to Female Genital Tumors.

1952 -- Richard Catell, Boston -- Carcinoma of the Colon and Rectum.

1953 -- Champ Lyons, Birmingham, AL -- Metabolic Aspects of Convalescence.

1954 -- Claude S. Beck, Cleveland, OH -- Operations for Coronary Disease.

1955 -- Charles W. Mayo, Rochester, Minn. -- The Role of Medicine and Doctors in International Relations.

1956 -- John B. Youmans, Nashville -- The Chronic Toxicity of Salt J(Sodium Chloride).

1957 -- Irvine H. Page, Cleveland -- The Treatment of Arterial Hypertension.

1958 -- R.C. Anderson, Columbus, OH -- What Should We Ask of Psychiatry?

1959 -- Thomas P. Findley, Augusta, Ga. -- Some Clinical Syndromes Due to Metabolic Dysfunctions of the Kidney.

1960 -- Joe Vincent Meigs, Boston, MA -- Changing Concepts in the Treatment of Cancer of the Cervix.

1961 -- Neal Owens, New Orleans, LA -- Hippocrates, a Physician and a Horse.

1962 -- A. Ashley Weech, Cincinnati, OH -- A Study in the Emotions of Childhood.

1963 -- Hugh H. Hussey, Jr. , Chicago, IL -- Medical Education and Medical Practice - Expectations and Realities.

1964 -- Luther L. Terry, Washington, DC -- In the Panoply of Our
Science.
1965 -- William M. Christopherson, Louisville, KY -- Early Diagnosis
of Cancer.
1966 -- Lester Dragstedt, Gainesville, FL -- The Pathogenesis and
Surgical Treatment of Gastric Ulcer.
1967 -- Robert Q. Marston, Bethesda, MD -- Progress of Regional
Medical Program.
1968 -- G. Gordon McHardy, New Orleans, LA --Changing Patterns of
Clinical Medicine.
1969 -- Alton Ochsner, New Orlean , LA -- The Increasing Menace of
Communism in the United States.
1970 -- W. Sterling Edwards, III, Albuquerque, NM -- Development of
Arterial Grafts and Vascular Surgery in Alabama.
1971 -- Luther L. Terry, Philadelphia, PA -- Health Care in the
Seventies -- Illusions and Realities.
1972 -- John W. Kirklin, Birmingham, AL -- Recent Advances in Heart
Surgery.
1973 -- Carl A. Hoffman, Huntington, WV -- Beyond the Fringe: The
New Imperatives.
1974 -- Tom E. Nesbit, Nashville, Tenn. -- Stars Fell on Alabama.
1975 -- Malcolm C. Todd, Long Beach, California -- Our Federated
Individuality.
1976 -- Howard C. Taylor, Jr., New York, N.Y. -- Maternal Health and
Family Planning.
1977 -- Howard L. Holley, Birmingham -- The Alabama Physician: A
Teacher Looks Back.
1978 -- William R. Willard, University Al. -- Family Practice
Movement. The Promises, Performances, & Prospects.
1979 -- Tom E. Nesbitt, Nashville, Tenn. -- Realities in Medical Care.
 1980 -- James D. Hardy, Jackson, Miss. -- An Alabama Student's
Investigation in Organ Replacement.
1981 -- James S. Todd, Ridgeway, New Jersey -- Medical Ethics.
1982 -- Dennis S. O'Leary , Washingtom, D.C. -- Medical Diary of an
Attempted Assassination.
1983 -- George M. Sheehan, Red Bank, NJ -- Exercise, the Third Force
in the Treatment of Disease.
1984 -- E. Henry Lamkin, Jr., Indianapolis, Indiana -- A Great and
Noble Profession is Dying -- America's March Toward Mediocrity.

1985 -- William L. Roper, Washington DC -- The Perspective of a Presidential Staff Advisor.
1986 -- Nicholas J. Pisacano, Lexington, KY -- Reconsecratio Medicine.
1987 -- Edward R. Annis, Miami, Florida -- Cost vs. Quality - The Challenge to Professional Freedom.
1988 -- George S. Allen, Nashville, Tenn. -- Adrenal Medullary Transplants - To Caudate Nucleus in Parkinson's Disease.
1989 -- Harriet P. Dustin, Birmingham, AL -- Diet and Drugs for Hypertension.
1990 -- Alan R. Nelson, Salt Lake City, Utah -- Medicine in America: What is its Future?
1991 -- Robert Bazell, New York, NY -- Science, Medicine and the Media.
1992 -- Charles A. LeMaistre, Houston TX -- Cancer - The End of the Beginning.
1993 -- John Lee Clowe, Schenectady, NY -- New Directions in Medicine.
1994 -- Edward R. Annis, Miami Shores, FL --Reform: New Challenges, New Opportunities.
1995 -- Robert E. McAfee, Portland, ME -- Quality in Health System Reform- I Know When I See It.
1996 -- Donald T. Lewers, Easton, M.D. National Managed Care Update.
1997-- George C. Lundberg, Chicago, IL -- Preserving Medical Professionalism in an Era of Managed Care.
1998

Index